Mind Maps

PHYSICS

First edition published 2020

UniPress Books Limited

Conceived, designed and produced by UniPress Books Limited

www.unipressbooks.com

Design, diagrams and doodles by Lindsey Johns

Project managed by Kate Duffy

Printed in China

ISBN: 978-1-9160-8963-1

1 2 3 4 5 6 7 8 9 10

Page 128 Red giant from an idea courtesy of *Astronomy*: Roen Kelly, after Klaus-Peter Schroeder and Robert Cannon Smith.

Mind Maps PHYSICS

How to Navigate the World of Science

DR. BEN STILL

unipress

Mind Maps

CONTENTS

Introduction.....p. 6

1 Motion and Measurement p. 10

2 Energy and Forces p. 24

3 Waves and Harmonic Motion p. 38

4 Electromagnetism p. 52

5 Matter and Materials p. 66

6 Thermodynamics p. 80

7 Quantum Ideas p. 94

8 Nuclear and Particle Physics p. 108

9 Astrophysics p. 122

10 Relativity p. 136

Glossary.....p. 150

Index.....p. 156

Acknowledgments.....p. 160

Introduction

Physics is a vast science that encompasses our entire universe: from the tiny subatomic world of particle physics to the cosmos of astrophysics and so much more in between. The ambition of this book is to guide the reader to discover the importance of physics day-to-day and to learn the language to talk about it confidently. We have distilled much of this hugely varied subject into a series of 10 mind maps. Each map not only covers the key vocabulary used to describe and explain each area of the subject, but also weaves connections between the ideas behind each term. The book is a springboard to encourage every reader to continue to explore this fascinating subject.

There is much new vocabulary, but each word is a key one for the topic being discussed. The complexity of the ideas progress as we go through the book. We start our journey in the civilizations of the ancient world and their early attempts to benchmark the world we live in, and finish in the modern world of relativity, which governs the evolution of our universe on the grandest scales. Along the way, we cover familiar topics of energy, electromagnetism, and waves, before exploring particle physics and the quantum realm.

So forget what you think you feel about physics and delve deep into this book, for the world is full of physics you just haven't seen yet!

What is a mind map?

A mind map is a visual method that aims to assist learning by structuring terms used regularly in a particular field to demonstrate their link to other keywords. The maps are powerful tools that go beyond mere rote learning of word definitions and allow the reader to wade deep into the ideas behind the words, as well as the logical evolution of the field in question.

Each map begins with an important term before weaving paths that link to other concepts. These key terms are highlighted in the text. While it may seem that each branch from this start point reaches a dead end this is, in fact, not so. While there are 10 separate maps, they do not exist in isolation but are part of a much larger global map that weaves the rich tapestry of the science that is physics.

These maps are seeds that sprout into exciting fields of science and branches that reach far beyond the limits set by the confines of one book. We have pruned the wider web of connections to select those we felt important to discuss in this book.

Those close to the start of their physics career will hopefully enjoy the extended explanations of each key term. Those a little further along this path will hopefully benefit from the web of connections laid out in each map as they pull together the themes of physics.

How to Use This Book

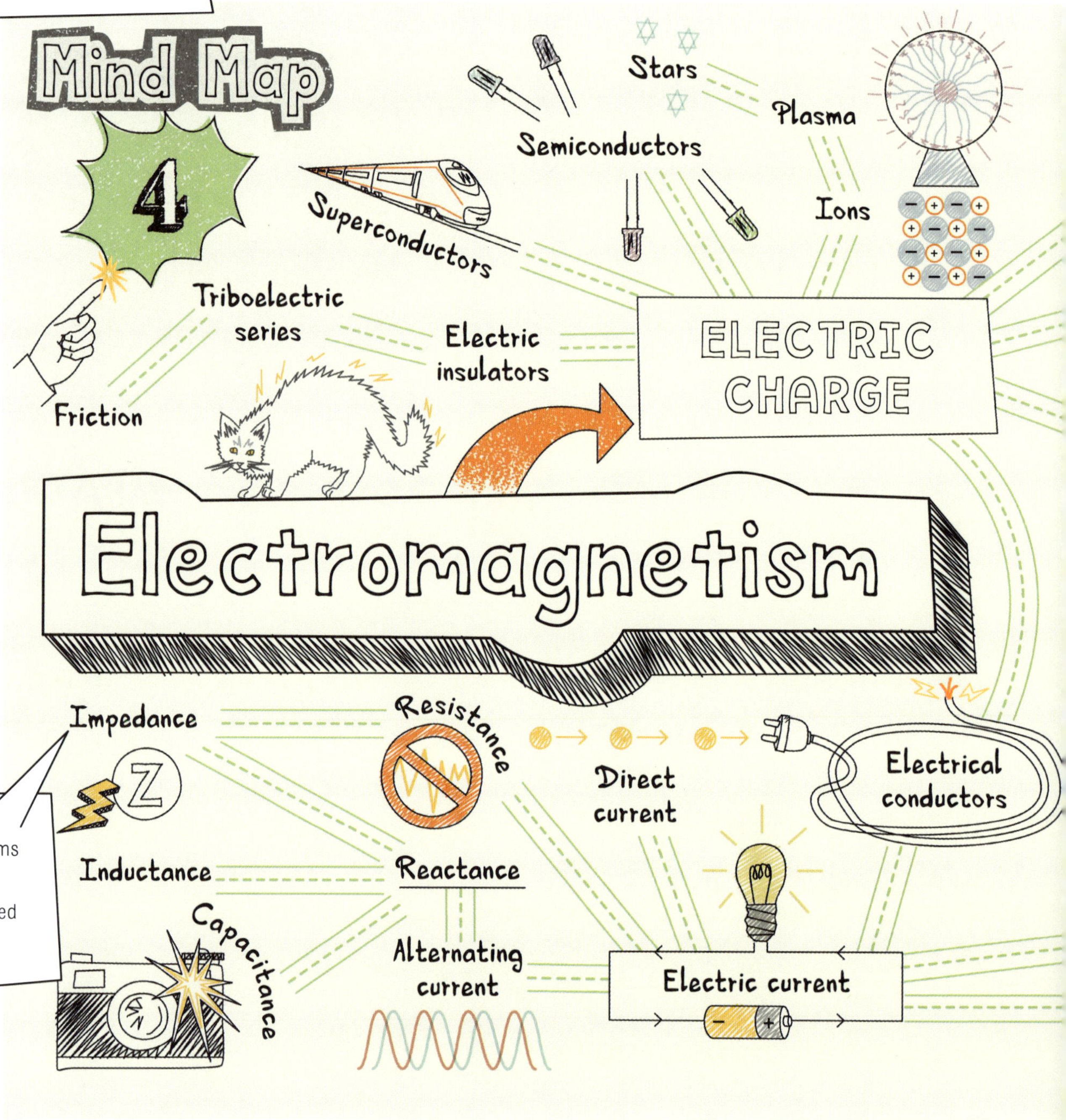

The important terms are emphasized in **bold** and explained in the text.

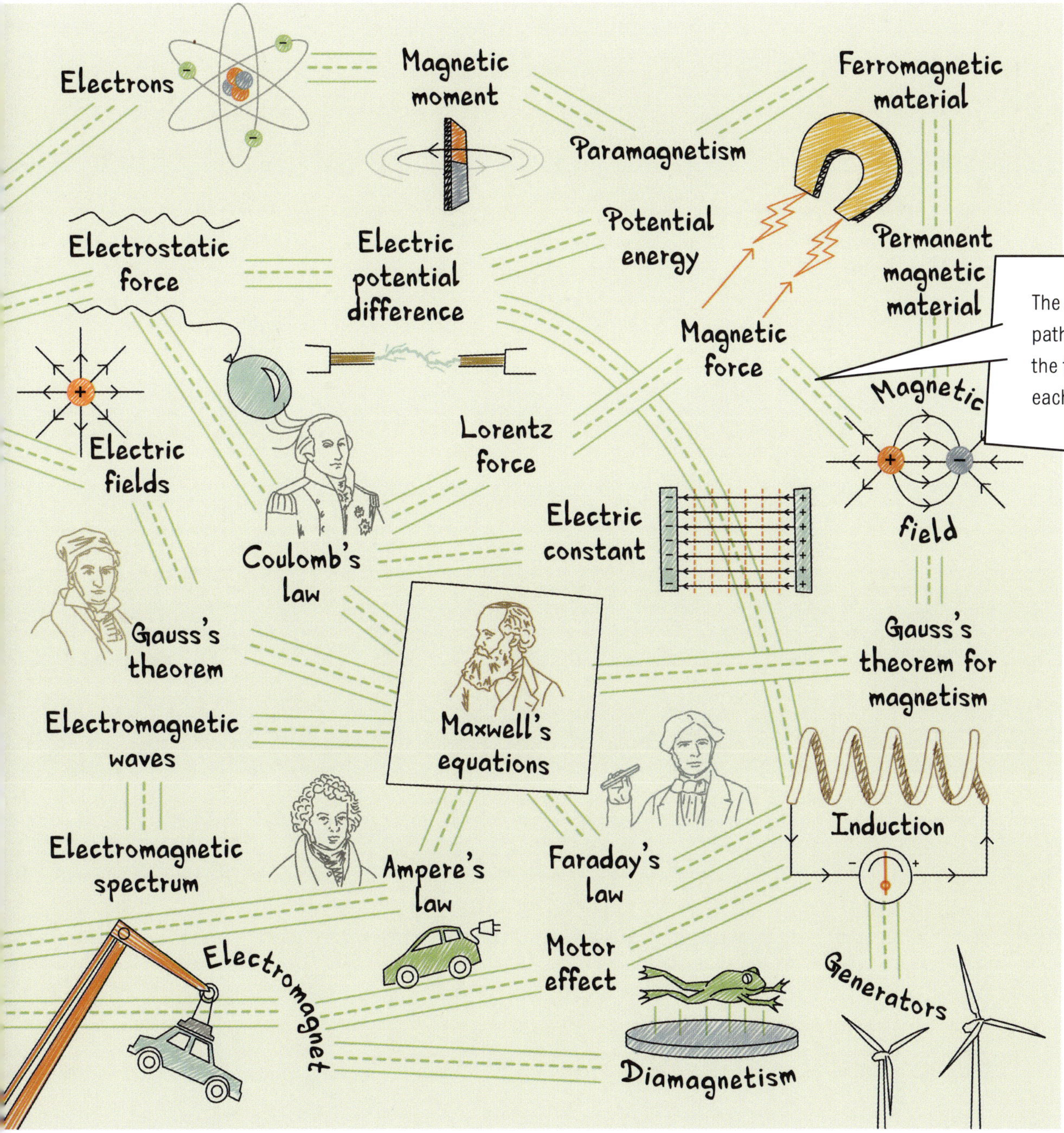

The arrows and pathways show how the topics link to each other.

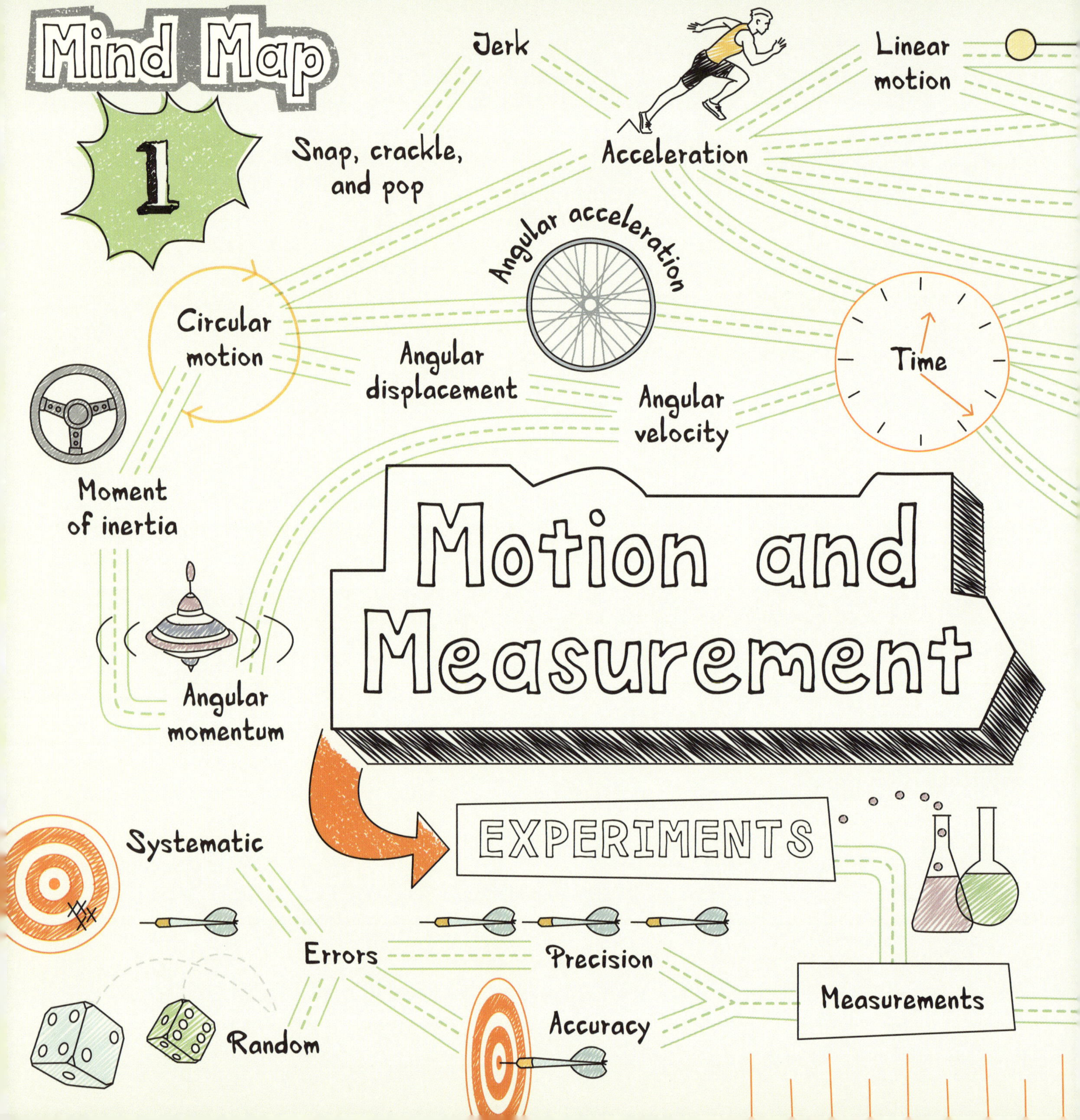
Mind Map
1
Motion and Measurement
Jerk
Snap, crackle, and pop
Acceleration
Linear motion
Angular acceleration
Circular motion
Angular displacement
Angular velocity
Time
Moment of inertia
Angular momentum
EXPERIMENTS
Systematic
Errors
Random
Precision
Accuracy
Measurements

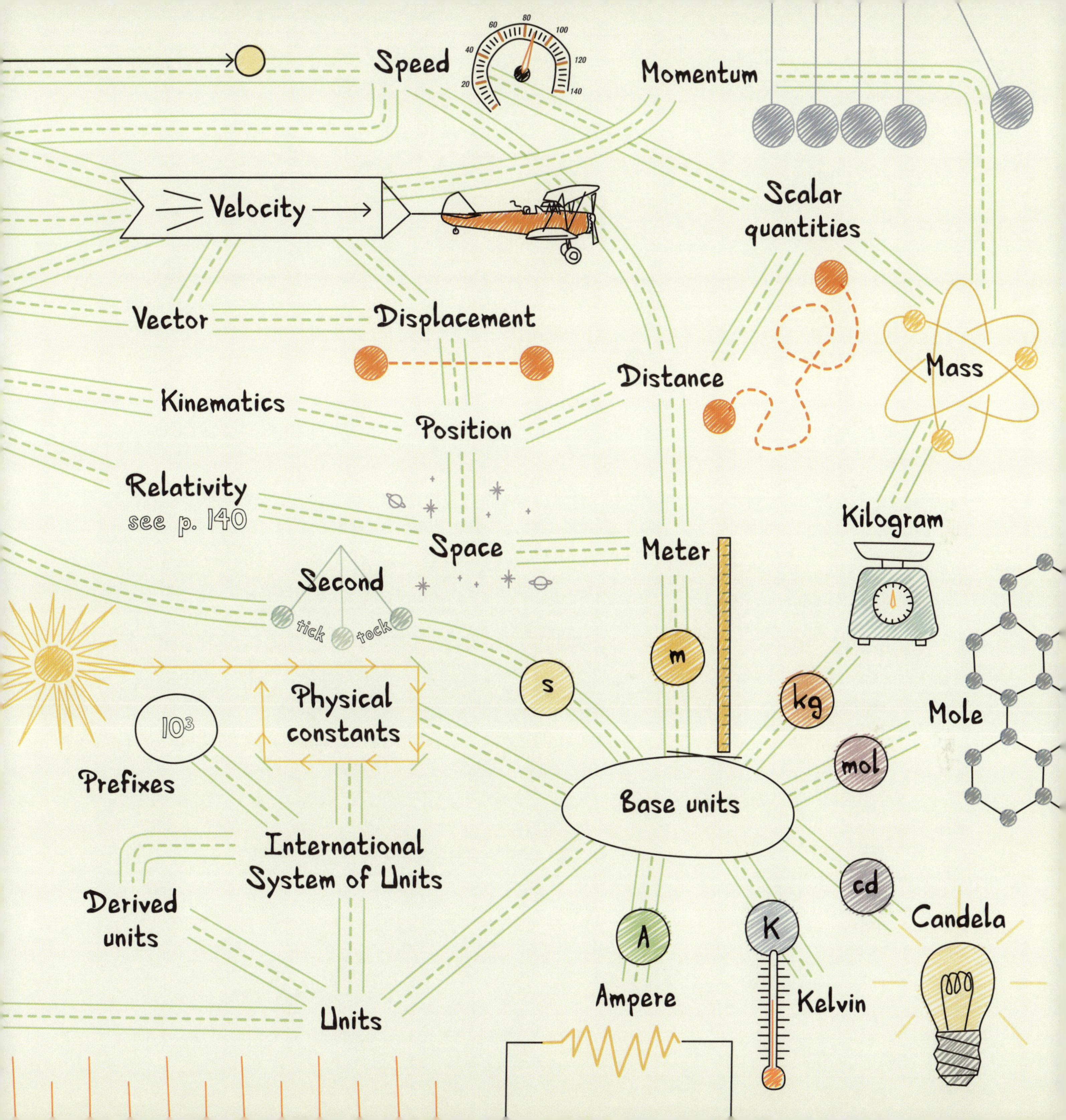
Speed
Momentum
Velocity
Scalar quantities
Vector
Displacement
Distance
Mass
Kinematics
Position
Relativity
see p. 140
Space
Meter
Kilogram
Second
tick
tock
s
m
kg
Mole
mol
10^3
Physical constants
Prefixes
Base units
International System of Units
Derived units
cd
Candela
A
K
Ampere
Kelvin
Units

Measuring the World

The goal of science is to understand the workings of nature. To achieve this, we must observe nature carefully and draw conclusions from our observations. Nature is so complex that it is difficult to figure out everything that is going on from simply sitting and watching the world. Instead, scientists use setups that test just a few elements of nature at a time. In these setups, scientists do their best to simplify the complexities by controlling the things that change and the things that remain constant. These are **experiments** and each one tells a different part of the story of nature. The outcome of each experiment is woven together by scientists into a coherent, complex narrative.

Different people may have different opinions on whatever they see. To ensure that individual opinion does not change the outcome of an experiment, scientists take **measurements** of different quantities in nature. These quantities could be one of many things, such as distance, time, or temperature. Through these measurements, scientists hope to observe nature in a universal way that is not dependent on the person conducting the experiment. Numbers are assigned to each of these quantities, so that we can compare the results of one experiment with another. The numbers are analyzed by looking for patterns, and these patterns guide our understanding of how nature works in very specific environments. These patterns are tested repeatedly, through new experiments in new places and in new environments to see if they represent the true behavior of nature.

Measuring our world

Humans invented different systems to measure and define the world in which they lived. From distance to time, our species has used numbers and units to describe each of our experiences on our planet.

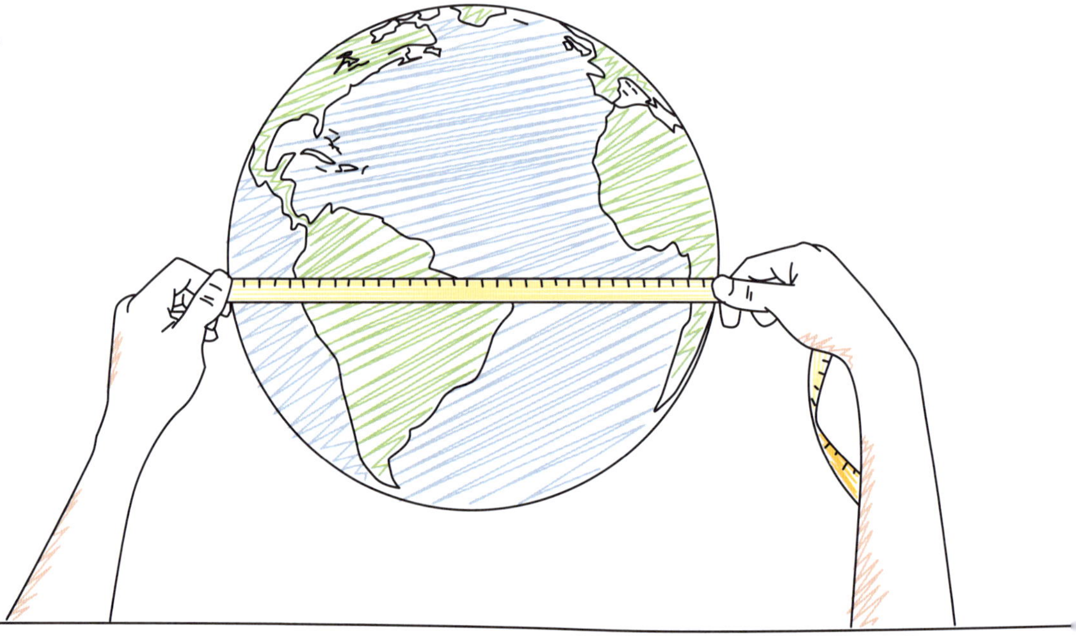

Precision of a measurement depends on how repeatable a certain measurement is from experiment to experiment. If the measurement returns the same value every time an experiment is run, then the measurement is precise; if it is very different each time then it is imprecise.

Accuracy of a measurement tells us how close a measurement is to nature's chosen true value. Two experiments may disagree on a measurement and show it as inaccurate because of unknown differences in their experimental setup. If two experiments measure the same quantity very precisely, but disagree on the value, then one or both experiments are likely to be inaccurate. The true value nature has chosen might lie between the two, or be closer to one experiment than the other. Only more experiments will settle the debate.

Accuracy and precision can be described using the analogy of archery, where the true value is represented by the center bull's-eye. Accurate and precise experiments return the same value, which is close to the true value nature has chosen, meaning all the arrows are in the bull's-eye. Some experiments may not be precise—the arrows are all over the target—but can still be accurate, as the average of the measurements gives close to the true value; the average position of these arrows is the center.

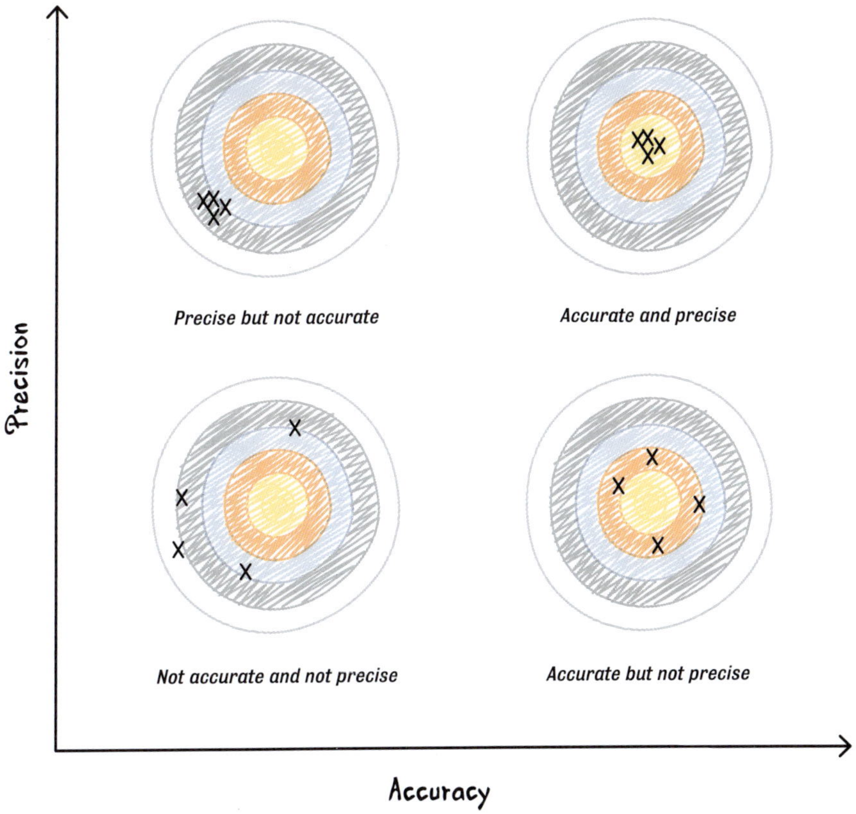

Precision and accuracy

A measurement can be accurate (close to the true value), or precise (measure the same value each time), or a combination of the two.

Some experiments can be precise but not accurate—the arrows are clustered together, but away from the center—such experiments usually have an unaccounted for systematic error. Some experiments are both inaccurate and imprecise.

Errors

Errors place a numerical value on any uncertainty of a measurement that we have taken. It is understood that it is impossible to know something with true certainty, in fact it is a fundamental law of nature (see page 94). There will always be some level of imprecision or inaccuracy. So to be universal and truthful of any measured quantity, we must be honest about how accurate the number we have obtained actually is.

Some errors are **random**, arising from small unpredictable changes in the setup of an experiment that have an effect on the outcome. Repeating an experiment in exactly the same environment and drawing patterns of measurements that represent the average outcome of every experiment can improve such errors. Experiments with uncontrolled random errors are imprecise, but they can become precise if the average values of enough experiments are taken.

Other errors are **systematic** and part of the way in which the experiment is conducted. These errors cannot be improved by repetition. Systematic errors can be improved only by an increased understanding of the experimental environment or increased accuracy of the devices used to take the measurements. Precise experiments that are inaccurate tend to have a shift in measured values due to an unaccounted for systematic error.

If numbers assigned to a measurement are to make sense to another person, we must choose our numbers carefully. Each number must be assigned a unit. **Units** translate each number into a common language that allows a reader to understand what the number means physically in the real world. If someone talked to you for two minutes, you would have some idea of how long that took, because you have an idea of the unit of a minute and its duration in time.

Numbers, units, and errors

When physicists quote any measured value they do so in three parts: first a number defines a magnitude, then an uncertainty is usually quoted as a number before a unit is written to explain what the numbers mean. This man is 1.82 meters tall with an uncertainty of plus or minus 0.01 meters, which means he is truly a height somewhere between 1.81 and 1.83 meters tall according to our measurement.

Units

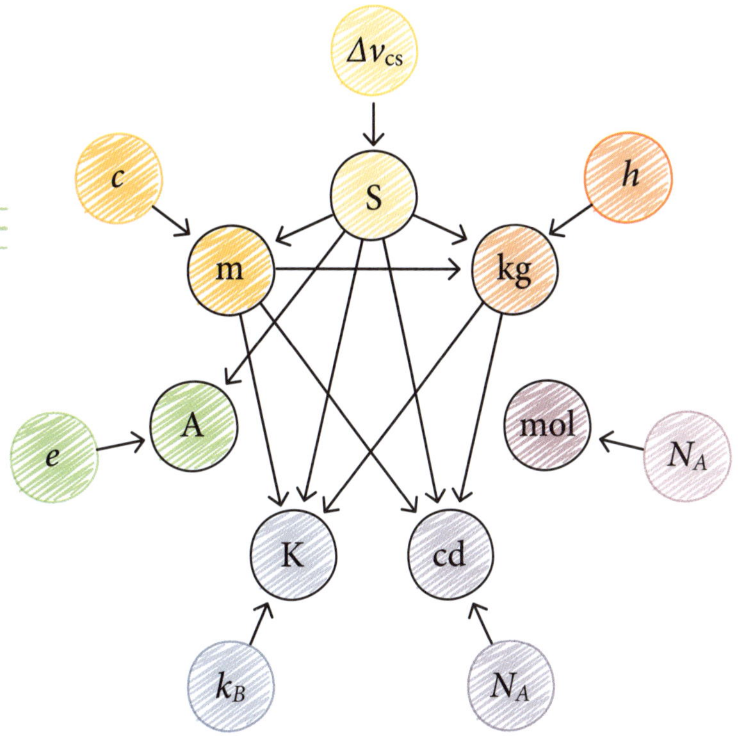

SI units

Each of the base units of the SI are linked to a fundamental constant of nature (around the outside) as well as being linked to one another.

There are various units used by many cultures to measure the world they live in. For example, feet and inches are used for measuring a person's height in the United States, while meters and centimeters are most commonly used in Europe. To avoid confusion, scientists have defined an International System of Units as their common language. These units mean the same across all languages and cultures. As the standard was first laid down in the French language, these are sometimes referred to as SI units from the French *Système International*.

International System of Units

The International System of Units was initially based on the metric system of units, but has since evolved. In 2019, scientists agreed that the units used to define everything in our universe should be based upon a handful of physical constants. **Physical constants** are things that do not change over time and would be the same when measured by any person anywhere in the universe. The speed at which light moves through empty space is a good example of a physical constant, as it does not change wherever or whenever you are measuring it—this is an important factor in **relativity** (see page 140).

Every quantity it is possible to measure in our universe can be assigned a combination of one or more **base units**. There are seven base units in the International System of Units, each represented by their own symbol: the meter *m*, the second *s*, the kilogram *kg*, the mole *mol*, the candela *cd*, the kelvin *K*, and the ampere *A*.

Derived units

All other standard units can be formed using some combination of these seven base units. These are known as derived units. The newton unit of force, with symbol *N*, is a derived unit that is a combination of kilograms multiplied by meters and divided by seconds squared. Derived units can be used to make measured numbers sensible, where they would otherwise be very large or small.

Base units and derived units

Any measurable quantity has an associated unit that tells everyone what a measured value means. Base units are the simplest units from which other more complex derived units can be made. Base units owe their definition to the fundamental constants of nature, while derived units are defined by their combination of base units.

	Quantity	Standard unit	Unit symbol	Base units
Base units	*Time*	*Second*	*s*	*s*
	Distance	*Meter*	*m*	*m*
	Mass	*Kilogram*	*kg*	*kg*
	Amount of substance	*Mole*	*mol*	*mol*
	Luminous intensity	*Candela*	*cd*	*cd*
	Temperature	*Kelvin*	*K*	*K*
	Electric current	*Ampere*	*A*	*A*
Derived units	*Force*	*Newton*	*N*	$kg\ m / s^2$
	Energy	*Joule*	*J*	$kg\ m^2 / s^2$
	Pressure	*Pascal*	*Pa*	$kg / m\ s^2$
	Electrical potential	*Volt*	*V*	$kg\ m^2 / s^3\ A$
	Electrical resistance	*Ohm*	*Ω*	$kg\ m^2 / s^3\ A^2$
	Frequency	*Hertz*	*Hz*	$1 / s$
	Power	*Watt*	*W*	$kg\ m^2 / s^3$
	Electric charge	*Coulomb*	*C*	*A s*

Prefixes

As well as units, scientists often use **prefixes** to assist them when handling very large or small numbers. A prefix may be placed in front of a unit to represent a multiplication by a power of ten. Instead of writing lots of zeros, we replace them with a prefix. Prefixes are usually defined for every difference of one thousand, or 10^3 in shorthand; although there are exceptions, such as centi-, used in centimeters as one-hundredth of a meter.

Big and small

When dealing with scale, scientists use prefixes before SI units. A prefix defines a power of 10 that you would need to multiply the number by in order for it to be in the chosen SI unit, e.g. a millimeter is one-thousandth of a meter.

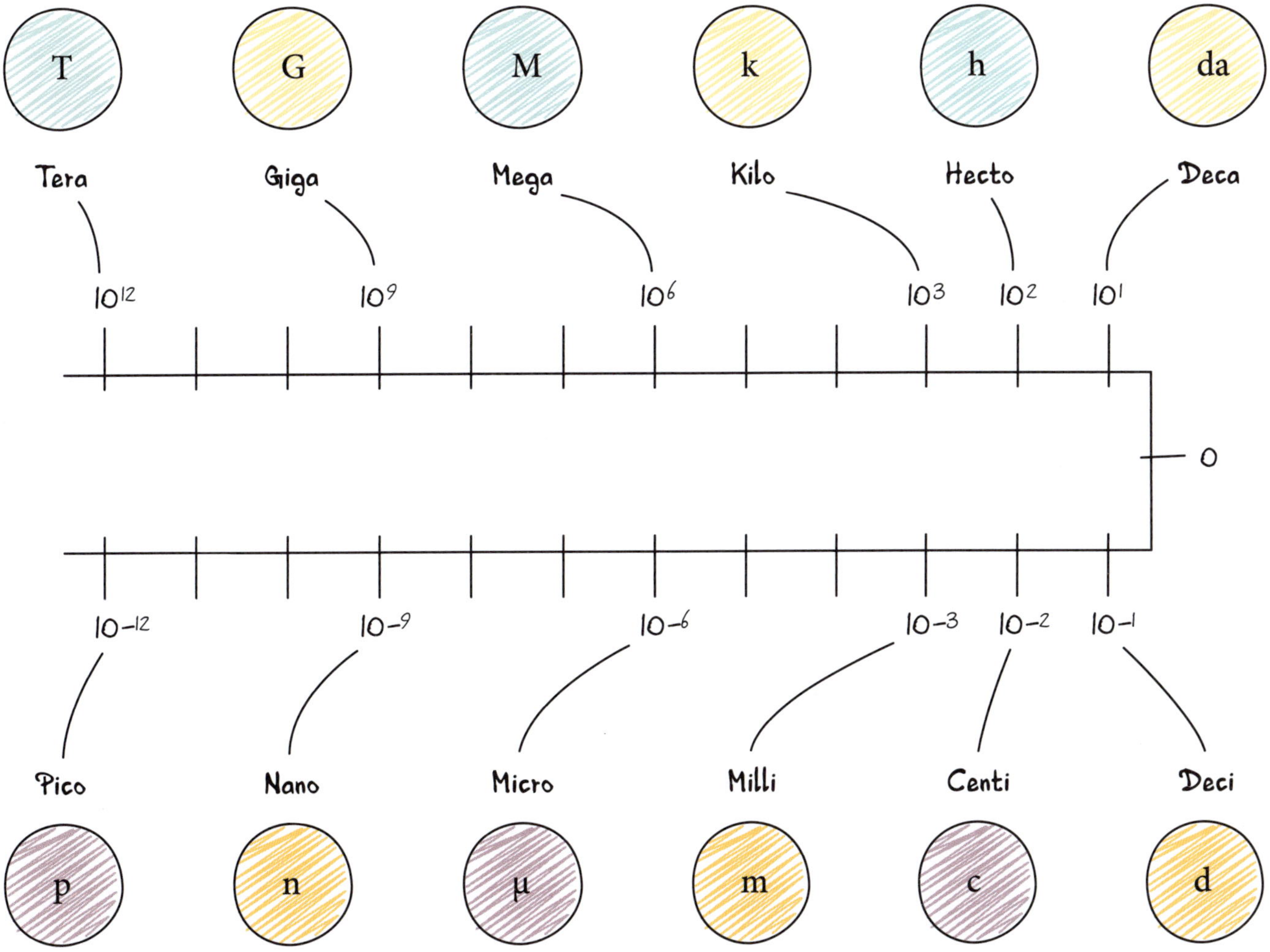

Base units

The **second** is the standard unit of time; it is a base unit given the symbol ***s***. While historically the second was defined by the length of a year on Earth, it is today defined very differently. Today, the second is defined by atomic physics. One second is exactly the time taken for electrons to bounce 9,192,631,770 times between two energy levels in an atom of Cesium-133. This strange number keeps the second at exactly the same magnitude as the old definition.

The base unit of the **meter**, with symbol ***m***, is the international standard for measuring the separation of two objects in space. It was previously defined as one ten-millionth of the distance between the equator and the North Pole on an imaginary line through Paris, France. Today, it is defined by the definition of a second and the ever-constant speed of light in empty space. One meter is the distance traveled by light in empty space in 1/299792458 of a second.

The **kilogram** is the base unit and standard measure of mass; it has the symbol ***kg***. It was first defined as the mass of one liter, or 0.001 meters cubed, of pure water close to its freezing point. This linked the kilogram to the meter and therefore the second. Today, it is defined by the meter, the second, and the Planck constant, h, which has a value set at exactly $6.62607015 \times 10^{-34}$ kilogram meters squared per second ($kg\ m^2/s$). **Mass** can take two different forms, it is either inertial or gravitational in behavior. Mass can determine the size of force required to change the velocity of an object, something known as inertia. Mass can also dictate the size of the gravitational force between two objects with mass.

The **ampere** is the standard base unit of electric current and has the symbol ***A***. It is named after the French electricity pioneer André-Marie Ampère. It was previously defined by the force of attraction felt between two wires carrying electric current. Today, its value is fixed by the constant value of the electric charge of an electron, *e*.

The meridian measure of the meter

The meter was first defined as one ten-millionth of the distance between the North Pole and the equator along the meridian line running through Paris.

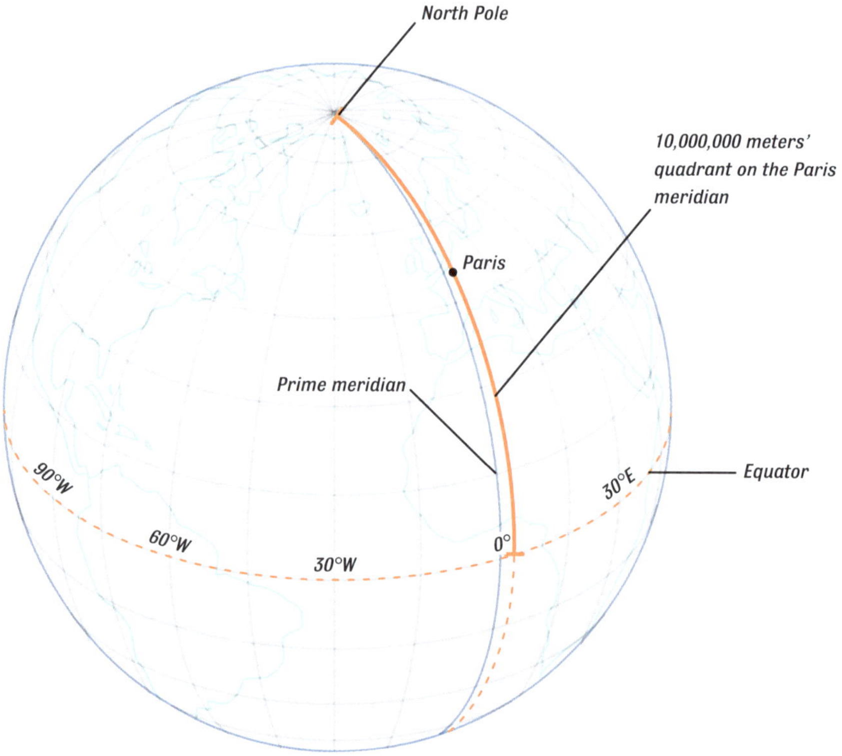

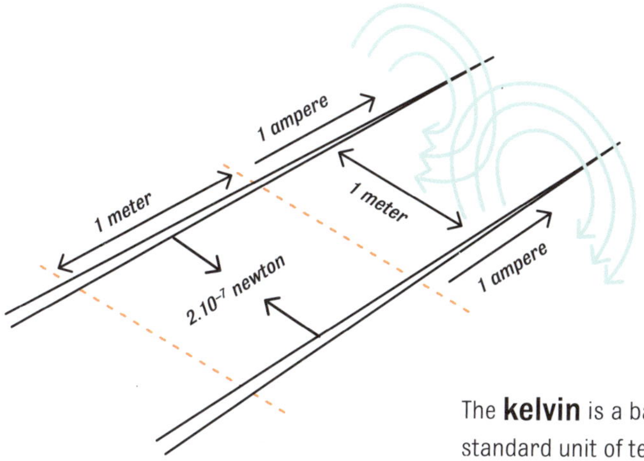

Ampere

Originally, Ampere defined the SI unit of electric current as the current required to produce a force of 2 x10^{-7} Newtons between two one-meter wires placed one meter apart.

Kelvin

One kelvin is equal to 1 degree Celsius, the only difference is their zero point: 0 K is at –273.15°C.

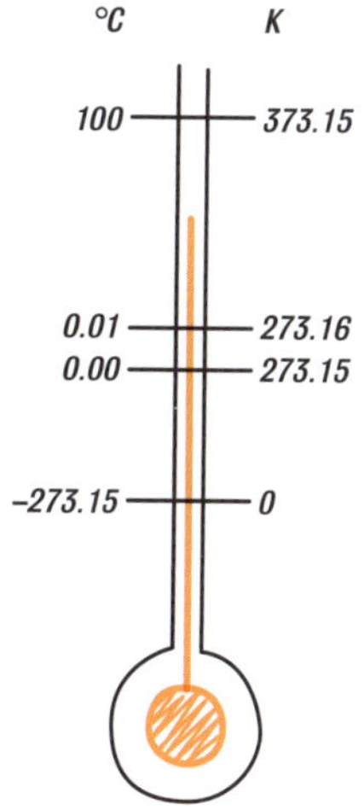

The **mole** defines the amount of a substance in any given sample of a material (see page 69); it is a base unit and has the symbol ***mol***. One mole was previously defined as the amount of a substance that contains as many individual things as there are carbon atoms in a sample of carbon of mass 0.012 kilograms. Today, it is defined entirely by the physical constant known as the Avogadro constant, N_A. One mole is the amount of a substance that contains exactly 6.02214076 × 10^{23} individual things.

The **kelvin** is a base unit and the standard unit of temperature, given the symbol ***K***. It is named after the nineteenth-century Scottish physicist William Thomson, 1st Baron Kelvin. Previously, temperature was measured in degrees Celsius (°C), which was defined as one-hundredth of the temperature difference between pure water freezing and boiling. It was realized that there was an absolute coldest temperature in nature of –273.15°C, and so the new Kelvin scale was defined with this as its zero point, but with each unit equal in size to a Celsius degree. Today, the definitions of the second, meter, and kilogram, along with Boltzmann's constant, k, fix the definition of the kelvin. Boltzmann's constant is fixed at 1.380649×10^{-23} kilograms meters squared per second squared per kelvin.

Candela

The candela is the standard unit of light intensity measuring a certain wavelength of green light.

The **candela** is the base unit and standard of measuring the luminous intensity of light in a given direction; it has the symbol ***cd***. It was previously defined by the amount of light emitted by a standard type of candle, and the sensitivity of the human eye to the light. Today, it is defined by a constant known as the luminous efficacy K_{cd} of certain green light, as well as the definitions of the kilogram, meter, and second.

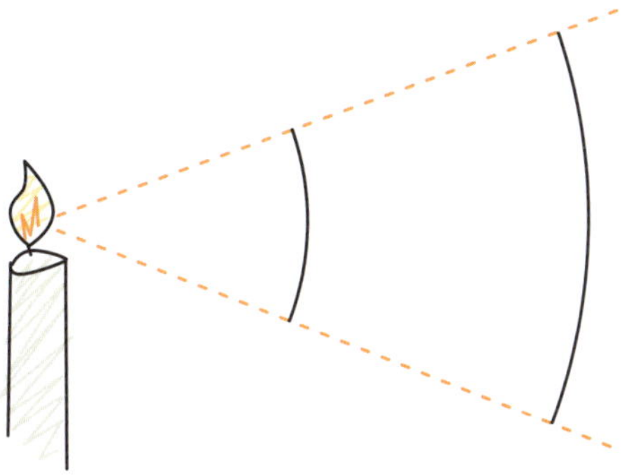

Space

Space is the vast expanse in which all things in our universe exist and move. It was created at the Big Bang at the beginning of the universe, along with time and huge sums of energy. It is represented in mathematics by coordinates and shape, most commonly flat with three dimensions: a height, a width, and a length.

An object's **position** is its location in space. It is usually represented by three numbers that define the location against another common reference position. In most cases, an origin is chosen to be a point defined as zero in all three dimensions of space.

Distance is a measure of how far something travels through space no matter the direction; represented by a dashed red line in the diagram below.

Distance traveled in a car is usually greater than the displacement between two points because of winding roads. The Romans tried to minimize the difference between the two by building roads as straight as possible.

Displacement is a measure of the separation between two positions in space, for example before and after an object has moved. Unlike distance, direction is an important part of the displacement. The red arrow shows the displacement as the object moves from left to right.

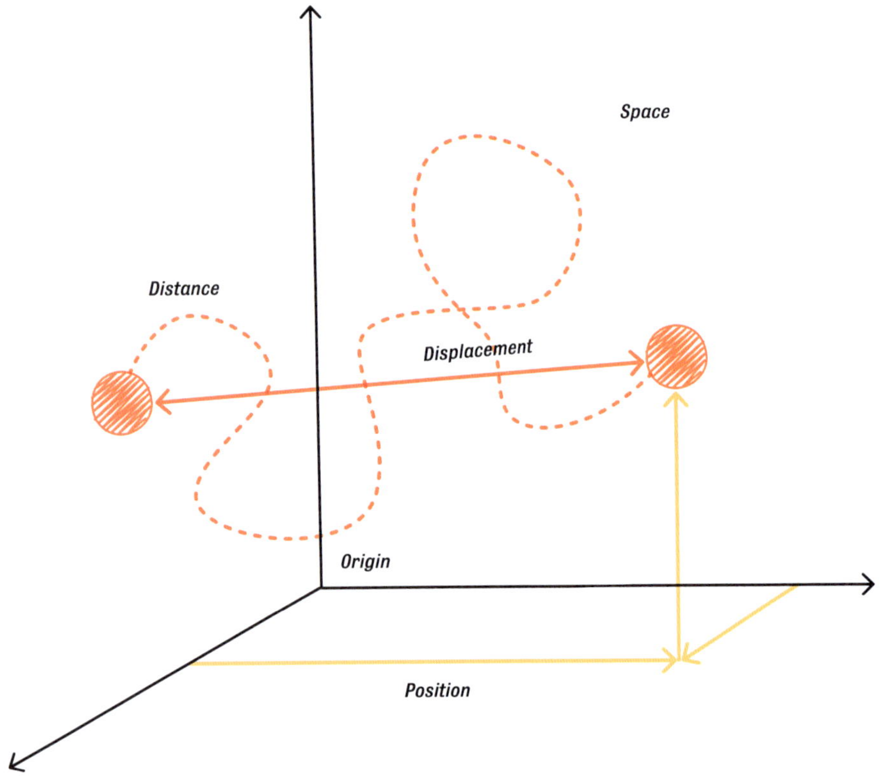

Combination of space, position, distance, and displacement

This diagram shows the relationship between position, distance, and displacement. Position is a single point in space, defined by three coordinates. Distance is the cumulative change in the position of an object as it moves through space no matter the directions. Displacement is a measure of the distance and direction following a straight line between any two points in space.

Scalar Quantities

Distance and speed are examples of **scalar quantities** that have a size but no particular orientation or direction in space. If an object moved a distance of 50 meters from its original position, we would not know its new position because there are many (infinite in fact) locations that satisfy a distance of 50 meters away.

Displacement, position, and velocity are **vector** quantities that not only have a size but also a direction associated with them. If we said that an object was displaced by 50 meters due north from its original position, then we would know the new position of the object exactly.

Scalar	Vector
Time	*Position*
Mass	*Velocity*
Temperature	*Acceleration*
Energy	*Force*
Distance	*Momentum*
Speed	*Jerk*
Mole	*Force field strength*
Luminosity	*Electric current*

Time enables things that exist within space to change. In the theory of relativity, space and time are not separate things, but instead are part of a four-dimensional fabric of space-time. Our position in the universe is then not just our location in space but also our moment in time. Time is a scalar as we can only travel through it in one direction.

Kinematics is the name given to the area of physics that looks at how an object's position changes with time.

Scalar and vector quantities

Some measured quantities only have a magnitude, these are known as scalar quantities. Other quantities have a specific direction in space as well as a magnitude, these are called vectors.

Speed is a measure of the rate at which an object travels a given distance. Rate here refers to the change of something each second. Speed is therefore calculated as the distance traveled divided by the time taken. Speed has no information about the direction the object has moved, and so it is a scalar quantity. For instance, we can say that an object is traveling at a speed of 20 meters per second. One second later this object will have moved a distance of 20 meters, but we will not know its new position, only that it is 20 meters away from where it started.

Velocity is the measure of the rate of change of position in a particular direction. It is calculated as the displacement of an object divided by the time that has passed. As it has information about the direction an object moves, it is a vector quantity. Stating that an object is moving with a velocity of 20 meters per second due east would mean that we would know the exact position of the object one, two, or many seconds later, providing that the velocity of the object does not change.

The **momentum** of an object is the product (multiplication) of an object's velocity and its mass. Momentum is one of a few things that seem to be conserved: it is the same before and after an event provided no forces were present. In the event that two objects collide, the sum of each of their momenta before the collision will always equal the sum of their momenta afterward. The velocities of the two objects may have changed dramatically, one may have sped up while the other slowed down, but the momenta does not change. This fact is used in many areas of physics, from the investigation of galaxies merging to the measurement of tiny, subatomic particles.

A change in direction or speed of an object is the result of **acceleration**. Acceleration is a measure of the rate of change of velocity; the difference in velocity divided by the time to change it. Accelerations may also change with time and the rate of change of acceleration is called **jerk**. Jerk is an important factor in engineering moving machines. **Snap** is the rate of change of jerk, **crackle** the rate of change of snap, and **pop** the rate of change of crackle. These take their name from cartoon characters used to advertise a popular breakfast cereal and have little use in physics or engineering.

Speed and velocity tell us about the **linear motion** of objects: how an object moves along straight lines in space. If acceleration is along the direction an object is moving, then its effect is only to change its speed in that linear direction.

If an acceleration of an object only acts to change the direction an object is moving, then it no longer moves in a straight line. If an acceleration remains at a constant value, and always at right angles to an object's motion, then an object will move in a circle. In this **circular motion**, an object's speed can remain constant, but its velocity is ever changing, because its direction is ever changing as it bends around a circle. Motion around a circle is described much in the same way as linear motion, but instead of a displacement change in position we consider a change in angle. All linear motion quantities have angular quantities that are defined in the same way but with position replaced with angle.

Circular motion

Motion in which the speed remains constant but the direction continually changes can be described as circular motion. The laws of circular motion are identical to the laws of linear motion, but with a translation between the change of position and the change of angle around a central point.

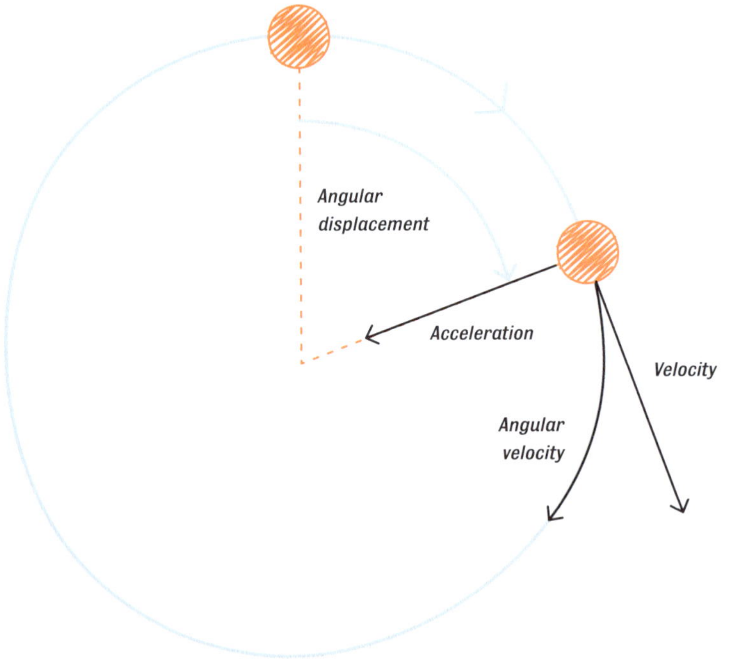

The change in angle of an object when moving around a circle is known as the **angular displacement**.

Angular velocity is the rate of change of angle in circular motion; it is a vector as it also has a direction (clockwise or anticlockwise) associated with it. **Angular acceleration** is the rate of change of angular velocity.

The **moment of inertia** is the circular motion version of mass. It is a measure of how easy or difficult it is to change the angular motion of an object. It is related to the object's mass and its position in relation to the center of the circle it is moving around.

Angular momentum is the product of an object's angular velocity and its moment of inertia. Like momentum in linear motion, angular momentum is a conserved quantity, taking the same value before and after an event. It is the reason the Earth spins on its axis to give us the passing of days; the Earth possesses angular momentum inherited from the disc of rocky material moving in circles around the Sun out of which it formed 4.5 billion years ago.

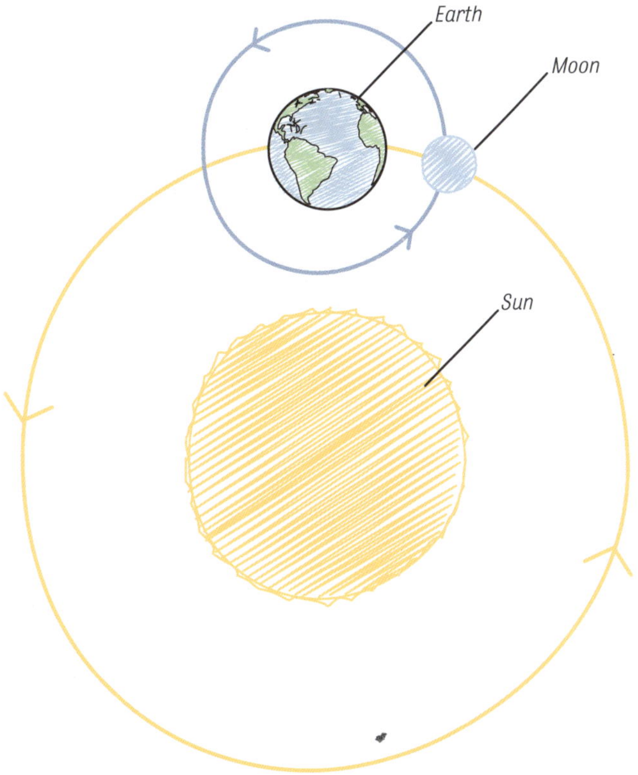

Experiments allow scientists to determine the behavior of nature. Units provide a common language with which scientists compare their experimental results. Discussions about different results allowed early scientists to identify links between the motion of objects. These are the basic building blocks from which the rest of the science of physics is built, and allows humans to make sense of the cosmos.

Spinning Earth

Just like linear momentum, angular momentum in circular motion is conserved. This is the reason that the Earth and all the planets orbit the Sun in the same direction, as they were all formed from the same rotating disk of material 4.5 billion years ago.

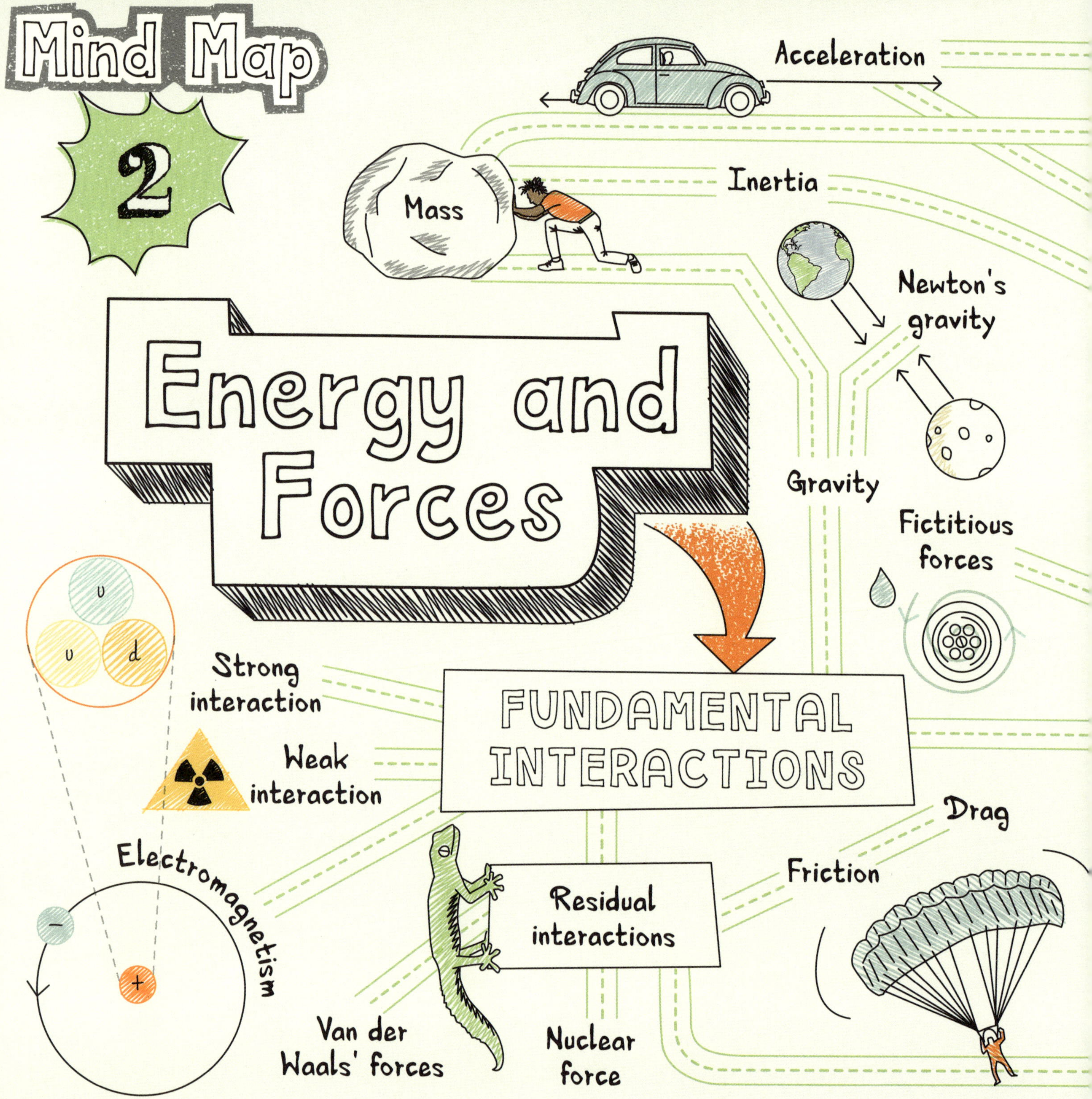
Mind Map
2
Energy and Forces
FUNDAMENTAL INTERACTIONS
Acceleration
Mass
Inertia
Newton's gravity
Gravity
Fictitious forces
Strong interaction
u
u
d
Weak interaction
Electromagnetism
−
+
Drag
Friction
Residual interactions
Van der Waals' forces
Nuclear force

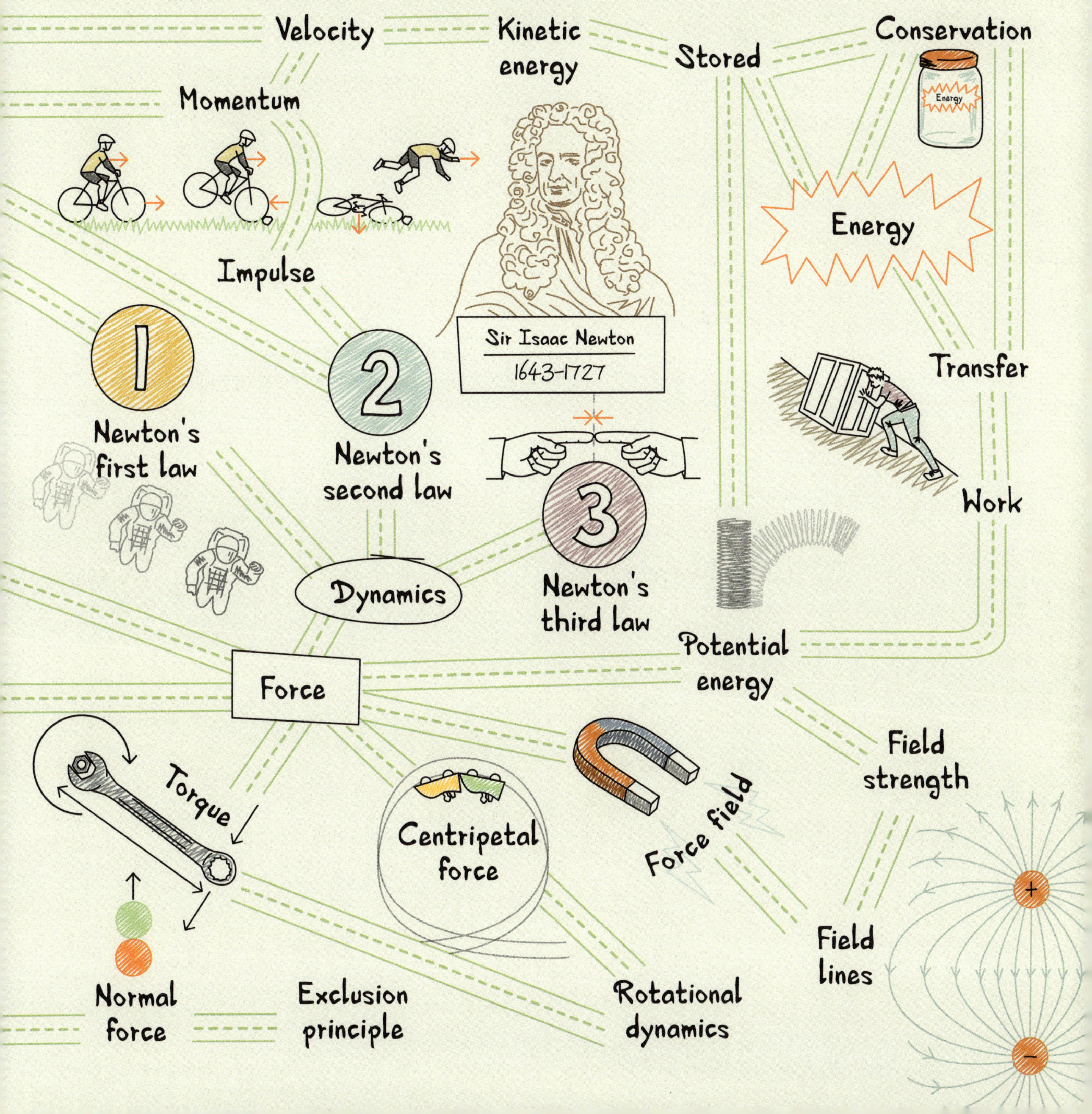
Velocity
Kinetic energy
Stored
Conservation
Energy
Momentum
Impulse
Energy
Sir Isaac Newton
1643–1727
Newton's first law
Newton's second law
Newton's third law
Transfer
Work
Dynamics
Potential energy
Force
Torque
Centripetal force
Force field
Field strength
Field lines
Normal force
Exclusion principle
Rotational dynamics
+
−

Fundamental Interactions

There seem to be four fundamental interactions that occur between any two or more objects that dictate all that happens in the universe. These four interactions—electromagnetism, strong, weak, and gravity—are fundamental because there is no deeper explanation to the source of the interaction other than that it happens. If an object possesses a particular property, then it can interact with other particles with similar properties. For example, all objects that have mass can interact with each other through gravity, and objects with electric charge interact through electromagnetism.

We do not know why there are only four fundamental interactions; their existence has been discovered from experiments. In advanced theories of our universe, it is thought that all four interactions are related to each other at a deeper level. Here, it is thought that they unite to become one indistinguishable force at very high energies, such as those shortly after the Big Bang (see page 124). Experiments have been unable to prove or disprove this idea. At moderately high energies, however, it has been shown that the electromagnetic and weak interactions become indistinguishable, forming one electroweak interaction.

A **force** is one type of interaction that can occur between any two objects, one that changes the motion of an object if unopposed by another force. Once all forces acting in all directions upon an object are taken into account, any force left over is called the resultant force. An overall resultant force will alter the speed or direction of an object. Forces can also bind objects together to form more complex structures, such as protons, atoms, and molecules.

Force

Forces are vectors that add together to produce a single resultant force. An object will only accelerate if there is a zero resultant force, e.g. if a push is larger than a frictional force.

Electromagnetism

The fundamental interaction of electromagnetism imposes forces upon objects that have an electric charge. The force can be attractive, pulling two objects with opposite charges together, or repulsive, pushing two objects with like charges apart. This interaction is infinite in its range of influence, although the force that is felt weakens dramatically with distance. Electromagnetism is responsible for shaping atoms, molecules and, by extension, life on Earth. It is also responsible for the wide range of technology we use every day, forming the basis of electronic circuits (see Mind Map 4).

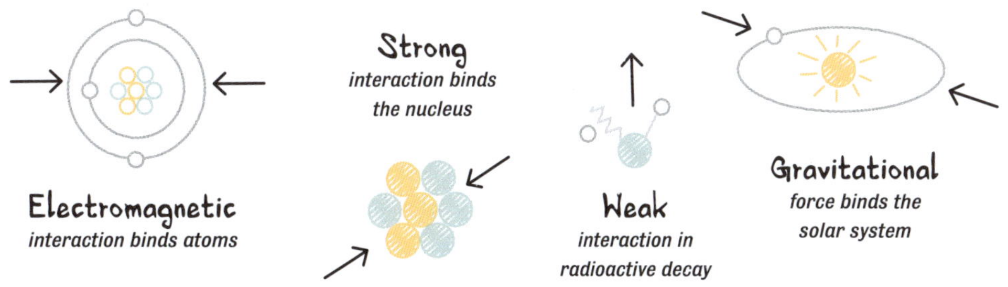

Strong and weak interactions

The **strong interaction** is a fundamental interaction that is strictly contained inside an atom, so we do not experience it directly. Despite its tiny range of influence, it's the strongest of all known interactions and the one to which all other interactions are compared. The strength of the strong interaction does not diminish with distance; it remains just as strong over its range of influence. It binds quark particles together to build the particles from which atoms are made—protons and neutrons.

The **weak interaction** is unlike the other fundamental interactions. It is not a force, it does not attract or repel, but instead brings about transformation. Like the strong interaction, it has no influence outside of the atom. Because of this, we do not experience it directly ourselves, day-to-day. Particles that build to make atoms can be changed by the weak interaction from one type to another. Radioactive beta decay is a result of the weak interaction at work.

Interaction	Range in meters	Strength relative to the strong interaction
Electromagnetic	*Infinite*	*1/137*
Gravitational	*Infinite*	$6 X 0^{-39}$
Weak interaction	10^{-17}	0^{-5}
Strong interaction	10^{-15}	*1*

Residual interactions

A residual interaction is something that can be explained by one or more fundamental interactions. They usually arise when many objects are each interacting with each other. The residual interaction can be thought of like a resultant force; once all interactions are balanced, there might be a small amount left over.

Van der Waals' forces are a group of residual interactions that result in force between molecules. They are named after the Dutch scientist Johannes Diderik van der Waals. Molecules are made from a collection of atoms bound together by chemical bonds. Molecules are electrically neutral, as they contain equal numbers of positive atomic nuclei and negatively charged electrons. At any one point in time, however, these electrically charged particles might be unevenly distributed, making one part of a molecule slightly positive and the other slightly negative. This small imbalance in electric charge can result in forces between the molecules. It is an echo, a residual, of the underlying fundamental force of electromagnetism that keeps the molecule together.

The **nuclear force** binds proton and neutron particles together to form the nucleus of an atom. It is a residual of the strong interaction that binds quark particles together to make protons and neutrons. Just like the residual electromagnetic for creating van der Waals forces between molecules, residual strong interactions produce an attractive force binding protons and neutrons together. Without the nuclear force there would be no nucleus to form atoms with, and therefore no us.

The **normal force** is the reason things feel solid; it is a reaction to an attempt to push two objects through each other. It is a combination of the electromagnetic interaction, with the electrons in atoms repelling each other, and the quantum physics **exclusion principle**, stating that no two electrons can be found in the same place. Without both of these present, the things we sit on and touch would not feel so solid.

Over 99% of an atom is empty space, in which electrons roam freely, surrounding a tiny, central nucleus. There is plenty of space for the particles in one atom to pass through another, like tennis- racket strings through air. But these two interactions prevent this from happening, making atoms seem solid to other atoms. This results in a normal force that acts directly upward from any surface an object pushes against.

Like the normal force, **friction** is a direct result of the electromagnetic interaction combined with the quantum exclusion principle. Instead of producing a force directly out from a surface, it produces a force that opposes movement along a surface. This is because no surface is truly smooth, but instead looks like a mountain range if you zoom in close enough. This means that when an object is moved, the surface will push back against the movement.

Van der Waals' forces

Van Der Waals' forces arise from a non-uniform distribution of electric charge within an object. Depending on the underlying structure of the object, these forces can be attractive or repulsive. Geckos use a form of these forces to stick to surfaces.

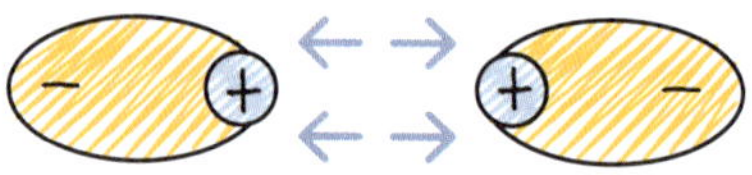

Repulsion

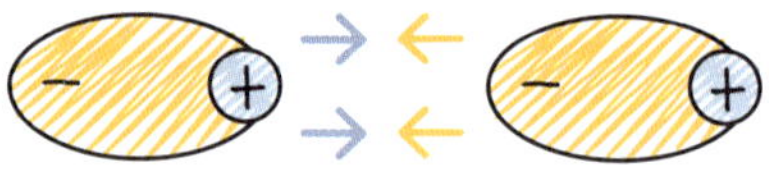

Attraction

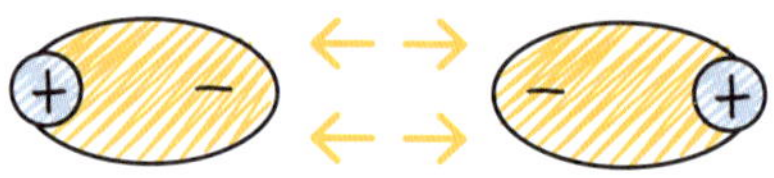

Repulsion

Normal force and friction

Frictional forces arise from the interlocking of two surfaces at the microscopic scale. If there is a larger, normal contact force between the surfaces then this leads to a greater interlocking and a larger component of frictional force, which opposes any motion.

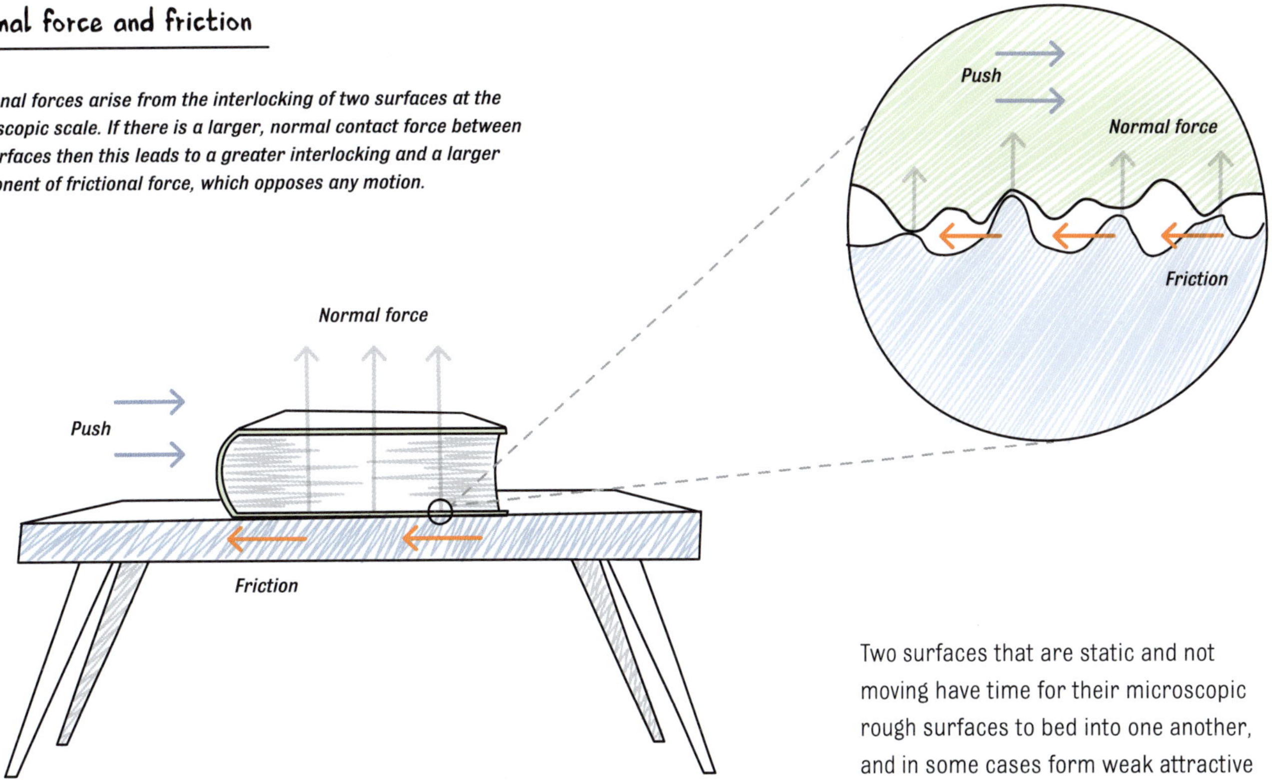

Friction is a small portion of the normal force acting on the object. The amount of normal force that is experienced as friction depends upon the surface. Surfaces that resist motion greatly are said to have a high coefficient of friction, and large percentages of the normal force are translated into friction. Lubricants reduce friction by adding a layer of material that fills in the craggy mountain range on the surface of the two objects. This allows the two surfaces to slide over each other more easily.

There are two types of friction usually experienced by any two surfaces: static and kinetic. Static friction is the frictional force that must be overcome to first set two surfaces in motion over one another. Kinetic friction is the frictional force experienced by two surfaces that are already in motion over one another.

Two surfaces that are static and not moving have time for their microscopic rough surfaces to bed into one another, and in some cases form weak attractive bonds. For this reason, static friction is almost always greater than kinetic friction, as many more microscopic forces must be overcome. Once moving, the two surfaces have less time to bed into one another or form weak bonds, and so kinetic friction is less than static friction. This is the reason why it is often better to keep something in motion, as you only have to overcome a smaller kinetic friction.

Drag is a special type of friction that produces a force that opposes the movement of an object through a fluid—a gas or a liquid. Different forms of drag arise from different features of an object moving through the fluid. Form drag comes from the shape of an object and the area facing the direction of motion—the larger the area, the greater the form drag—this is how parachutes work. Other forms of drag come from the friction between fluids moving over the surface of the object and are reduced by changing the way the fluid moves over the surface of the object. Golf balls have dimples on them to create a layer of turbulent air that reduces drag, smoother balls would not fly as far.

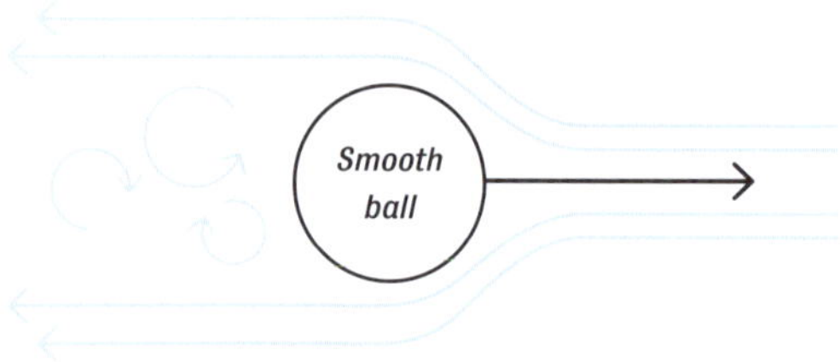

Air flows in a smooth and continuous laminar way over a smooth ball, ensuring drag is felt across the entire surface

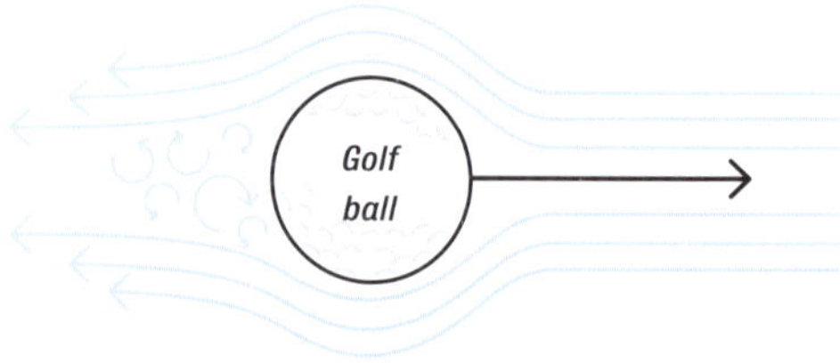

Dimples on a golf ball break up the air flowing over the surface, causing turbulence, and reducing the drag felt

Gravity

Gravity is the weakest of all four fundamental interactions. It requires huge masses, the size of planets and stars, to produce a force of any real influence. Despite its weakness, it is ever prevalent in our lives because it can be felt infinitely far away, right across the cosmos. Gravitational interaction produces an always-attractive force, which pulls together any two objects with gravitational mass.

Gravitational mass is subtly different to inertial mass, which appears in Newton's laws of motion. Gravitational mass can be thought of like the charge of the gravitational force, in the same way electric charge defines the strength of electromagnetic interactions. Gravitational mass is the property of an object that determines how strongly it interacts with other massive objects through gravity. Inertial mass on the other hand is a property that determines how difficult it is to change an object's motion with a force. As far as we can tell, the two masses are equivalent (see page 145).

Laminar and turbulent

Flow of a fluid over a surface can be changed by the shape of the surface to produce laminar or turbulent flow.

Newton's gravity states the relationship between the force two objects feel, the gravitational mass of the objects and the distance between them. The force is related to the product of the two masses, so the larger the masses of the objects, the larger the force of attraction between them. The force is also increased by reducing the distance between the objects—the closer two masses are, the larger the force between them. In fact, the force is related to the inverse of the distance squared. This means that halving the distance between two massive objects actually increases the force by a factor of four.

Newton's gravity

Two bodies each with gravitational mass will attract each other with an equal force that is dependent upon the product of their masses divided by the square of the distance between them.

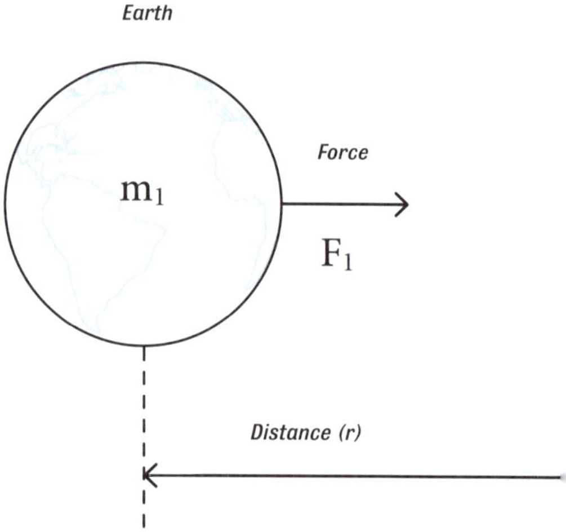

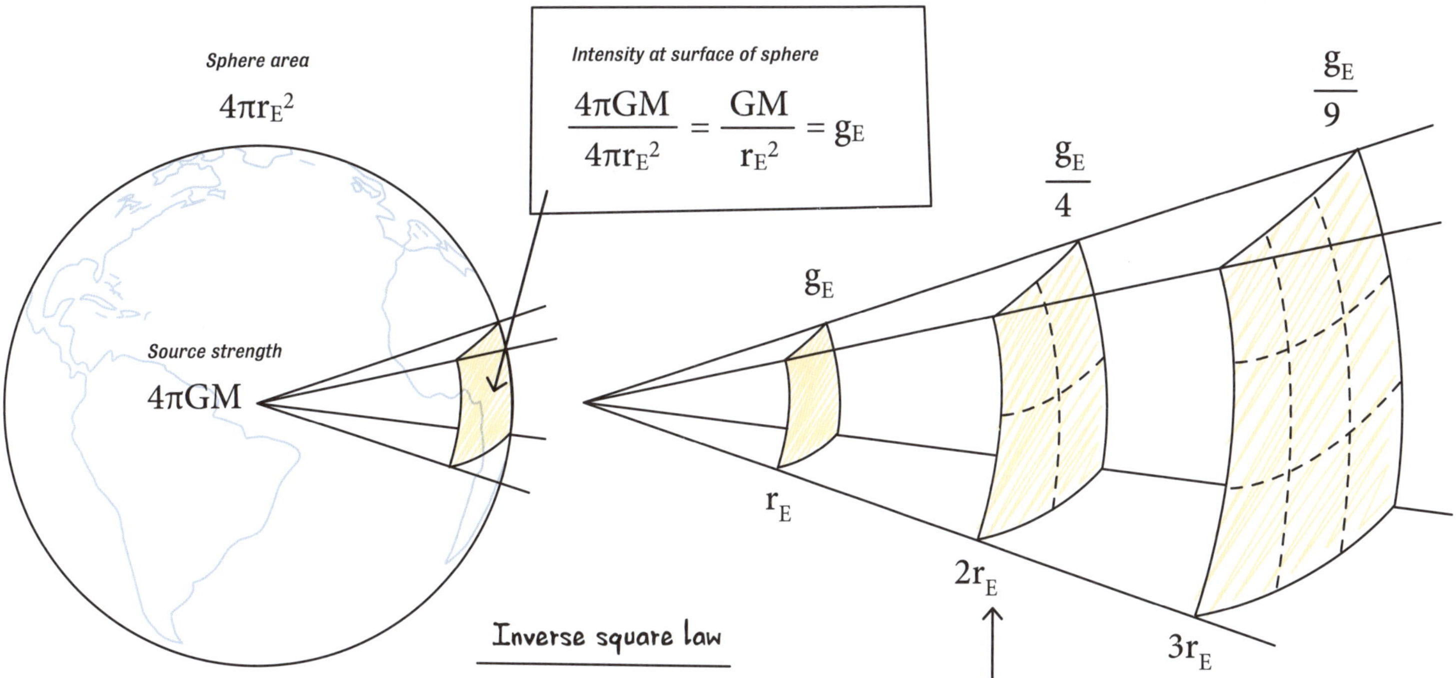

Inverse square law

The gravitational field twice as far from the source is spread over four times the area, hence one-fourth the intensity.

The subscript E indicates values at the surface of the Earth

$$F_1 = F_2 = G\frac{m_1 \times m_2}{r^2}$$

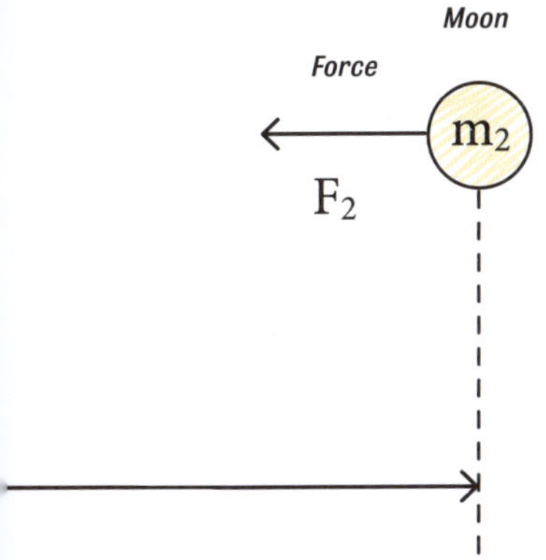

A **force field** is an imaginary and invisible region of space surrounding an object, within which the object is able to exert a force on other objects. A field is not physically real but a mathematical tool that helps to explain what is observed in experiments. The type of force field around an object depends upon the properties of that object. Something with an electric charge will be surrounded by an electric field. If a second object with an electric charge wanders into this field, then it will experience a force through the electromagnetic interaction. For example, a negative electrically charged object possesses an electric field around it that attracts any positively charged particle and repels any negatively charged particle that passes through it. Each fundamental interaction has a field associated with it. These fields stretch out as far as each force has an influence. For gravity and electromagnetism, this is all the way to infinity. Strong and weak force fields, however, do not extend beyond the nucleus of an atom.

Fields

Fields are imagined as a collection of **field lines**, also called flux, which provide a graphical way of representing the strength and direction of the force a passing object would feel if it entered the field. Just like the field, field lines are a made-up concept, although we can get a picture of what field lines might look like by sprinkling iron filings around a bar magnet. Field lines tell us how strong the force that might be felt is at every point in the field.

Force fields

The density of field lines represent the strength of a force around an object: the more densely packed, the stronger the force. Field lines also represent the direction a force will act.

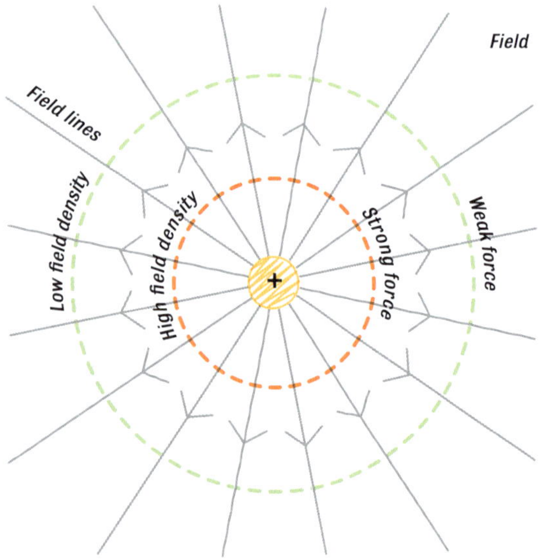

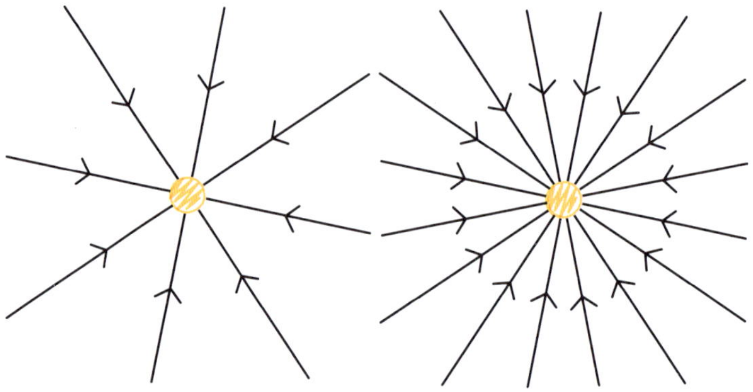

Field strength

Comparison of the field lines on a -1 (above left) and -2 charge (above right).

The strength of a force at any given point in the field is given by the **field strength**. Areas closely packed with field lines, reflecting a high field density, are regions of space where the force would be felt strongest. Areas where the lines are widely spaced apart, reflecting low field density, are regions of space where the force is weakest. An object's maximum field strength depends upon their properties. An object with double the electric charge of another would have twice the density of electric field lines at any distance from the object.

The deeper explanation for forces acting on objects is explained in physics with another imaginary concept called **energy**. Energy is an abstract idea that can't be seen or detected directly, but we do see the effect it has on things when it is transferred from one place to another. Despite the fact it is imaginary, energy is a powerful idea that is important in every field of physics.

Energy is like a force field, a mathematical idea that doesn't physically exist. We cannot hold energy or see it directly, only the changes in things when energy is transferred. Energy is like **momentum**, a conserved quantity in nature. The amount we start any event with will always equal the amount we end with. It can never be created or destroyed, but can be transferred into different forms. If we can determine the energy of a group of objects before an event has happened, then we know they will have the same energy afterward. The event, whatever it was, will have transferred energy, so that afterward it is stored in different ways and shared out differently across the objects. Taking this law of **conservation** to the extreme tells us that all of the energy in our universe today came from one place, the Big Bang. No extra energy has been made and none of it lost since the start of time, it has only been shared out among different forms.

Work is the **transfer** of energy by a force, from one store to another or one object to another. If an object is said to have done work, then it has transferred energy to another object by exerting a force upon that object. We say that this second object has had work done to it, as energy was transferred to the object. The force changes the velocity or position within a force field of both objects.

Conservation of energy

Any closed system will always have the same energy at all times, no matter what processes go on. Energy will be converted into different forms, but the total when added together will be constant.

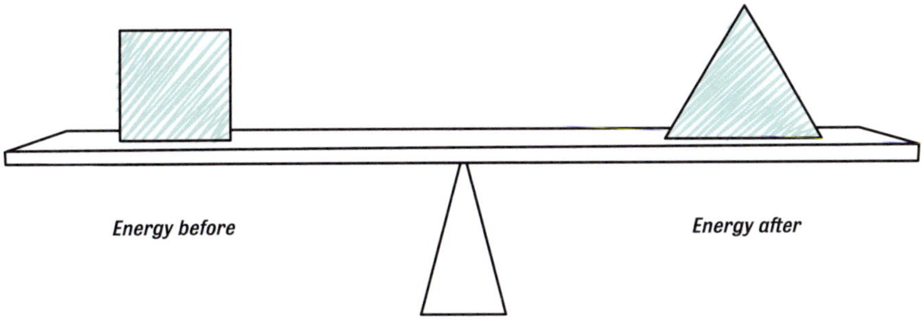

Transferring energy

Waves are one way energy is transferred. While we can see a water wave, we cannot directly see the energy it has. The true energy of a wave can be seen when a wave hits land.

Energy can be transferred between different stores and different objects in a number of ways. An applied force, transfer of a wave, or the exchange of heat are all methods of energy transfer between objects.

Energy can be **stored** in two distinct ways, either in the position of an object within a force field, or in the motion of an object. It is evident that energy is stored in an object if it is able to do work and energy is transferred from the object, or if work is done to it and energy is transferred to the object.

Newton's Laws of Motion

Dynamics is the name given to the area of physics that deals with the way forces affect the motion of everyday objects. **Sir Isaac Newton** first laid down all the main ideas relating to **dynamics** in his three laws of motion.

Newton's first law of motion states that any object will remain in the same linear motion unless acted upon by some force. This means that if an object is stationary (not moving) it will forever remain that way unless a resultant force acts upon it. If an object is moving with a certain velocity then it will continue moving at that velocity, with the same speed and straight-line direction, until a force acts upon it.

A ball remains stationary if there is no resultant force acting upon it

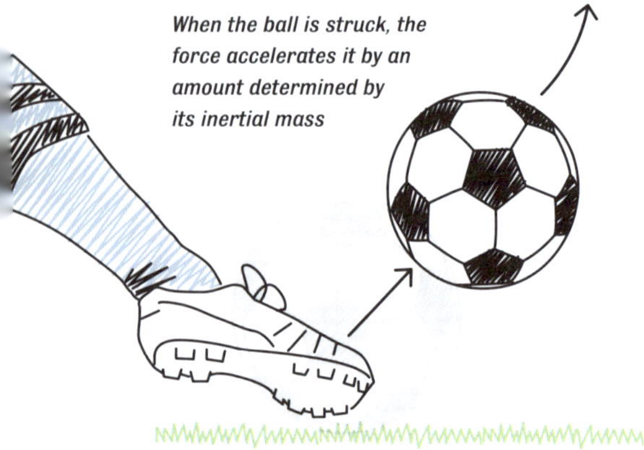

When the ball is struck, the force accelerates it by an amount determined by its inertial mass

Motion of different objects is affected differently when a force is applied. The measure of how easy or difficult it is to change an object's motion is known as **inertia**. In Newton's laws of motion, the **mass** of an object is directly related to its inertia, as it is the mass that dictates by how much an object's motion changes when a force is applied. Objects with a large mass require larger forces to change their movement than smaller objects, because a large mass means a large inertia—a large resistance to changing its movement when a force is applied.

Newton's first law

An object will remain at constant velocity unless a resultant force acts upon it.

Newton's second law of motion links the force applied to an object with an object's inertia and its change in motion. The relationship can be stated in two ways. Traditionally, the applied force is equated to the product of an object's mass and acceleration, $F = ma$. The second way of stating Newton's second law is the one he chose to write originally in his *Principia*—the force is equal to the rate of change of momentum. Put another way, the average force equals the change in momentum Δp divided by the time t that the force is applied for.

Modern cars make use of Newton's second law to keep us safe. For any given car driving at any given speed, there is a fixed momentum change that has to occur to bring the car to a stop. The only thing that can be changed is the time over which the impact between two cars takes place. If the impact is longer, then the force of the impact will be reduced. Modern cars increase the impact time by crumpling during a collision, reducing the force of impact and protecting the occupants of the cars.

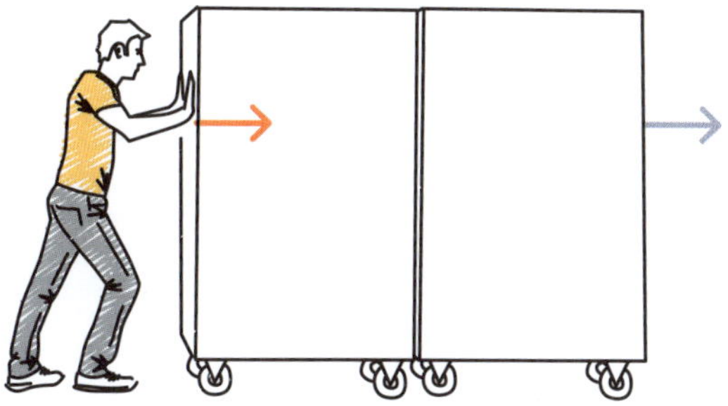

Applying a small force to a large mass produces a tiny acceleration

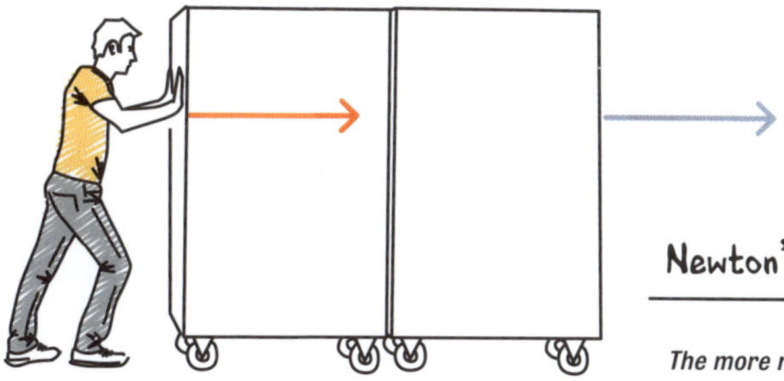

Applying a large force to a large mass produces a small acceleration

Newton's second law

The more massive an object is the larger the force required to produce a certain acceleration. The less massive an object is the greater an acceleration will occur for the same force.

$$F = ma$$

Applying a small force to a small mass will produce a small acceleration

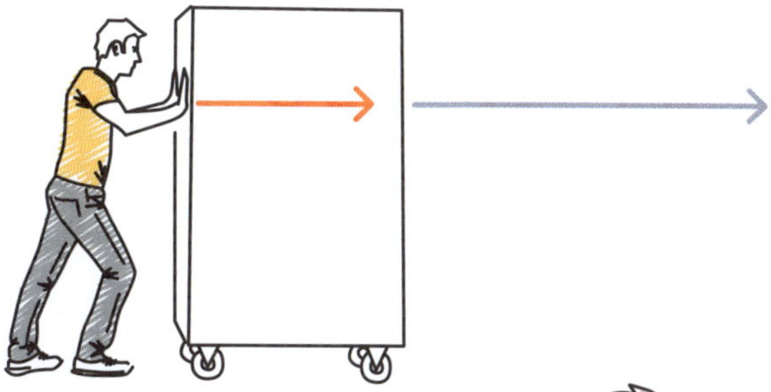

Applying a large force to a small mass will produce a large acceleration

Newton's third law tells us about the symmetry of force experienced when two objects interact. If an interaction generates a force between two objects, then the force is felt equally by each object but in opposite directions. If two objects are attracted to each other, then each object pulls on the other with equal force; there is not just one object pulling on the other, they both pull toward each other equally. We often think of the Earth being pulled toward the Sun, but the Sun is also pulled toward the Earth with exactly the same size of force. Also, if we fall, gravity is pulling the Earth toward us with exactly the same force as we are being pulled toward the Earth. The reason we don't think of the Earth being pulled toward us is because of the huge inertia of the Earth. Its mass is so large that the force produces only a tiny acceleration. As we have a much smaller inertia, our motion is dramatically affected as we accelerate greatly. In truth, the Earth is accelerating toward us because of an equal pull, but the acceleration is so small that it is undetectable.

Newton's third law

Every force acting on an object has an equal and opposite force that acts upon another object.

Kinetic and potential energy

Kinetic energy is the energy stored in the speed of an object. The faster an object is moving, the greater its kinetic energy. Kinetic energy stored in an object can be changed by a force acting upon it, or if it exerts a force upon something else. Both of these scenarios can result in a change of speed and therefore **kinetic energy**.

Potential energy is the energy that can potentially be transferred if an object is moved between different positions in a force field. An object generally has higher potential energy in a region of low field strength and low potential energy in a region of high field strength. Moving from a region of low field strength to high field strength transfers potential energy into kinetic energy. This is evident when lifting something up on Earth and then dropping it. Lifting the object takes it from an area of high field strength to lower field strength, and this increases the potential energy stored. When the object is then dropped, this potential energy is transferred into kinetic energy as it falls from an area of low field strength to higher field strength. The higher an object is lifted, the greater the change in field strength, and, therefore, the potential energy stored. In full mathematical language, forces that an object feels are related to the gradient of the potential energy.

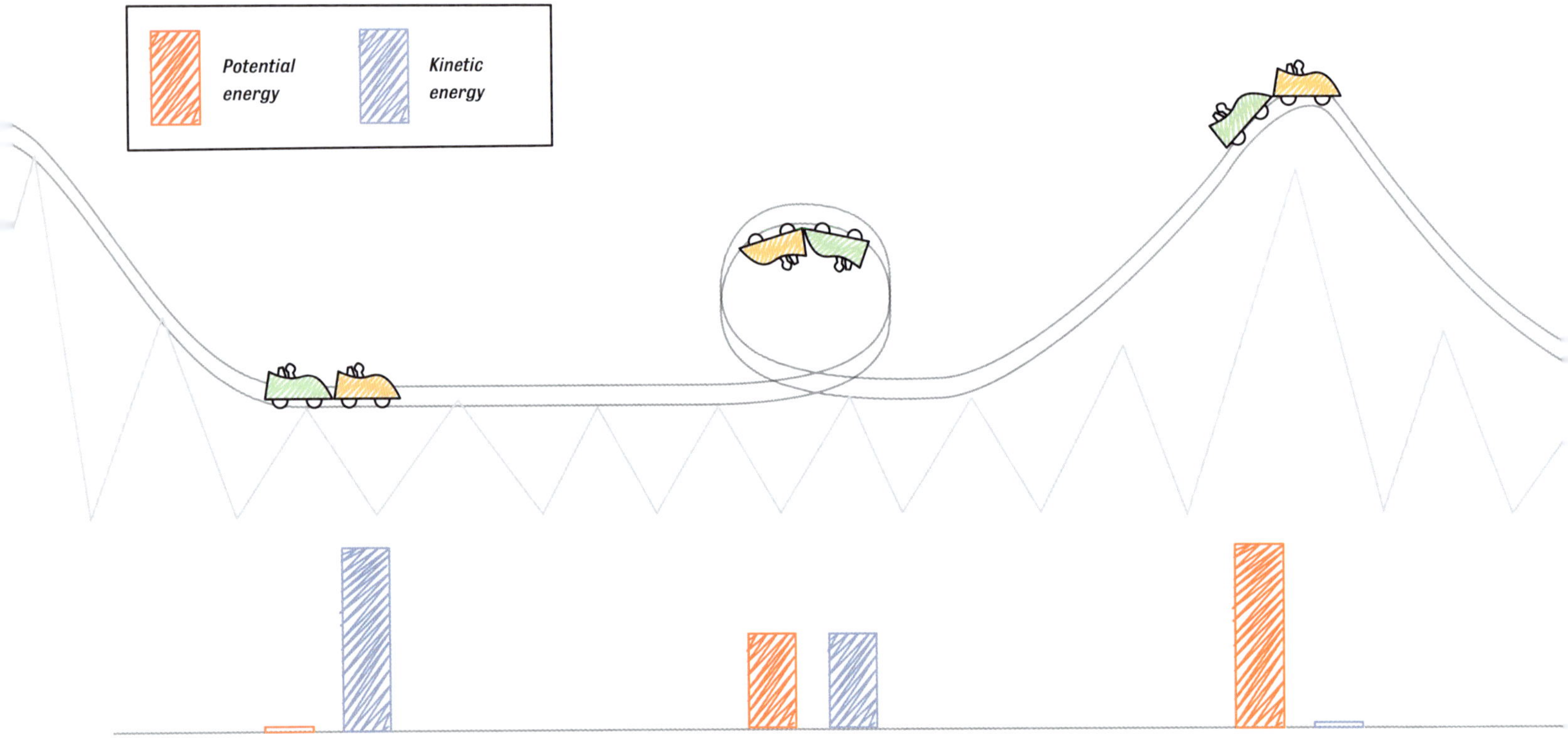

Acceleration is a change in **velocity** (speed or direction) in a certain time. A large acceleration causes a dramatic change in motion over a short time period, smaller accelerations produce a more gentle change in motion over longer time periods. The magnitude of an acceleration experienced by an object depends upon the magnitude of the force applied to it and the object's mass. A large force may only provide a moderate acceleration if the object is very massive. The same large force would produce a large acceleration of a low mass object. The size of the acceleration is determined by the ratio of the force and mass.

The momentum change of an object when a force is applied for a given time is called the **impulse**. The longer the impact time, the lower the force needs to be to produce the same impulse.

Fictitious forces only exist if we try to describe the motion of an object when we ourselves are not traveling at a constant velocity. Objects that are rotating are constantly changing velocity. On the rotating surface of the Earth, these produce a fictitious force, usually referred to as the Coriolis force, after French scientist Gaspard-Gustave de Coriolis. The Coriolis force influences the direction of prevailing winds and ocean currents.

Centripetal force is the resultant force that always acts toward a central point at right angles to an object's motion. It continually changes an object's direction of motion but not its speed. Centripetal forces cause an object to move in a circular motion. Different interactions may be the source of a centripetal force. For example, friction provides a centripetal force to keep a person on a spinning merry-go-round.

Rotational dynamics is the circular motion partner of linear dynamics. Rotating objects obey Newton's laws the same as objects moving in linear motion. As with moving from linear to rotational motion in kinematics, we just need to make translations between variables. The rotational equivalent of force is torque. A **torque** produces a turning or angular acceleration when applied to an object.

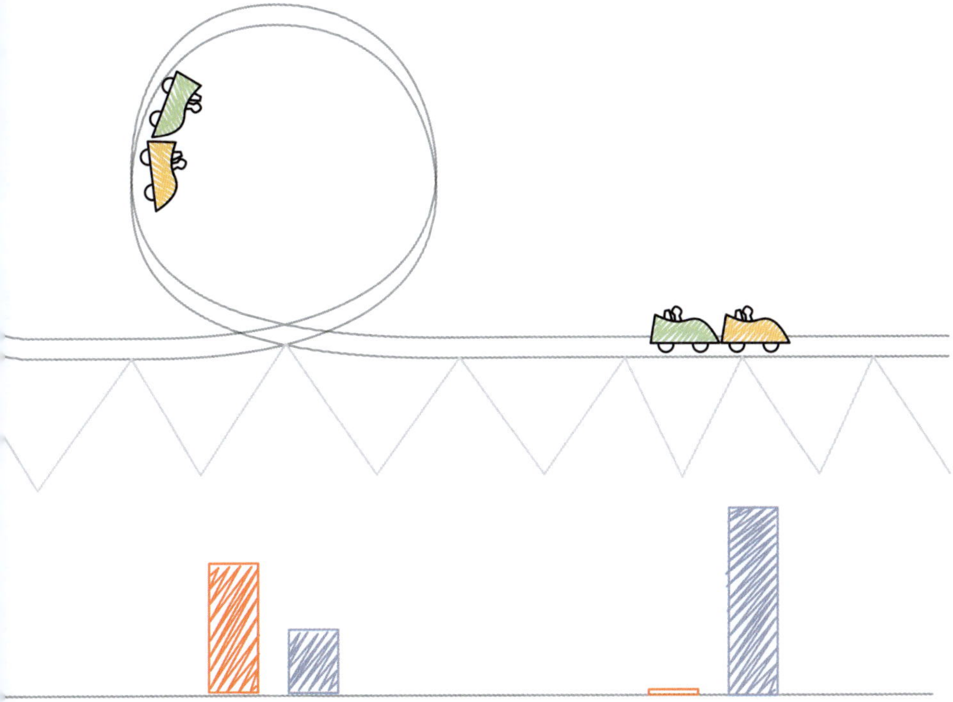

A rollercoaster ride

At different times during a rollercoaster ride the cars will possess different amounts of kinetic and gravitational potential energy. The cars potential energy is greatest when it is farthest from the ground and least when it is lower. Where the cars move fastest they have the most kinetic energy.

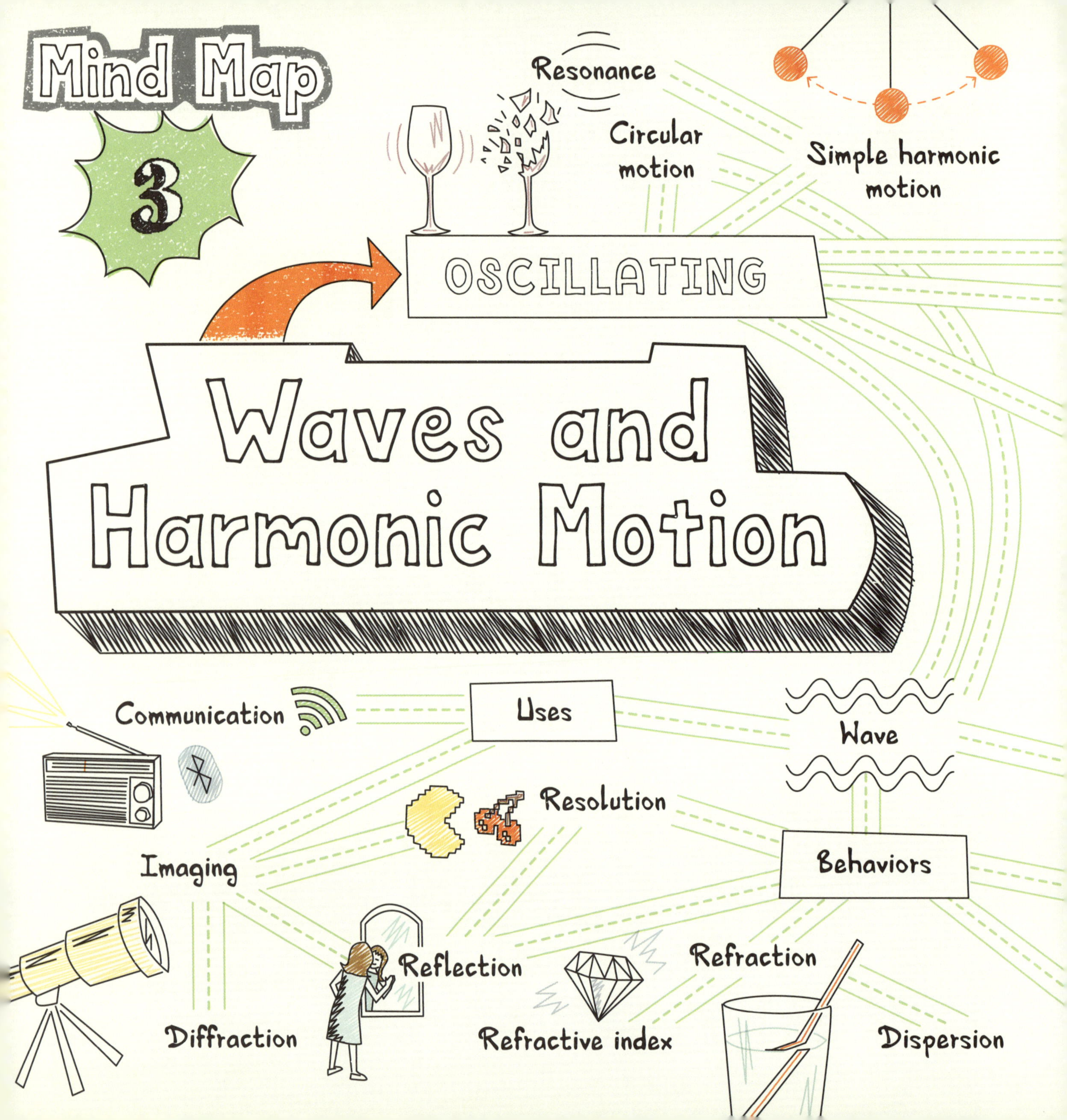
Mind Map
3
Waves and Harmonic Motion
OSCILLATING
Resonance
Circular motion
Simple harmonic motion
Uses
Communication
Imaging
Resolution
Wave
Behaviors
Diffraction
Reflection
Refractive index
Refraction
Dispersion

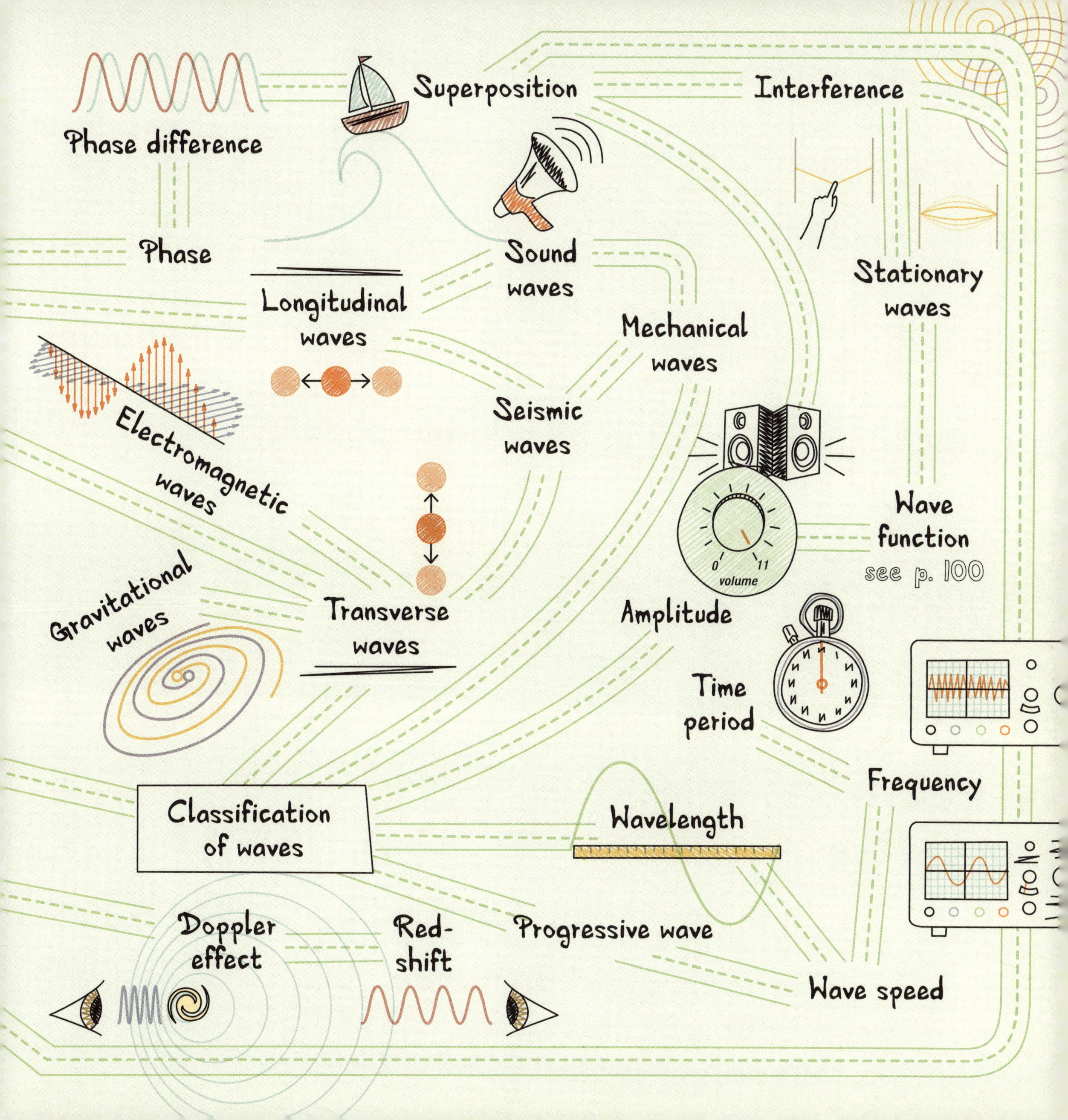
Phase difference
Superposition
Interference
Phase
Sound waves
Stationary waves
Longitudinal waves
Mechanical waves
Seismic waves
Electromagnetic waves
Wave function
see p. 100
0
11
volume
Gravitational waves
Transverse waves
Amplitude
Time period
Frequency
Classification of waves
Wavelength
Doppler effect
Red-shift
Progressive wave
Wave speed

Oscillating

An object is oscillating if it is moving regularly back and forth around a single position. Whereas oscillation is periodic repeating movement in one dimension, **circular motion** is periodic repeating motion in two dimensions. Tracing the position of an object undergoing circular motion in just one dimension would show the particle to be oscillating back and forth in that dimension.

One complete circular motion is when an object has completed one full circle, 360° or 2π radians. A complete oscillation is when an object returns to its original position and also is moving in the same direction as originally. An object would pass through any point in an oscillation twice but each time it would be moving in opposite directions.

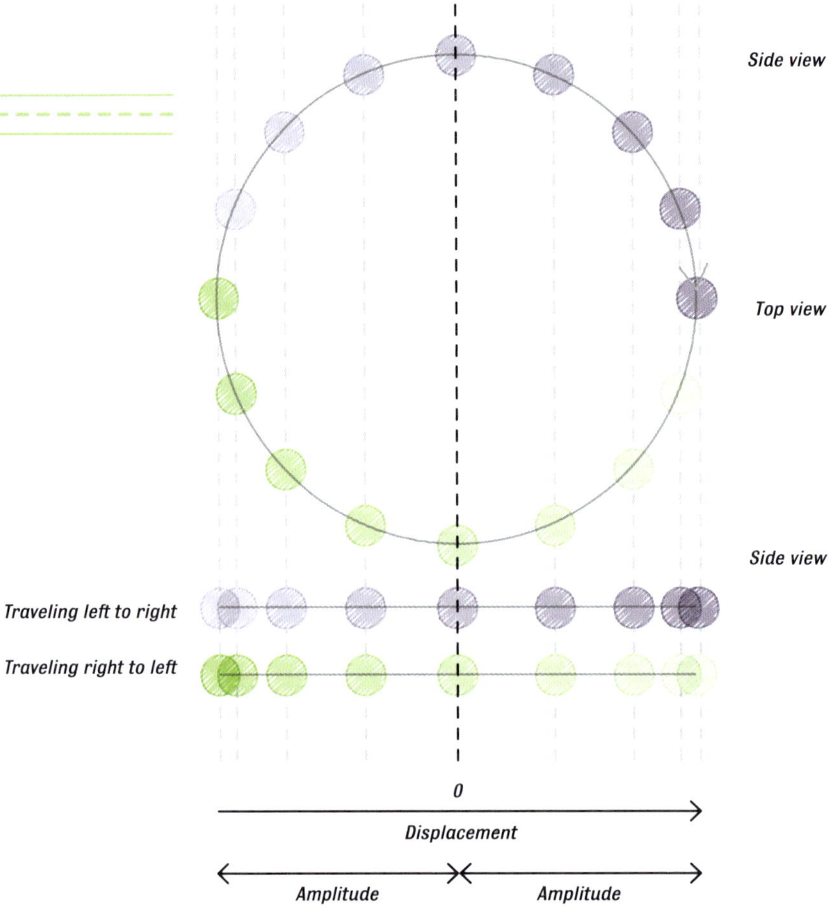

Oscillating and amplitude

This diagram demonstrates the link between circular and simple harmonic motion (SHM). A full rotation of an object moving in a circle would look to move one full oscillation under SHM if viewed from the side.

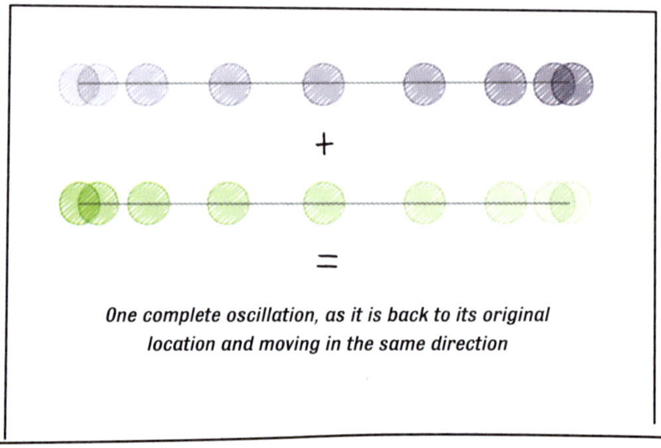

A **wave** is an oscillation of a force field or particles of a material that transfers energy from one location to another. A complete wave is said to have passed if the field or particle at a fixed location has experienced a full cycle of oscillation. A wave may oscillate material or force fields in the direction of its motion, or at right angles to its direction of motion.

The **amplitude** of a wave is the magnitude of maximum displacement of an oscillating object from the central oscillation point. The amplitude of different waves relates to different things for different waves.

Mechanical waves require something to travel through, called a medium. Medium is a phrase that encompasses all types of materials made from particles that can be solid, liquid, gas, or even plasma. Mechanical waves transfer energy by the propagation of oscillation between particles that make up the medium. Amplitude of a mechanical wave is directly related to the magnitude of energy being transferred by the wave.

In some waves, the particles oscillate back and forth along the same direction as the waves move. This type of wave is called a **longitudinal wave** and energy is passed on primarily through collisions between particles in the medium. Waves are forced from ever-changing regions in the medium that alternate between high-density compressions, which are packed full of particles, and rarefactions of low density. Compression regions are named as such because they are where the pressure of the wave is highest and rarefactions are where the pressure is lowest.

In other waves, the oscillation of particles or the force fields are at right angles to the direction the wave is moving; these are known as **transverse waves**. All electromagnetic waves are transverse in nature as the electric, magnetic, and wave direction are all at right angles to each other. The regions of a wave that change as the wave propagates are peaks with the largest positive displacement and troughs with the largest negative displacement. The magnitude of each represents the amplitude of the wave.

Longitudinal and transverse waves

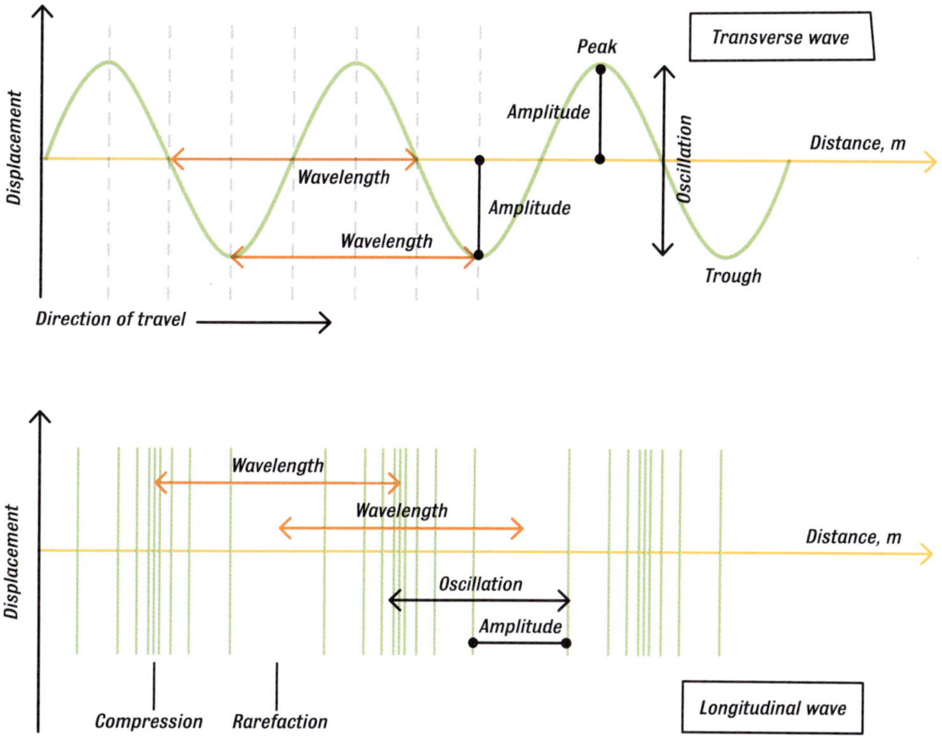

This diagram demonstrates the two distinct types of wave propagation: transverse and longitudinal. Also labeled are the key features of each wave, including the direction of oscillation that defines them.

Classification of waves

Sound waves are longitudinal mechanical waves. Particles in a medium are oscillated by some surface, such as a speaker cone bouncing air molecules back and forth. Oscillations are then passed between particles, and the wave is propagated, through collisions that set a new set of particles oscillating. This continues, setting up regions of compression and rarefaction as the wave transfers energy. The greater the amount of air that is moved in oscillation, the greater the amount of energy transferred; this is what we refer to usually as the volume of the sound. When talking musically about sound waves, the word pitch is often used in place of frequency, but both mean the same thing.

Seismic waves are those responsible for earthquakes and are usually created by rapid movement of the thin crust of rock on which we all live. Body waves are seismic waves that travel through the body of the Earth, transferring energy from the point the

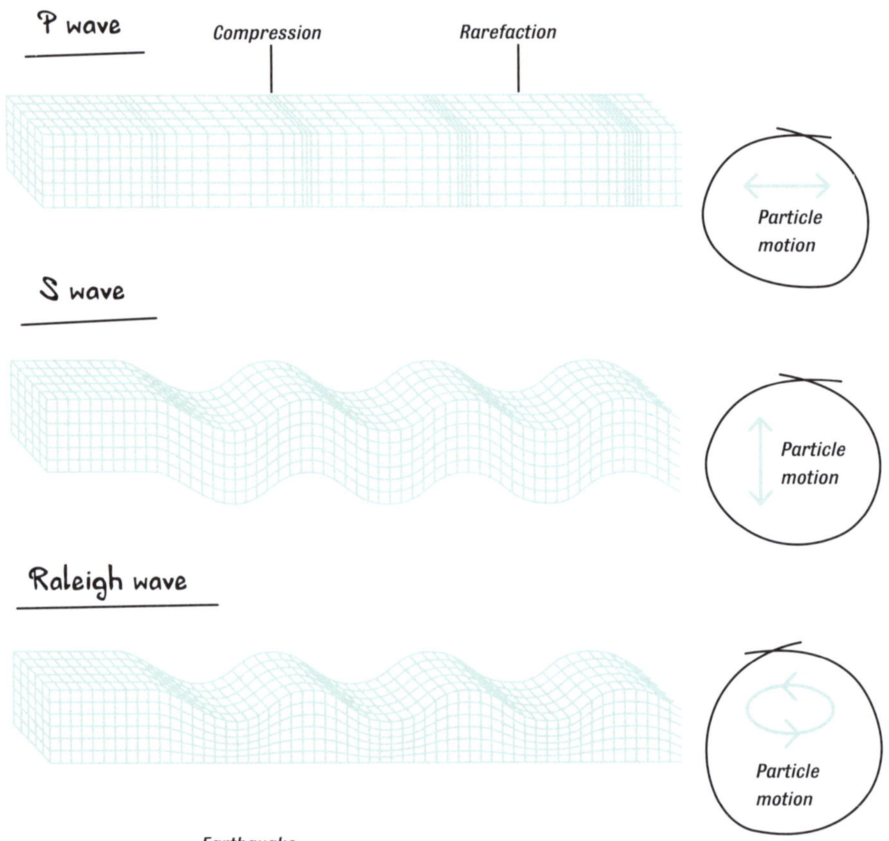

Seismic waves

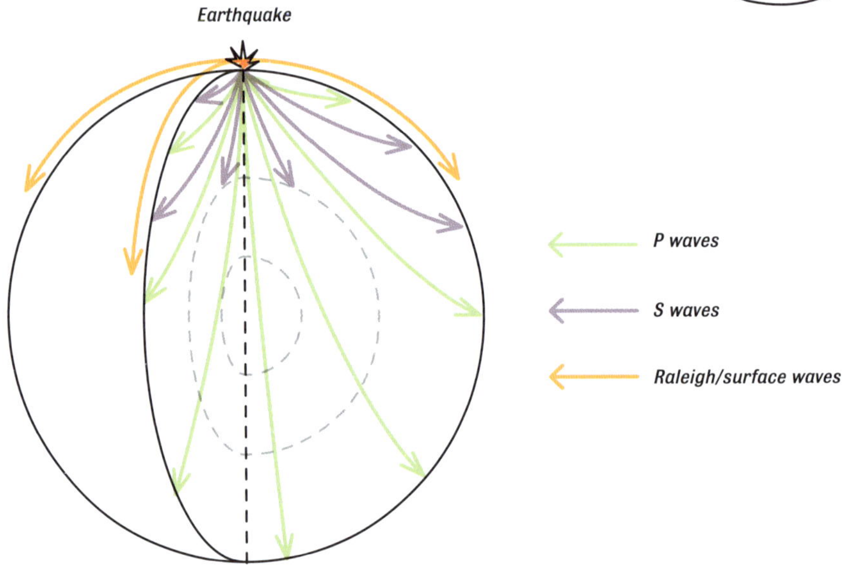

Seismic waves, responsible for earthquakes, come in different types. Transverse P waves travel fastest through the Earth, while longitudinal S waves are slower. Raleigh waves are a combination, causing the rotation of matter.

earthquake is created to the surface, where surface waves are formed. Primary seismic waves, or P waves for short, are longitudinal waves that propagate fastest through the Earth. Secondary seismic waves, or S waves, travel at about half the speed of the P waves and are transverse.

Electromagnetic waves

transfer energy through the oscillation of combined electric and magnetic fields. As they do not require particles to oscillate, electromagnetic waves do not require a medium to travel through; they can transfer energy through a vacuum that contains nothing at all. We commonly call electromagnetic waves light, which is why we say that all electromagnetic waves travel at the speed of light through a vacuum. This is the fastest speed possible in our universe, at around 984 million feet (300 million meters) per second. Because of their many uses, we give different frequencies of electromagnetic wave special names (see page 65).

At a boundary, where two different media meet, such as the boundary between air and a block of glass, waves can display different **behaviors**.

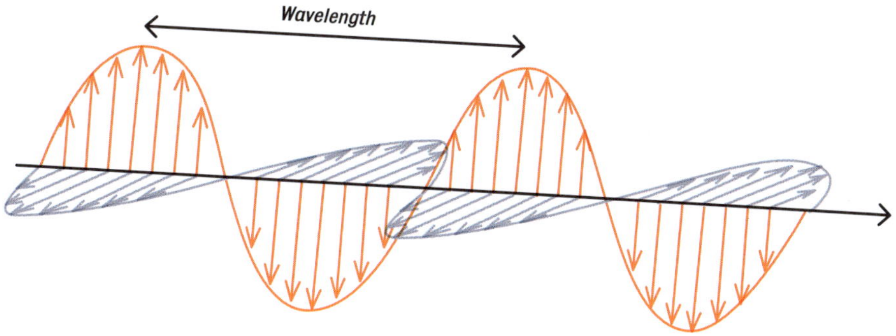

Electromagnetic waves

Electromagnetic waves, which we commonly refer to as light, are formed from oscillating electric and magnetic fields. The wave direction, electric field oscillation, and magnetic field oscillation are all perpendicular to one another.

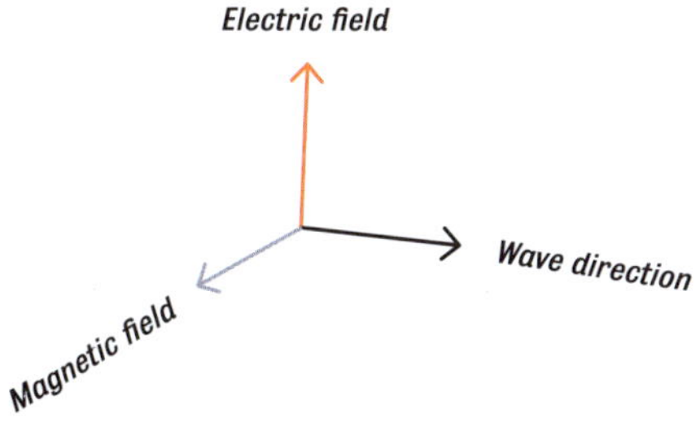

Waves may reflect at the boundary between one medium and another. **Reflection** is the bouncing back of the wave, so that it remains in the medium it was originally traveling through. The angle that a wave approaches is measured against an imaginary line that sticks out of the boundary at right angles, which is called the normal. This angle of incidence, as the wave is incident, or incoming, upon the boundary, is always exactly the same as the angle it reflects back away from the boundary. This statement that the angle of incidence equals the angle of reflection is known as "the law of reflection." To conserve the momentum of the particle or field that is oscillating at the boundary, the phase of the wave changes by exactly one half-wave, or π radians. This is because an upward oscillation of a wave traveling left to right is equal to a downward oscillation of a wave traveling in the opposite direction. And so, the oscillation is shifted by exactly half a wave.

Refraction

Waves that cross a boundary are said to have been transmitted. Transmitted waves may change speed as they pass from one medium into the other. If this happens, the direction the wave is traveling can change in a process called **refraction**. The change of direction can be understood with an analogy of a racing car. If the car goes from a tarmac track onto dirt then it will slow down. If just the left-hand side of the car veers off the track onto dirt then just the left-hand side slows down while the right-hand side of the car remains traveling fast. This has the effect of turning the car to the left. As a wave travels into a region of lower speed, it is affected in the same way and the wave changes direction as it crosses the boundary. The opposite happens if the wave goes from moving slowly through one medium to fast through another. The angle at which the wave is refracted is smaller than the incident angle if the wave slows down across the boundary, and larger if the wave speeds up.

The speed a wave travels through a certain medium is defined by the **refractive index**. This benchmarks how fast a wave moves through a medium with respect to the fastest possible speed for that wave. The higher the refractive index, the slower the wave travels through that medium. It is only usually used when looking at the refraction of light, where the maximum speed is fixed as the speed of light waves in a vacuum. The difference in refractive index between two mediums on either side of a boundary dictates the size of the change in direction when a wave refracts. The value of the refractive index depends upon the medium and the frequency of the wave.

Dispersion is the separation of different frequencies of light. It can occur at a boundary between two different media because the different frequencies of a wave will each experience a different refractive index. This means that they will each change direction by a different amount as they cross the boundary. Different frequencies of a wave are fanned out to travel in differing directions. This is commonly done with white light and a triangular glass block called a prism. White light is a mixture of all the colors of the rainbow, each of which represents a different frequency of electromagnetic wave. As white light crosses the boundary between air and glass,

Reflection and refraction

When a wave strikes a boundary between two different mediums it can reflect or refract. Reflection is when the wave bounces off the boundary back into the medium it was originally traveling through. Refraction is a change in the direction the wave is moving because of a change in its speed.

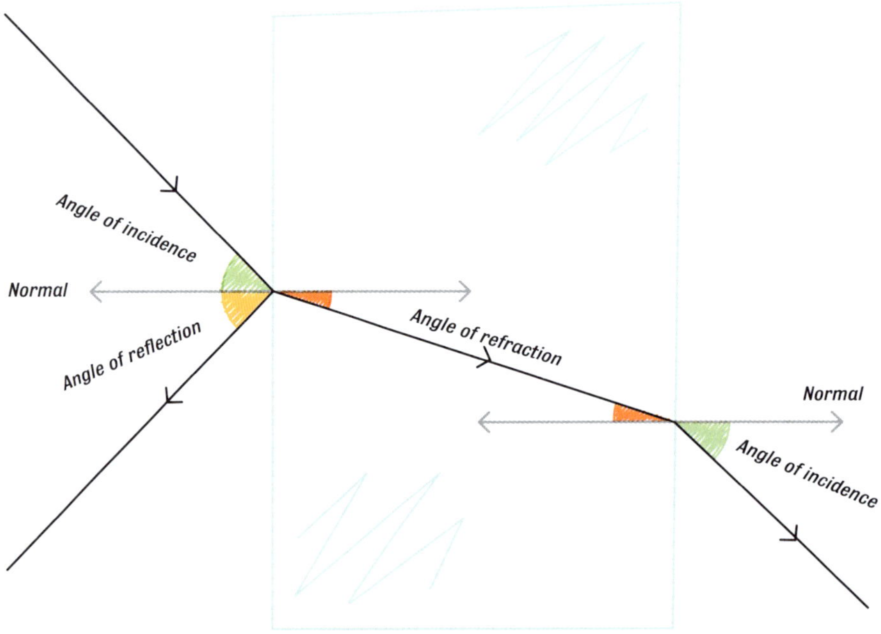

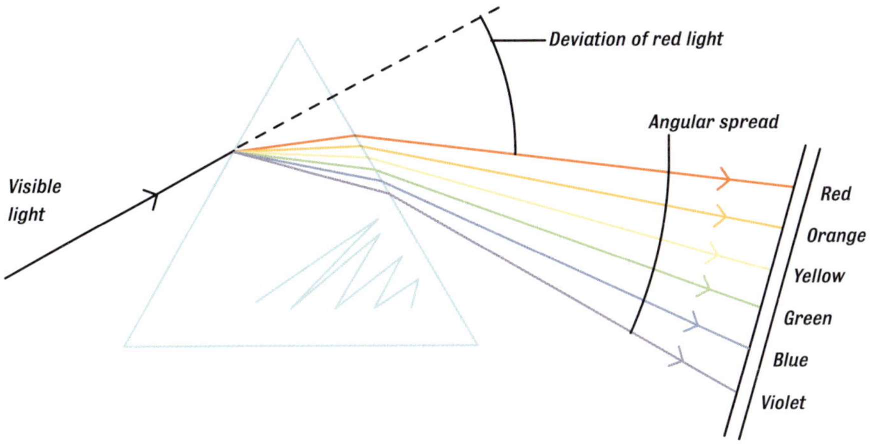

Dispersion

Different frequencies of light experience slightly different refractive indices when entering a medium. This leads to a different change in direction for different colors of light, setting them each on their own paths.

each color of light refracts at a slightly different angle, sending each color on a different path. This is enhanced as the light refracts for a second time as it comes out of the prism, crossing the boundary from glass to air. The result is a rainbow of colors, as each of the colors of light are now on their own paths with unique directions. The direction of each path is determined by the material of the prism, which is common to all of the light, and the frequency of the light, which varies for different colors.

Dispersion can also be seen when using lenses. White light disperses a little as it passes through a lens that uses refraction to focus light. This can leave rainbow halos around lens-focussed images.

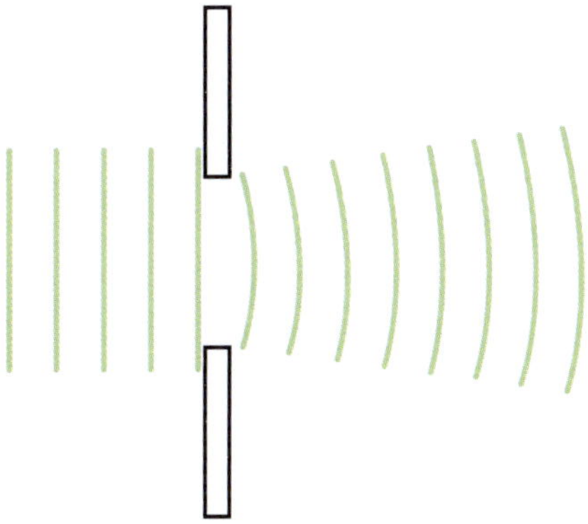

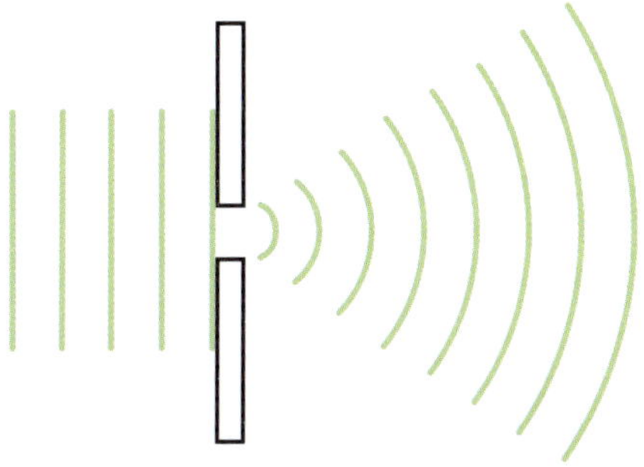

Diffraction

If a wave strikes an edge then it will spread out a little, this is known as diffraction. If two edges are used to create a slit, then this effect is enhanced.

If a wave encounters a barrier it cannot be transmitted through, it can only be reflected or absorbed. A wave that passes the edge of a barrier will spread around the edge in a process called **diffraction**. Diffraction can be enhanced, and waves made to spread more, by bringing two edges together to form a slit. The closer the edges are brought together, the greater the amount of diffraction that occurs. Waves diffract maximally when the width of a slit is close to the wave's wavelength.

The uses of waves

Waves have many **uses**, not just the transfer of energy from one location to another. **Communication** of information is a major use of electromagnetic waves. Information can be transferred either as an analog or digital signal. Analog signals are comprised of a stream of data that can take any value from a continuous range of values, and has no loss of original information. Digital signals take samples of the data at a certain rate and assign each sample a discrete number. Both signals can be encoded into a wave in two distinct ways. Frequency modulation, or FM for short, encodes a signal into the frequency of a wave, which is changed in response to the signal being encoded. Amplitude modulation, or AM for short, encodes a signal into the amplitude of a wave, with a different amplitude encoding a different piece of data.

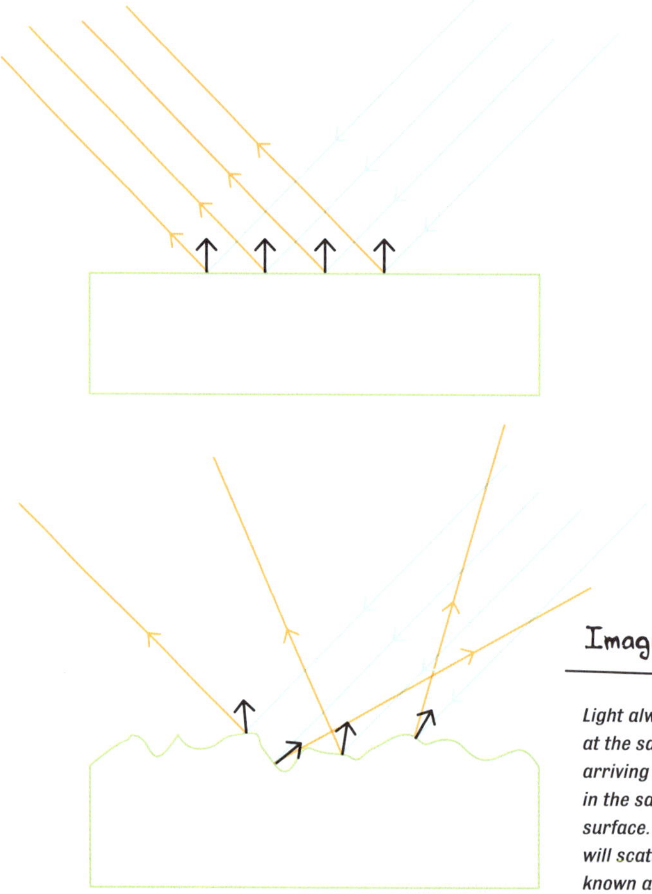

Imaging

Light always reflects from a surface at the same angle it is incident. Light arriving in the same direction will leave in the same direction from a smooth surface. However, a rough surface will scatter the light in a process known as diffuse reflection.

We can use the reflection of waves for **imaging** objects. By taking advantage of the law of reflection, our eyes can reconstruct the path of many light waves reflected from external objects, and piece together this information about the different directions to form a picture.

Resolution is the smallest size of object it is possible to see with a certain wave. If imaging something by measuring the waves reflected from an object, you could only use a wave to see objects if their size is equal to or larger than the wavelength of the wave used. A good way to think of this is trying to figure out the shape of an egg carton by firing things at it and looking at how they bounce off. If we chose to fire Ping-Pong balls at the egg carton, then they would fly off in different directions. If we recorded each of the flying Ping-Pong balls then we could, using the law of reflection, reconstruct the surface shape of the egg carton. Imagine we try to use a beach ball to achieve the same task—it just wouldn't work. The beach ball is so large that it would, no matter where it hit, just bounce of the egg carton at the same angle it hit it. The features of the egg

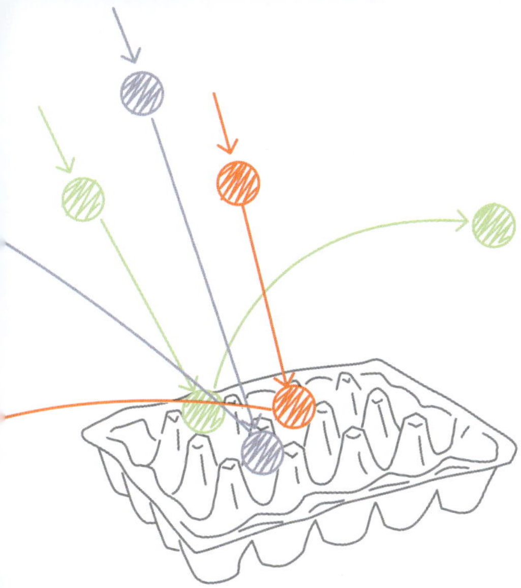

carton are too small to be resolved using the beach ball, in the same way that small objects cannot be resolved by waves with too large a wavelength.

If a source emitting waves is moving relative to you then the frequency of the waves you experience will be different to the frequency emitted by the source. This behavior is known as the **Doppler effect**, after Austrian physicist Christian Doppler, and occurs whenever an emergency vehicle passes us with sirens on. As the siren approaches, we experience every wave it emits as constantly catching up a little bit with the wave emitted before it. This means that the same point on successive waves become bunched up in front of the siren by its movement. The opposite happens when the siren is moving away—the waves are stretched out.

This movement causes a change in the wavelength experienced by the person stood listening to the siren. The wavelength of the wave in front of the siren is smaller and the wavelength behind the siren is longer. More waves hit our ears each second in front of the siren as they are tightly bunched up; behind the siren, less waves per second hit our ear as they are stretched out. Our ears hear this as high-frequency sound when the siren is moving toward us and lower-frequency sound when moving away. This is the reason for the change in pitch (a word that denotes frequency of sound waves) when an emergency vehicle passes us.

Doppler effect

If a wave's source is moving with respect to us then we experience a change in the wave's wavelength. Moving toward us shortens the wavelength and increases the frequency and moving away does the opposite.

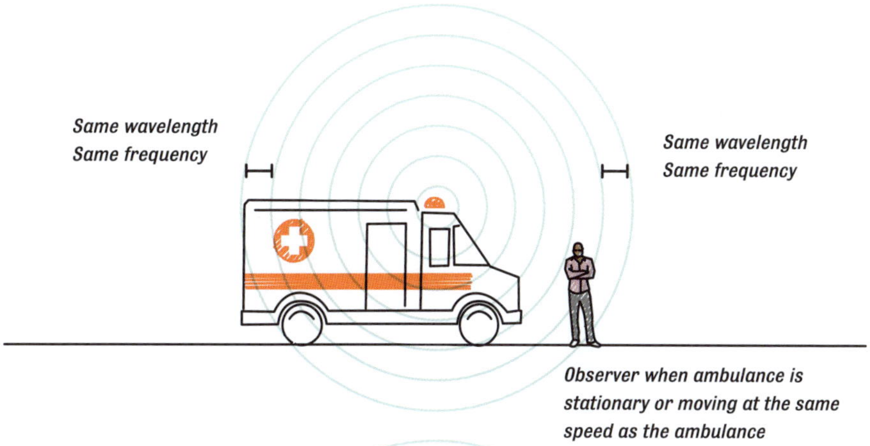

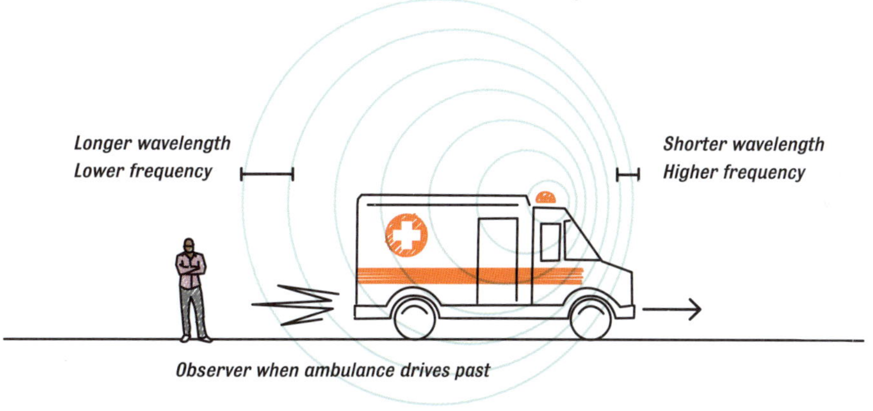

Redshift is the electromagnetic wave version of the Doppler effect. If an object is emitting light and moving away from us, the wavelength of light we see is stretched out, becoming lower in frequency and therefore redder in color—hence the name redshift. If an object emitting light is moving toward us then the light is bunched up and shorter in wavelength, therefore appearing higher in frequency and bluer in color, sometimes called blueshift.

Astronomers can determine if and to what extent light emitted by distant stars and galaxies is redshifted or blueshifted, which can tell us about the motion of that star or galaxy relative to our own. Things get complicated by the fact that the universe is expanding, something which also tends to stretch out the wavelength of light as it travels across the cosmos. The longer light travels, the greater its wavelength is stretched and the redder it would look through telescopes on Earth. This is usually referred to as cosmological redshift (see page 125).

Gravitational waves can also pass through a vacuum, because gravitational waves move as oscillations of the fabric of space-time. Space–time is the stage on which everything in the universe is played out, but it is a stage that can be stretched and bent like an elastic sheet. Gravitational waves are a prediction of the general theory of relativity, which states that all gravitational interactions are not a force but a consequence of the curving of space-time (see page 144).

The **time period** of a wave is the time taken for one part of a wave to begin a new cycle of oscillation. If the trace of a wave is taken over some time, the time period can be deduced as the difference in time between two identical points on waves neighboring in time.

The **frequency** of a wave is a measure of how many full waves pass a fixed position each second. It can be calculated as the number of waves that have passed a position divided by the time taken for those waves to pass. More waves of a high frequency wave pass a fixed point each second than of a lower frequency wave.

The **wavelength** of a wave is the distance between identical points in the current and preceding or succeeding wave. For progressive waves, this is also the distance that one wave travels in one time period.

Wavelength

The distance between two identical points or phases in a wave is known as the wavelength.

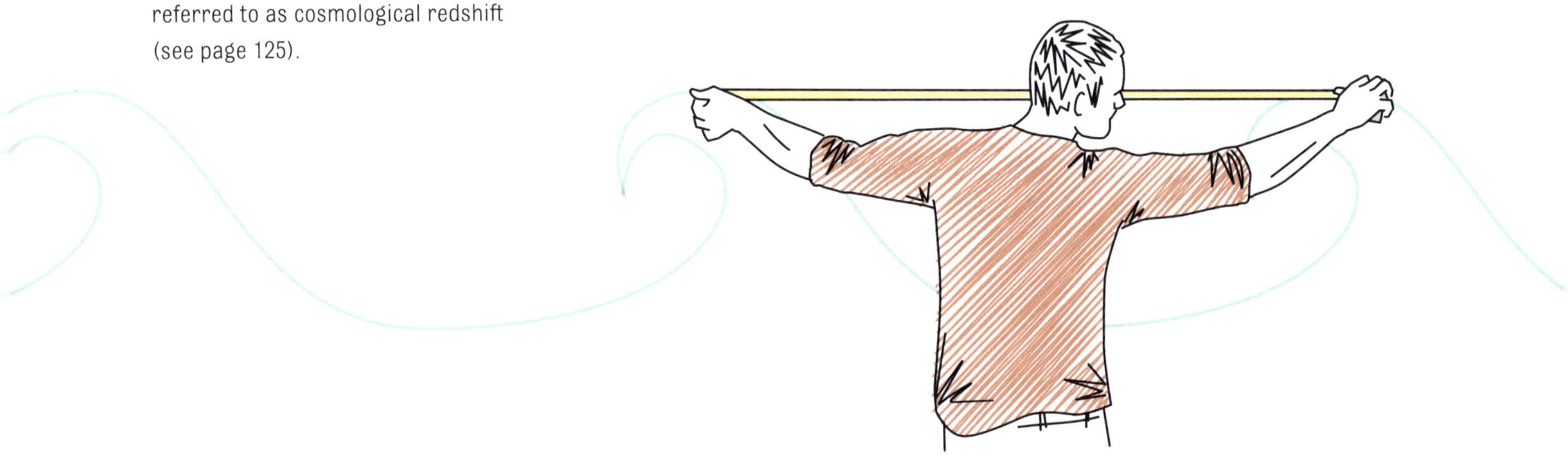

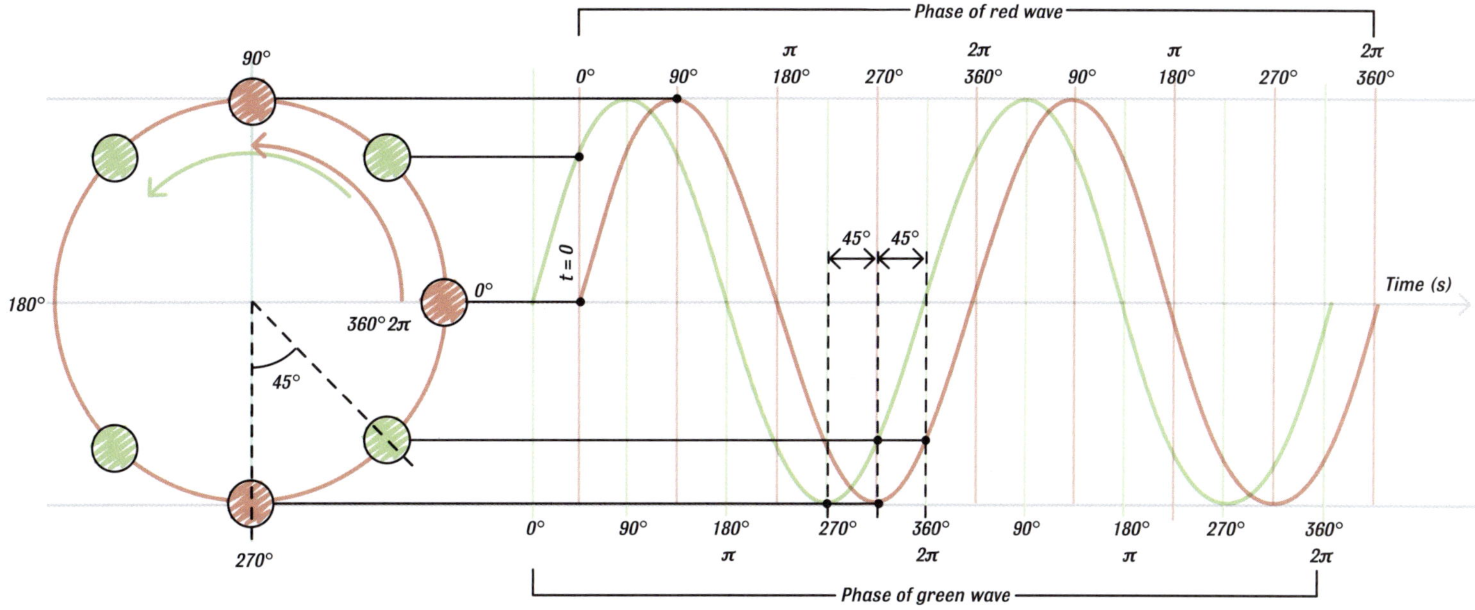

The **wave speed** is the speed at which waves pass a given point. It can be calculated by multiplying the wavelength and frequency together. Wave speeds are different in different mediums because of different material properties.

A **progressive wave** moves through space from one position to another, moving at the wave speed. A progressive wave transfers energy from one location in space to another.

Phase tells us the point an object is at in a cycle of oscillation. It is very much like the angle that an object in circular motion has passed around a circle. The starting point for any oscillation, including waves, is usually chosen as the point that an object is at maximum positive displacement from the central oscillation point. Adopting the circular motion idea of oscillation, an angle is used to represent the phase of oscillation from 0 at the beginning to 360° or 2π radians at the end of its oscillation. If an object has moved through just half of its oscillation cycle then it will have a phase of π radians.

The **phase difference** tells us the mismatch in phase between two waves of the same frequency. If one wave is further through a cycle of oscillation, has a greater phase, than another wave, then the first wave is said to be leading the other. If a wave is behind another wave in its oscillation phase then it is said to lag that wave.

Phase

The place a wave is at within one oscillation cycle is known as the phase. As oscillation is analogous to circular motion, each oscillation is split into 360° or 2π radians. Therefore, a wave's phase is quoted as being between 0–360° or 0–2π radians.

Two waves may be out of phase by a phase difference. In this diagram, the green wave is out of phase with the red wave by 45 degrees or π/4 radians. We say that the green wave leads the red. The reason for this is easily seen if we look at the circular motion diagram where the green dot is ahead of the red.

Superposition occurs when any two or more waves travel through the same space at the same time. The displacement of all waves at any point in space sum together to form a single value of displacement. The displacement experienced by an oscillating object at that point is this new superimposed displacement. Superposition may not result in a wave, as the cycle of oscillation might not periodically repeat.

Interference is the superposition of two waves with a constant phase difference. Waves with a constant phase difference must have the same frequency and are said to be coherent. The resulting superposition produces a new wave with the same frequency as the original waves, but a shift in phase equal to half the phase difference between the two original waves. The amplitude of the waves is also modified by the phase difference, reaching a maximum of the sum of the two original amplitudes when the waves are in phase and zero when they are exactly π out of phase. If the amplitudes produce an amplitude larger than the original, then the interference is said to be constructive. If the amplitude is smaller than the original, then the interference is said to be destructive.

Stationary waves are produced when two coherent waves of the same amplitude pass through the same space in exactly opposite directions. The waves interfere to produce a wave with a pattern of oscillation that is fixed in space. The progressive nature of the waves cancel each other out and so stationary waves do not transfer energy between two different positions, rather they trap energy. Stationary waves have fixed points where there is no displacement at all (called nodes) and points exactly between these of maximum displacement (antinodes). The amplitude of this stationary wave

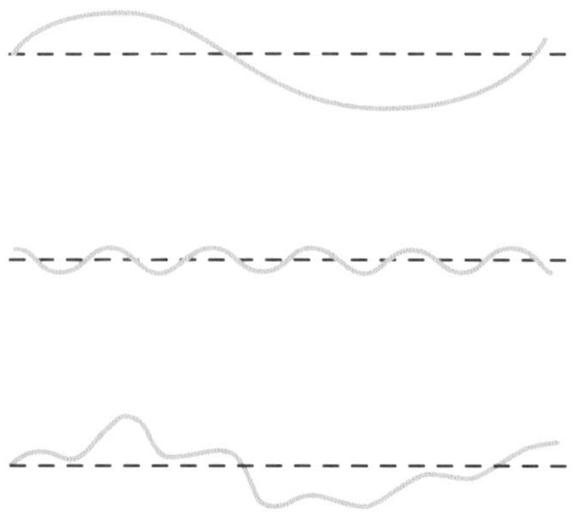

Superposition

Superposition is the combining of any two or more waves to form a single wave.

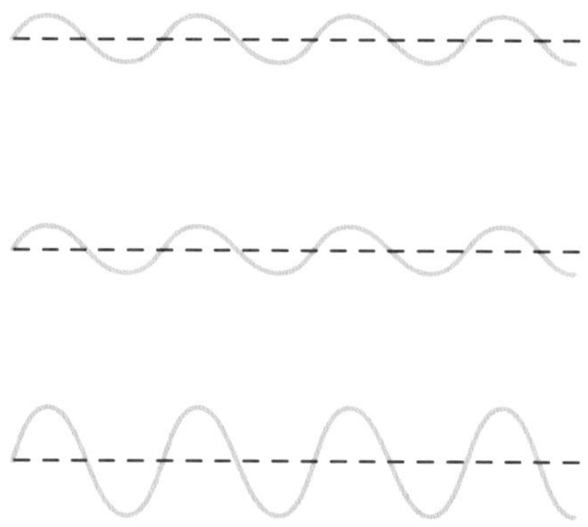

Constructive interference

Coherent waves of the same frequency and phase interfere constructively to form waves with higher amplitudes.

Destructive interference

Coherent waves of the same frequency and exactly π or 180° out of phase perfectly cancel each other out in destructive interference.

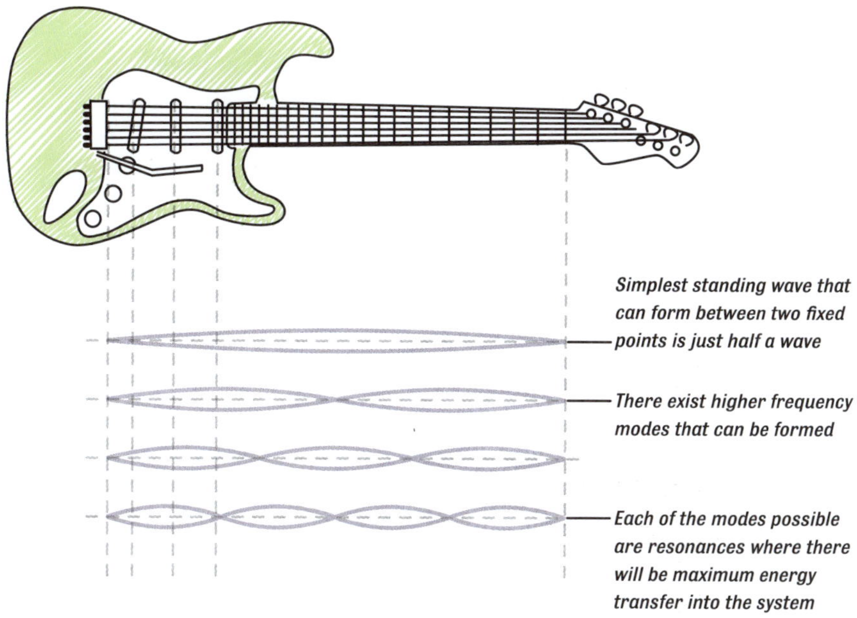

Stationary wave

Stationary waves of different resonant frequencies can form between any two fixed points.

is the sum of the amplitude of the two original progressive waves. The wavelength of the wave remains the same but the frequency and wave speed of this group of waves has become zero. Stationary waves are formed on stringed instruments like a guitar, where the original wave created from plucking the guitar reflects at the fixed ends of the string. The wave passing down the string and the reflected wave are coherent with a phase difference of π radians (180°), and interfere to produce a standing wave. The same happens for standing wave forms within air in musical wind instruments.

An object moves in **simple harmonic motion** if it oscillates because of a single restoring force that pulls it back toward a central position. The magnitude of the acceleration provided by the force is directly related to its displacement from the central position. A larger displacement produces a larger acceleration always back toward the central point. Simple harmonic motion is an important concept in physics because many things in nature move in this way. A simple swinging pendulum is accelerated toward its lowest central hanging point by gravity. Atoms in solid materials vibrate under simple harmonic motion about positions determined by chemical bonding.

Resonance occurs when an oscillator is driven at its natural frequency. When the two are matched, the maximum amount of energy is transferred by the force into the kinetic energy of the oscillating object. This causes the oscillation speed to grow in magnitude rapidly. If the frequency of the driving force is different to the natural frequency, then a smaller amount of energy is transferred by the force into the kinetic energy store of the oscillator. A good example is an opera singer shattering a glass when the correct note is struck, as all of the sound energy is transferred into vibrating the glass, so much so that it breaks.

If an object is hit with a hammer, then it is made to oscillate at many different frequencies. While most of these frequencies are not absorbed by the object a small number of resonant frequencies are. These frequencies set the object in motion and the object then emits sound of certain pitch. This why different bells can be struck with the same hammer but produce distinctly different sounds.

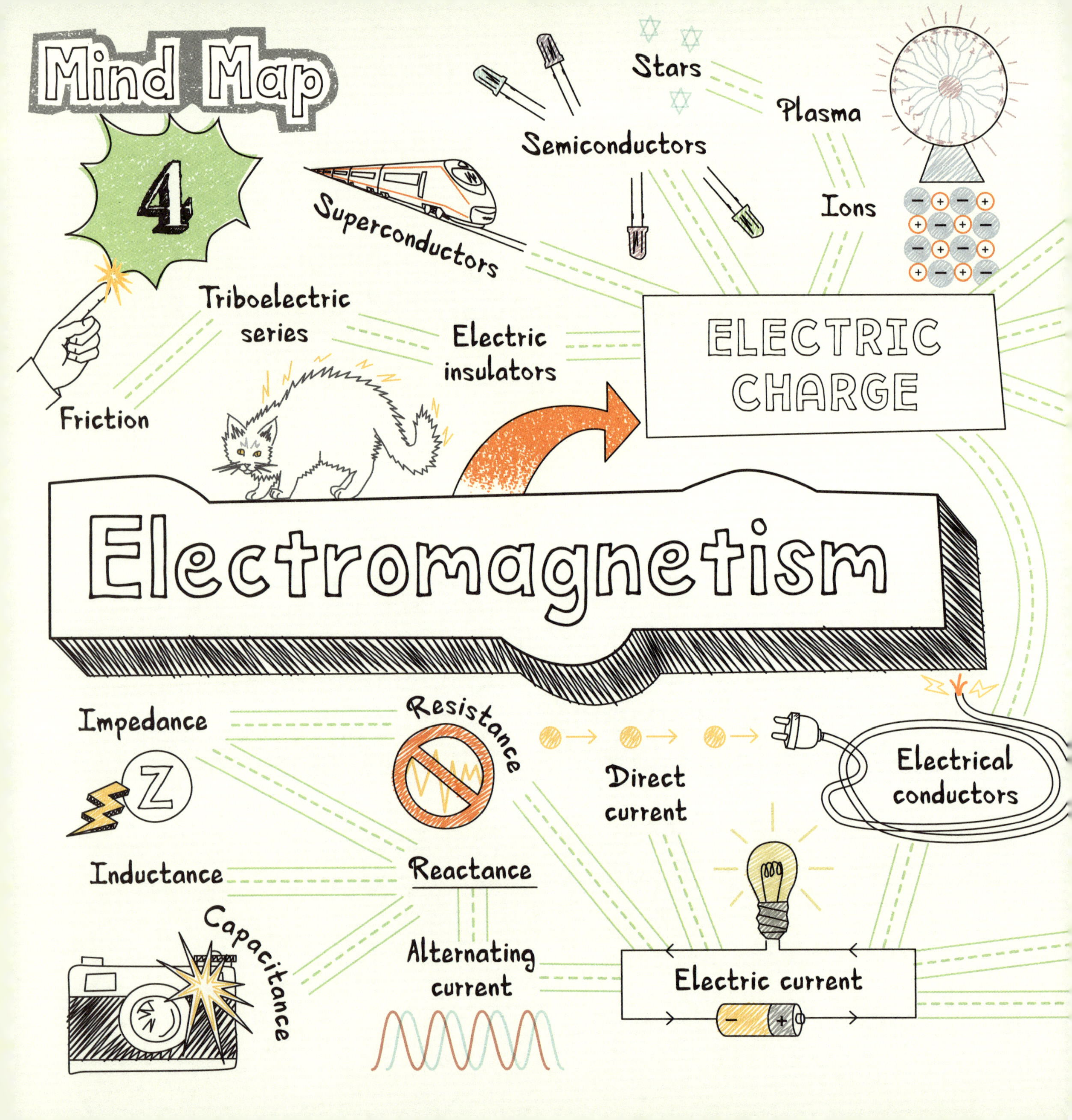

Mind Map
4
Electromagnetism
ELECTRIC CHARGE
Stars
Plasma
Semiconductors
Ions
Superconductors
Triboelectric series
Electric insulators
Friction
Impedance
Resistance
Direct current
Electrical conductors
Inductance
Reactance
Capacitance
Alternating current
Electric current

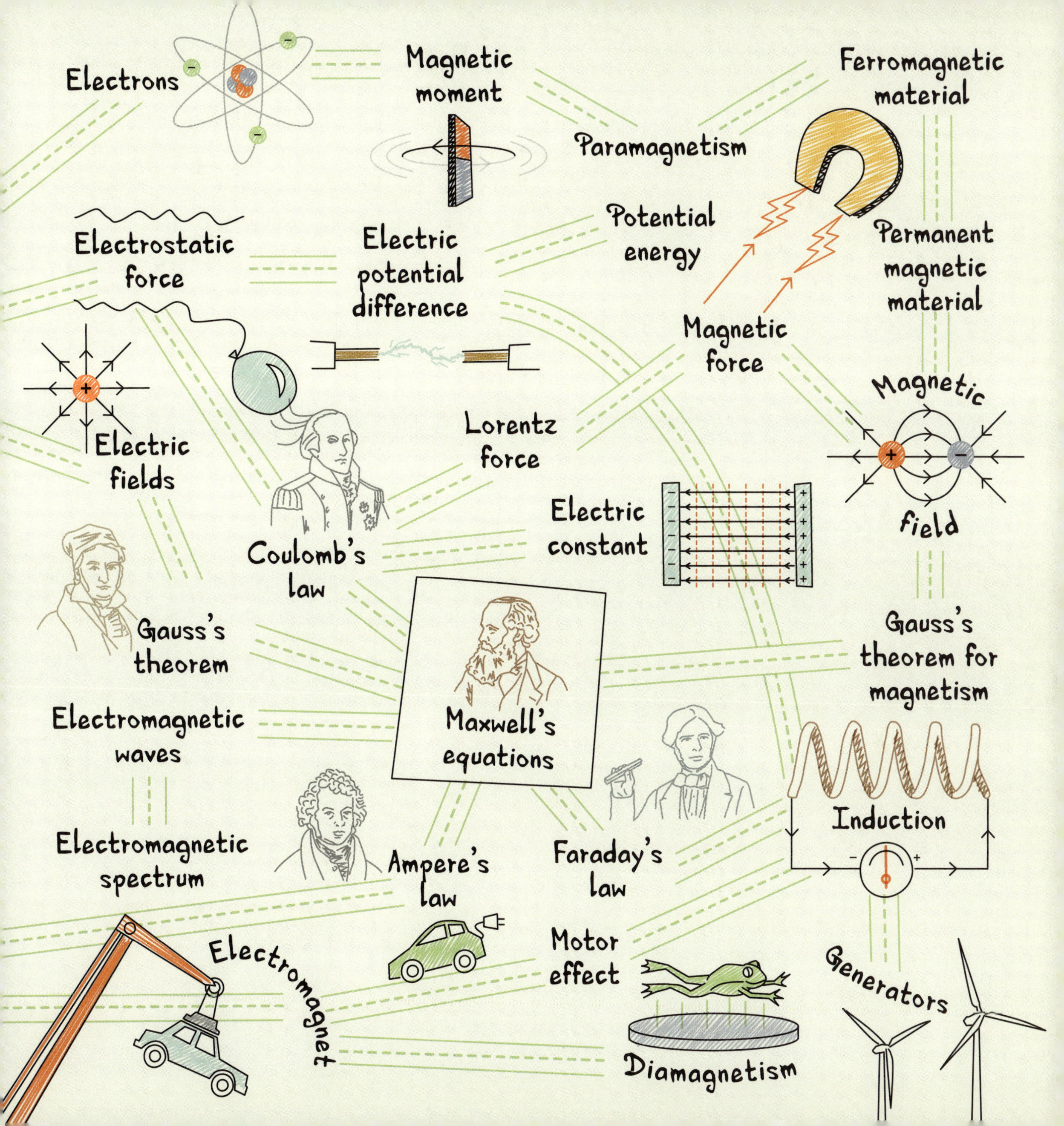
Electrons
Magnetic moment
Ferromagnetic material
Paramagnetism
Potential energy
Permanent magnetic material
Electrostatic force
Electric potential difference
Magnetic force
Magnetic field
Electric fields
Lorentz force
Electric constant
Coulomb's law
Gauss's theorem
Gauss's theorem for magnetism
Maxwell's equations
Electromagnetic waves
Induction
Electromagnetic spectrum
Ampere's law
Faraday's law
Motor effect
Electromagnet
Generators
Diamagnetism

Electric Charge

Electric charge is a property that tells us how an object is influenced by the electrostatic force. Electric charges on large objects come from adding together the electric charge of the many different subatomic particles it is made from. Most materials around us have an even balance of positive and negative charge, and so have zero electric charge; they are electrically neutral. Neutrons found in the nucleus of an atom are electrically neutral. Protons that are also found in the nucleus are said to have a positive electric charge. The charge of each proton is balanced by the negative charge of **electrons** that surround the nucleus of an atom, to make atoms overall electrically neutral.

Electric charge is an abstract concept, which means nothing to our senses. Until the nineteenth century, people would talk of two different types of electricity. It was not until the work of Benjamin Franklin that we realized these types of electricity to be polar opposite. Franklin assigned these different types of electricity mathematical identities as positive and negative, which allowed scientists to quantify electric charge rather than just talking of it qualitatively.

Atoms are usually electrically neutral, but in special circumstances, such as chemical reactions, or at extremely hot temperatures, they can lose or gain electrons. Electrically charged atoms are called **ions**.

If a gas is heated up to very high temperatures, all the electrons gain enough energy to escape the atoms, leaving just ions behind and forming a fourth state of matter called a **plasma**. **Stars** are balls of hot plasma.

Electric charge of atoms and ions

The electric charge of atoms and ions are defined by the collection of subatomic particles they are made from.

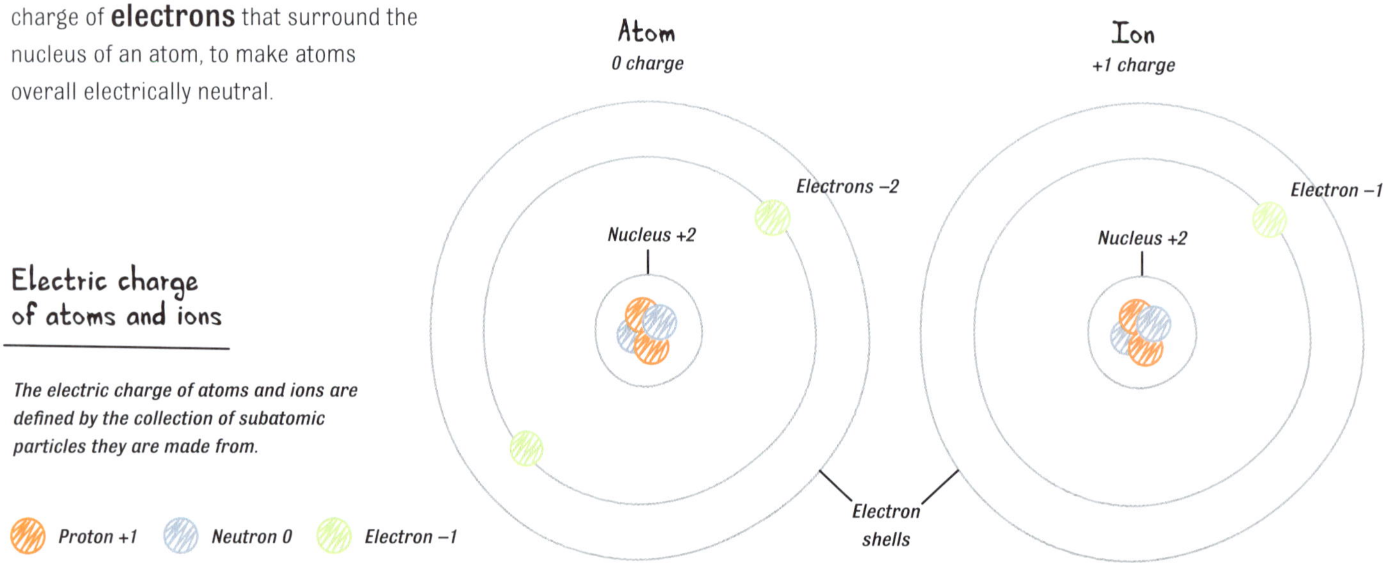

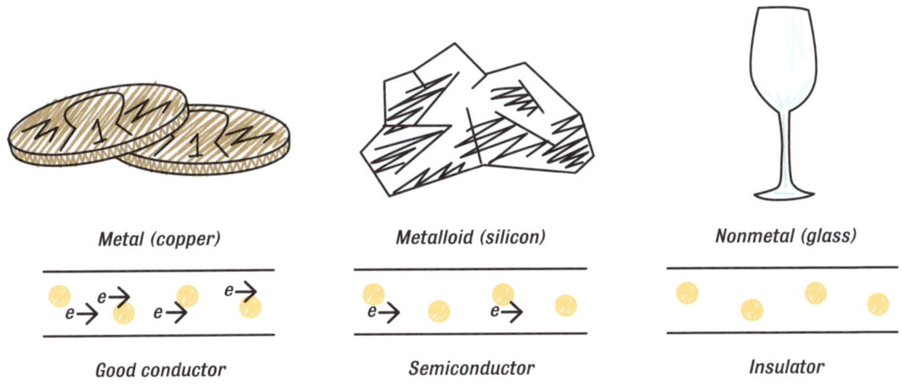

Electrical conductors

Materials can be categorized by how well they allow electric current to flow through them. Conductors allow flow easily, semiconductors less so, and insulators do not allow current to flow at all.

Materials containing charges that are free to move are **electrical conductors**, as an electric current of moving electric charges can easily be formed in them. Most metals are classed as electrical conductors, as they contain electrons that are able to move freely through a fixed background of charged ions. Ionic liquids or solutions, such as salt water, and plasmas are also electrical conductors, as both negative electrons and positive ions can move and carry electric current.

Semiconductors are materials with a small number of electric charges that are free to move, far less than an electrical conductor. By adding different chemical elements, the properties of semiconductor materials can be designed to suit many different applications. Semiconductors such as silicon are used in modern electronics to make everything from computer processors to the light-sensitive photodetectors in digital cameras.

Electrical insulators are materials that do not allow particles with an electric charge to move freely. Electric charges that build up on an electrical insulator cannot move and give rise to static electricity.

Charge by friction

Electrons are exchanged between the surfaces of two insulating materials when rubbed together. This leaves the surfaces with opposite electric charges.

Static electricity

When two electrical insulators are rubbed together, the force of **friction** between the surfaces can exchange electrons between the materials. If the two insulators are made of very different materials, then more electrons will be exchanged one way than the other. The result is that of the two surfaces that were originally neutral, one loses electrons to become positively charged while the other gains those electrons to become negatively charged.

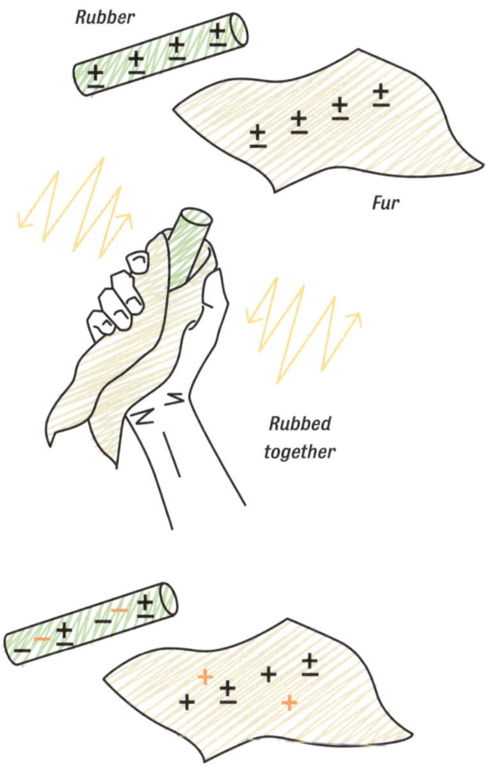

Insulating materials are ranked on the **triboelectric series** according to how freely they exchange electrons through friction. An example list is given here from positive, most likely to give up electrons, to negative, least likely to give up electrons: rabbit's fur | Lucite | Bakelite | acetate | glass | quartz | mica | nylon | wool | cat's fur | silk | paper | cotton | wood | amber | resins | polystyrene | polyethylene | Teflon.

Rubbing rabbit fur against Teflon would leave the rabbit fur quite positive as more of its electrons would have been exchanged and given to the Teflon.

Electric current

Electric current is the movement of electric charge from one location to another. Historically, before the discovery of the electron, electric current was defined as the direction positive electric charges moved in. In most electric conductors, however, it is negatively charged electrons that are free to move, not positive charges. Today, we are left with the historical idea of moving positive charges as the direction of current, despite knowing that it is the movement of electrons in the opposite direction that is truly moving electric charge in most materials.

A **direct current** is formed when all of the moving electric charges press on in just one direction through a material.

An **alternating current** is formed when electric charges change their direction of movement through a material at regular intervals. This oscillating back and forth of the electric charges can form electromagnetic waves.

Moving charges experience **resistance** to their movement as they pass through a material. Collisions with other electrons or ions in the materials deflect an electron from the direction of the electric current. This hinders the progress of electric current through the material, which is measured as electrical resistance of the material. Resistance transfers energy from the electric current into waste thermal energy, which is why all electronics heat up when used.

Direct and alternating currents

Electric current is the flow of electric charge. A direct current is the continuous movement of charge in one direction while alternating current alters the direction the charges move in.

Direct current (DC)

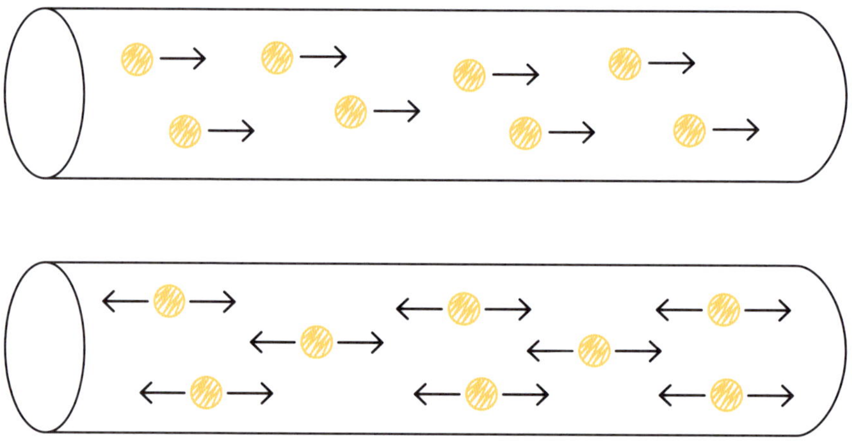

Alternating current (AC)

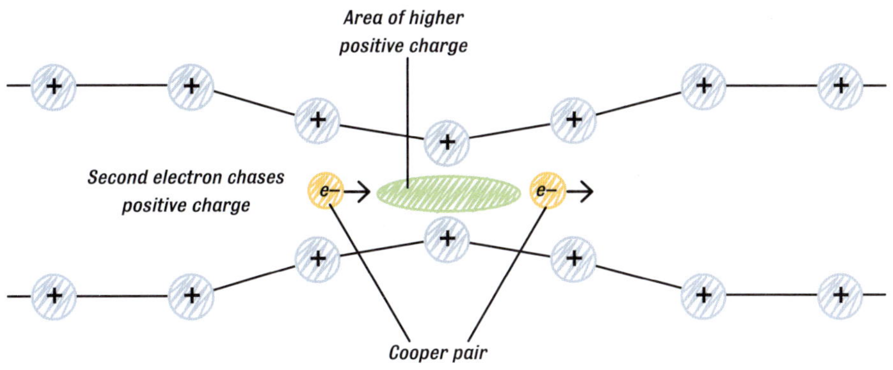

Superconductors are materials in which electric charges can move through the material with zero electrical resistance. Thirty pure metals become superconductors if they are cooled down to near absolute zero (see page 85). At these low temperatures, electrons in the metal pair up into what are called Cooper pairs and disguise themselves as boson particles (see page 121) similar to light. Bosons can all have the same energy, one that allows them to completely avoid collisions with the ions in the material, flowing through unhindered. Pure metals are called type-I or "soft" semiconductors, as they require very cold temperatures. Type-II or "hard" semiconductors, which are made from alloy mixtures of metals and nonmetal elements, retain their superconductivity at much higher temperatures. The highest temperature superconductors at normal pressure are made from copper-oxide alloys and become

Superconductivity

Some materials become superconducting at low temperatures, leaving them with zero electrical resistance.

superconductive at around -284°F (-140°C). This is useful because it is above the boiling temperature of liquid nitrogen, which is a relatively cheap way of cooling a material down.

Reactance is a different form of opposition to the flow of electric current than standard resistance. Energy from alternating electric currents is stored and released by some electronic components as magnetic and electric fields. The process of energy storage opposes the movement of the electric charges through these components.

Capacitance when combined with the frequency of the alternating current is a measure of the reactance of electronic components called capacitors. They store energy into, and release energy from, an electric field by keeping apart collections of opposite electric charges.

Inductance when combined with the frequency of the alternating current is a measure of the reactance of electronic components called inductors. They store energy into, and release energy from, a magnetic field within circuits carrying an alternating current.

Impedance is the vector combination of both resistance and reactance; it is the total opposition to the flow of an alternating electric current.

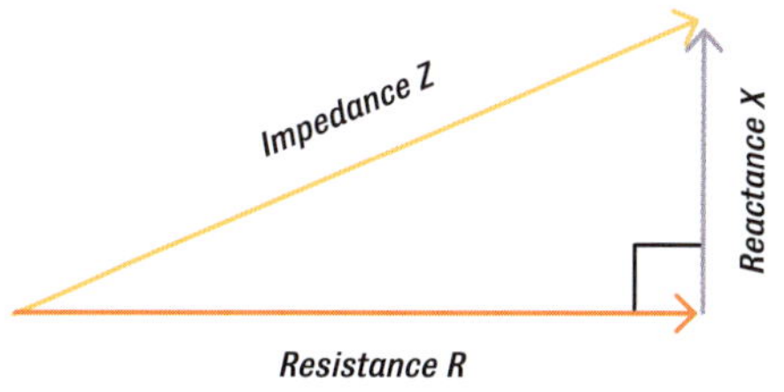

Impedance

Opposition to alternating currents comes from both resistance and reactance. The two are added in quadrature to calculate a total opposition to alternating electric current called impedance.

The **electrostatic force** is the force felt between two objects because of their electric charge. The force can be attractive, pulling charges of opposite sign (+ – or – +) together. It can also be repulsive, pushing charges of the same sign (+ + or – –) apart.

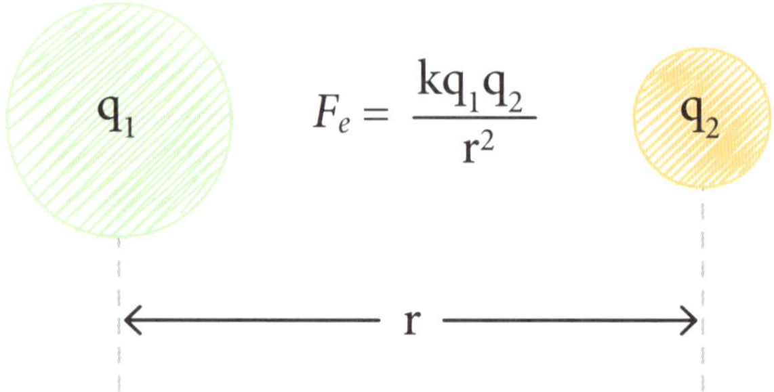

$$F_e = \frac{kq_1q_2}{r^2}$$

Coulomb's law

Coulomb's law is the electromagnetic version of Newton's law of gravity. It tells us that the force of attraction or repulsion between two objects of electric charge is related to the product of the electric charges divided by the square of the distance between them.

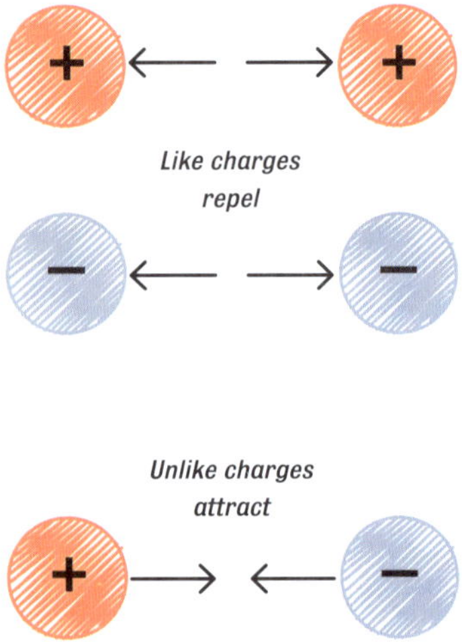

Electrostatic force

A force of attraction or repulsion arises between objects with electric charge; this is called the electrostatic force.

Coulomb's law provides an equation for calculating the magnitude of the force between any two charges q_1 and q_2 separated by a distance r.

French physicist Charles-Augustin de Coulomb derived it from experimental observation in 1784 and the constant k that determines the strength of the force is known as Coulomb's constant.

Electric fields

An electric field is an imagined network of lines issuing from an object with electric charge that reflects the strength and direction of the electrostatic force. For the same historical reasons as the direction of electric current, arrows on electric field lines point the way in which positive electric charges would move.

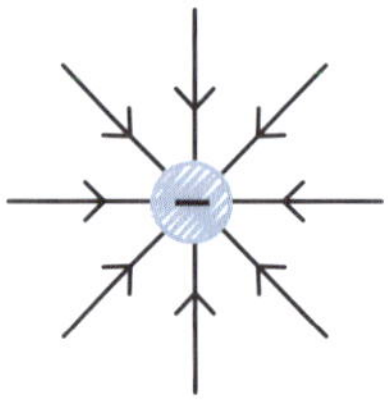

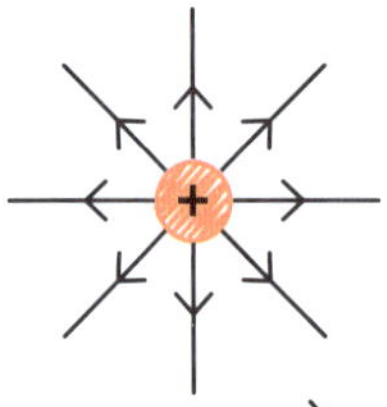

Electric field lines

Electric field lines map out the strength and direction a positive electric charge would take after experiencing the force field.

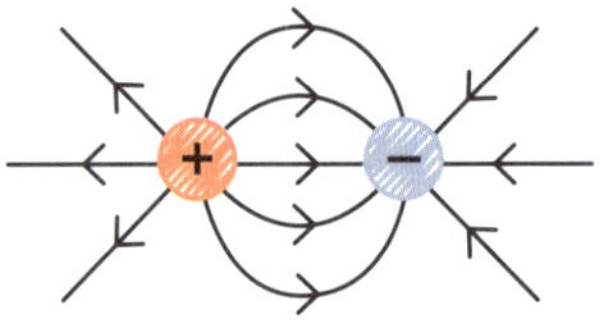

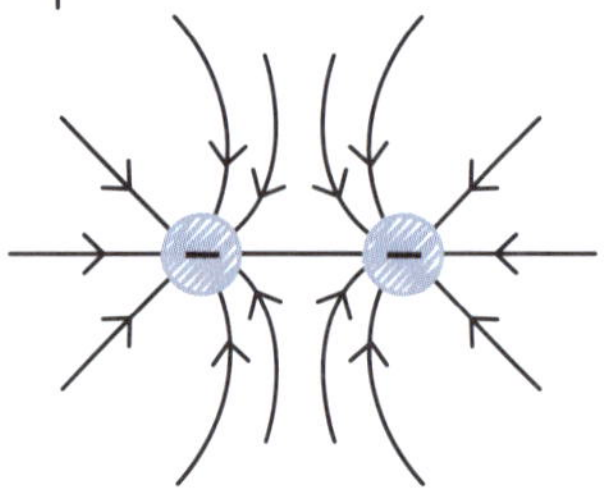

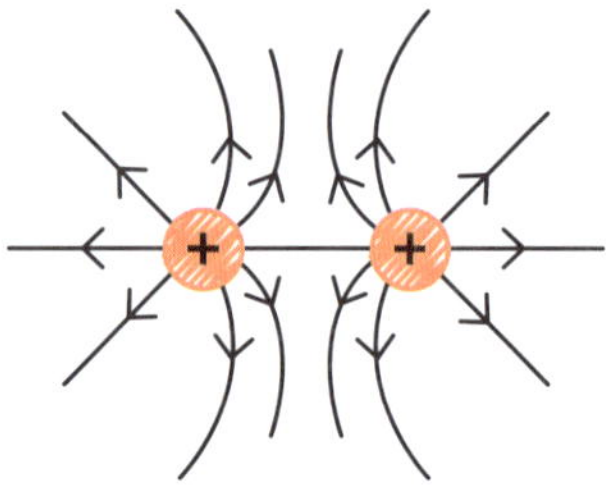

The strength of the force is shown by how densely packed the field lines are at a certain point—more field lines in a smaller space equals a stronger force. Electric flux is the name given to a group of electric field lines passing through a particular area.

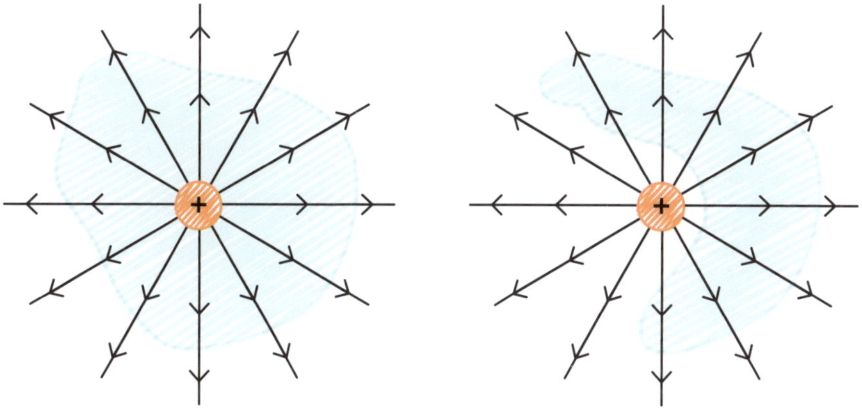

Gauss's theorem

Gauss's theorem relates the charge contained within a region of space with the total number of field lines entering or exiting that region.

Gauss's theorem gives the mathematical relationship between the total electric flux passing through a closed surface like a sphere (one that does not have an edge or hole), and the electric charge that is inside the surface. It is a more general form of the electric field equation of a point charge that is derived from Coulomb's law. The constant that relates these two laws is the electric constant ε_0. Gauss's theorem was derived by the German mathematical physicist Carl Friedrich Gauss and is one of the four Maxwell's equations.

The **electric constant** ε_0 is a measure of how easily electric field lines are permitted to form in a vacuum, or totally empty space. For this reason, it has also been referred to as the permittivity of free space, or vacuum permittivity, among many other names. It is a fundamental constant of nature with a fixed value. Coulomb's constant, it turns out, is just a special spherical version of the electric constant.

To work against the electrostatic force and pull two opposite charges apart or push two like charges together requires work. The work done in moving any electric charge some distance through an electric field changes the charge's **potential energy**. The potential energy change of each unit of charge that is moved in an electric field is called the **electric potential difference**, but is commonly referred to as the voltage. A voltage can exist between any separated static charges. The voltage is equal to the energy that each unit charge would transfer into or out of the electric field if the charges were free to move.

A potential energy can be transferred to electric charges by a chemical reaction in a cell or through the magnetic force by induction. The potential difference (voltage) generated is traditionally called an electromotive force (EMF), although it is not a force at all. As explained above, it is the potential energy per unit charge that has been transferred to the electric charges. It is the energy that has become available to the charged particle experiencing the EMF, which is usually then transferred into kinetic energy and movement, creating an electric current.

Magnetism

Magnetism can be traced to the subatomic level. Each subatomic particle has a small **magnetic moment** associated with it, which can be thought of as its own little internal bar magnet. Just like electric charge, a particle's magnetic moment is a fundamental property of a particle; it is related to a particle's spin (see page 99), but there is no deeper level of understanding to its origin. Electrons with opposite spin and magnetic moment direction pair up in energy levels around an atomic nucleus. This cancels out the magnetism contributed by the magnetic moment from most electrons in an atom. Magnetism is a property mainly of atoms with one or more unpaired electrons. These orbit a nucleus alone and are free to align their magnetic moments with external magnetic fields. The more the moments of these unpaired electrons align together, the stronger the experienced magnetism of the atom.

A **magnetic field** is a region of space where any other magnetic object would experience a magnetic force. Like all fields, it is invisible and a made-up idea, but it allows us to calculate the strength and direction of the magnetic force that a magnetic object would experience if it entered this region of space. Magnetic flux is the name given to a group of magnetic field lines passing through a particular area.

Magnetic moment

The magnetic moment is an inherent property of subatomic particles that dictates how they react in magnetic fields.

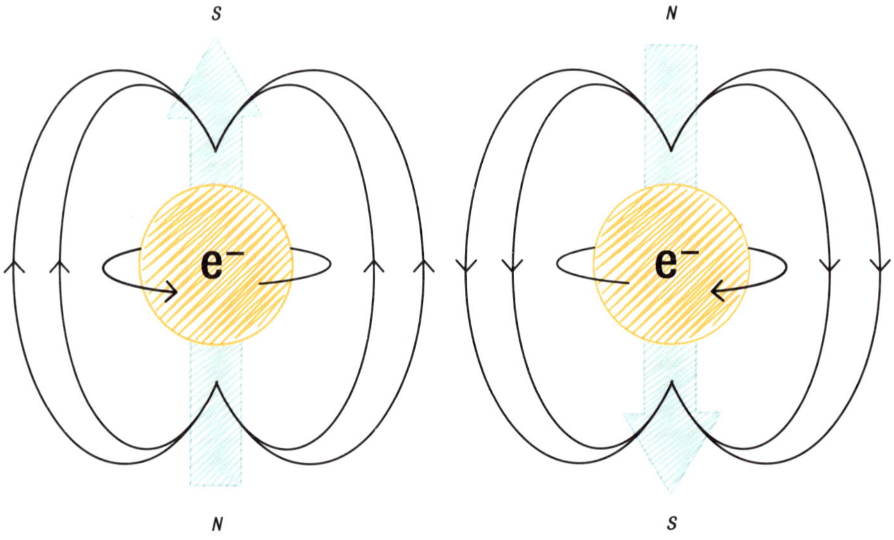

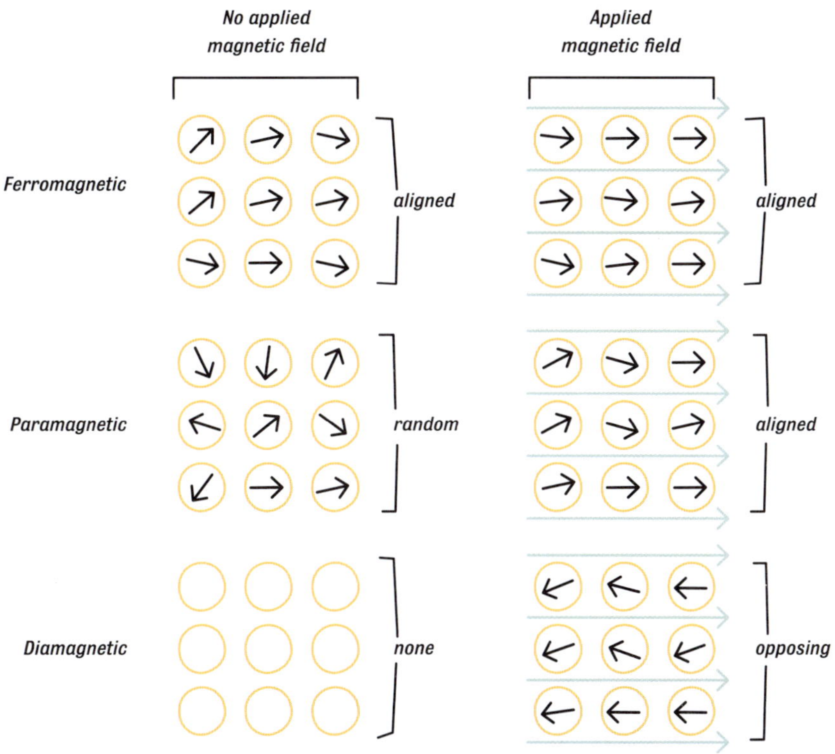

Paramagnetism, diamagnetism, and ferromagnetism

Electrons in atoms either align or oppose external magnetic fields which leads to three distinct types of magnetic behavior.

An external magnetic field will align the magnetic moments of any unpaired electrons, an effect known as **paramagnetism**. This alignment attracts the material toward the source of the magnetism. In most elements, this is the dominant form of magnetism and so elemental materials are usually attracted toward magnets.

Elemental nickel, iron, and cobalt have a large number of lone unpaired electrons. When placed inside a magnetic field, the magnetic moments of all of these electrons line up. This produces a much larger magnetic field in each atom than happens with paramagnetic materials. Increased paramagnetism means a much stronger attraction to the source of magnetism. This unique behavior classes these elements and many of their combinations with other elements as a **ferromagnetic material**.

Some ferromagnetic materials, such as steel, are said to be magnetically hard, as they retain their magnetism even after the magnetic field is removed. Soft ferromagnetic materials lose their magnetism quickly once an applied magnetic field is removed. To demagnetize hard magnetic materials, they must be heated to high temperatures or physically knocked about to shake up the aligned magnetic moments of the atoms. Soft magnetic materials require only a gentle hit or warm temperatures for them to become unmagnetized once more.

A **permanent magnetic material** is one in which the magnetic moments of a large number of electrons are fixed in the same direction. It has a constant magnetic field, which means that permanent magnets are usually made from hard magnetic materials. Permanent magnets are formed when an external magnetic field aligns the moments of electrons in the material. Heat usually plays a role by shaking electrons up until they align their magnetic moments with whatever magnetic field there is. You can make a magnet yourself by rubbing another magnet over a piece of steel, each pass aligns more and more electron magnetic moments.

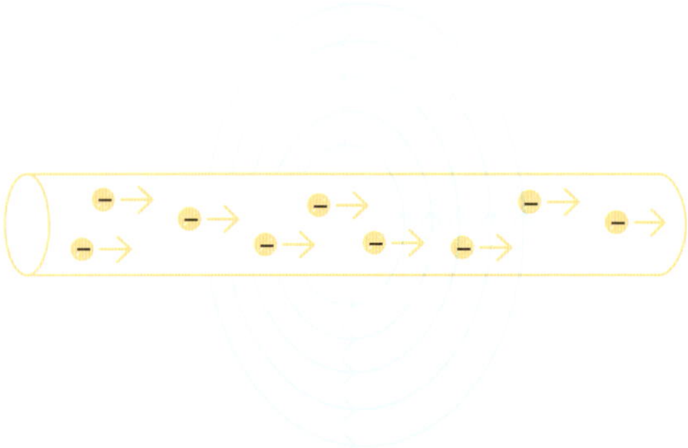

Electric current and magnetic fields

Any flowing electric current will produce a magnetic field at 90° to the direction of flow.

In 2000, scientists demonstrated the diamagnetism of water molecules by levitating a frog above a superconducting electromagnet.

The force a current-carrying wire feels in a magnetic field is known as the **motor effect**. It is used in electric motors to transfer electrical potential energy into kinetic energy.

Danish physicist Hans Christian Ørsted noticed that wires carrying an electric current generate their own magnetic field because they exert force upon permanent magnets. He showed that a circular magnetic field is generated by a current-carrying wire at 90° to the motion of the electric current. This was the first hint that there was a link between electricity and magnetism. The magnetic field produced by an electric current is amplified by looping the wire around many times to create a coil. Many wires stacked on top of one another carry current and therefore produce a magnetic field in a single direction. This is how you make an **electromagnet**: a device that has a magnetic field only when an electric current is flowing. The magnetic field is also given a boost in most electromagnets by putting a soft ferromagnetic material, such as iron, through the middle of the coil. The magnetic moments of electrons in the iron are aligned by the magnetic field of the electromagnet to produce a more powerful magnetic field.

When a magnetic field is applied to a material, the motion of electrons around an atom steps into sync. This generates a small magnetic field in the atom, which is oppositely aligned to the external field, repelling it away from the source of magnetism. This magnetism is called **diamagnetism** and is present in all materials.

Electric potential energy creates an electric current through a coiled wire to create an electromagnet. This coil is mounted on an axle through its center, allowing it to spin. The magnetic field of this electromagnet interacts with the field of a permanent magnet to generate a force that turns the coil

Motor effect

The magnetic field produced by a loop of wire carrying electric current interacts with a permanent magnetic field, resulting in a turning force.

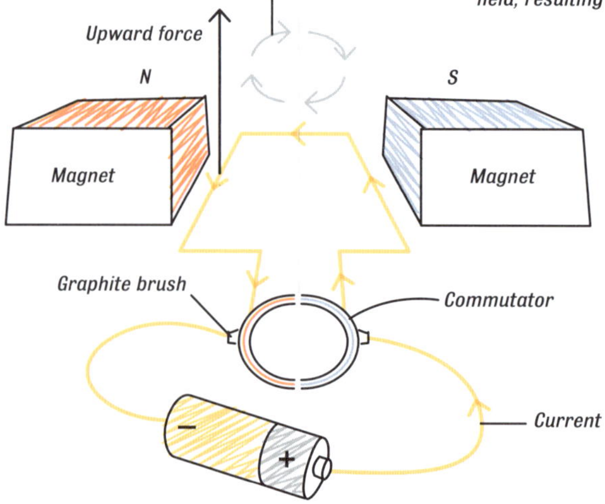

Induction

A changing magnetic field, created by moving a magnet, will induce a potential difference in a wire that will result in an electric current if it is part of a complete circuit.

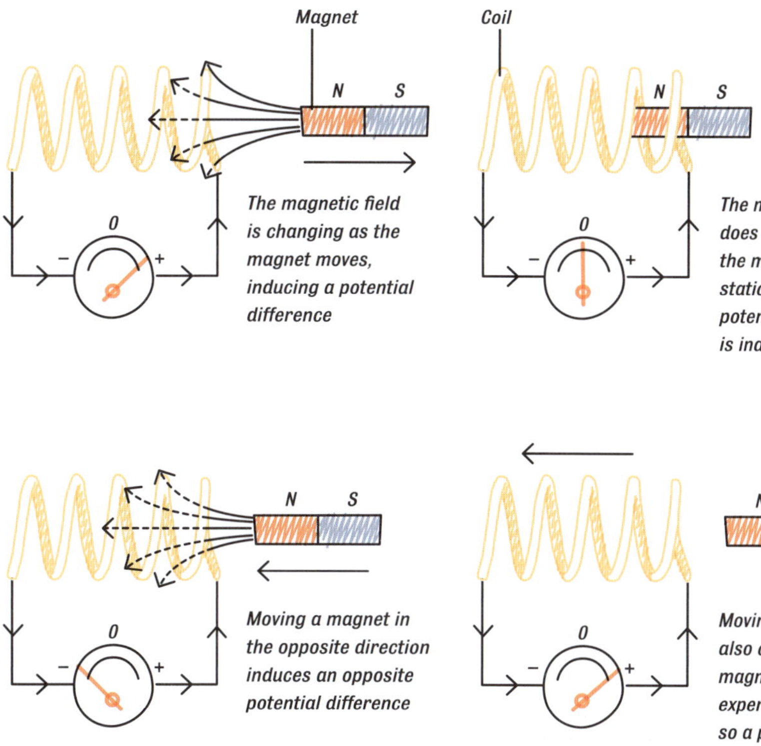

The magnetic field is changing as the magnet moves, inducing a potential difference

The magnetic field does not change if the magnet is stationary, so no potential difference is induced

Moving a magnet in the opposite direction induces an opposite potential difference

Moving the coil also changes the magnetic field it experiences and so a potential difference is also induced

around the axle. This turning force must always act in the same direction, otherwise the motor will not continue to turn. Despite turning, the magnetic field of the electromagnet must always point in the same direction, which is achieved if the current flowing around the coil changes its direction every half turn. This is achieved by passing the current to the coil using commutators (rotary electric switches). These ensure that even as the coil turns, the current changes direction around the coil every half turn so that the magnetic field the coil generates is always in the same direction compared to the permanent magnet.

Electric current passing through a coil of wire in a magnetic field causes movement and movement in a coil of wire in a magnetic field can produce an electric current. If we imagine electron magnetic moments to be tiny bar magnets, then it makes sense that a moving magnetic field would move electrons. This process is known as **induction**, as the motion induces an electric potential difference, which if connected to a complete circuit will produce an electric current.

Generators use the principle of induction to transfer kinetic energy into electrical potential energy, eventually producing an electric current. Generators are the main way both renewable and nonrenewable energy sources produce electricity. A coil of wire is placed inside a permanent magnet. Kinetic (movement) energy is transferred to rotate either the coil or the magnet so that the wire in the coil experiences a changing magnetic field. An electric potential is induced in the coil, which can be used to create an electric current for powering electrical devices. The kinetic energy may come directly from blowing wind or lapping waves, but most commonly comes from steam expanding after water has been boiled. Water can be heated by renewable sources such as sunlight or biofuels, or by nonrenewable sources such as oil, gas, coal, or radioactivity.

Faraday's law, developed by pioneering British physicist Michael Faraday, is an equation that describes the link between electric potential difference induced and the changing magnetic field. It tells us that the rate of change in the number of field lines is directly related to the potential difference; double the rate of change and double the potential difference induced. This can be done by doubling the area exposed to the magnetic field by adding a second loop of wire into the changing magnetic field, doubling the speed at which the wire moves through the magnetic field (or vice versa) or by doubling the strength of the magnetic field. Faraday's law is always combined with Lenz's law, named after Russian physicist Emil Lenz. Lenz noted that the potential difference induced in a coil was always induced in a way that opposed the change in magnetic field. This is shown simply as a negative sign in the potential with respect to the changing magnetic field lines.

Gauss's theorem for magnetism is the magnetic version of Gauss's theorem. It gives the mathematical relationship between the total magnetic flux passing through a surface and the magnet surrounded by the surface. It is important, as it states there is no such thing as magnetic charge. A magnet cannot exist as a monopole; it cannot be just north or just south, but must be a dipole with both a north and south pole. Under Gauss's theorem of magnetism, the total flux through a surface surrounding a magnet must always be zero. Any flux coming out from a north pole must be perfectly balanced by flux pointing in the opposite direction going into the south pole.

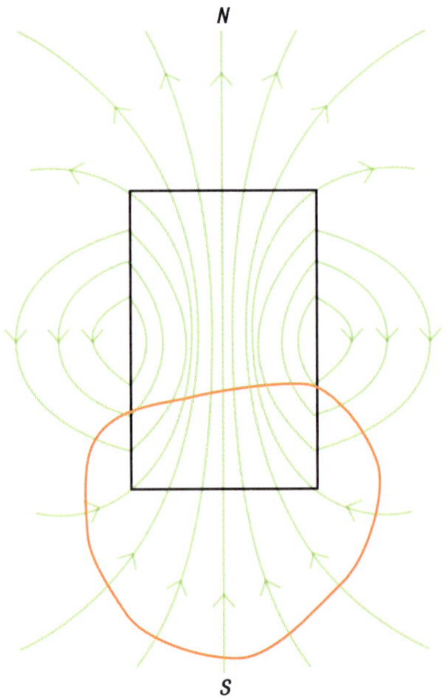

Gauss's theorem for magnetism

The magnetic field lines of a bar magnet form closed loops. Note that the net magnetic flux through the closed surface (red line) surrounding one of the poles (or any other closed surface) is zero.

A **magnetic force** is experienced when the magnetic fields of two magnetic objects interact. If the field lines connect, then the force is attractive and pulls the objects together, if the field lines oppose each other and wish to pass through each other, then the magnetic force pushes the objects apart.

Hendrik Lorentz combined the electrostatic force of Coulomb and the magnetic force on moving charges investigated by Ampère into a single equation called the **Lorentz force**. This equation describes the total force and its direction on any electrically charged object moving simultaneously through both electric and magnetic fields. It is a vector equation as it involves the vector quantities of force (F), electric field (E), magnetic field (B), and velocity (v).

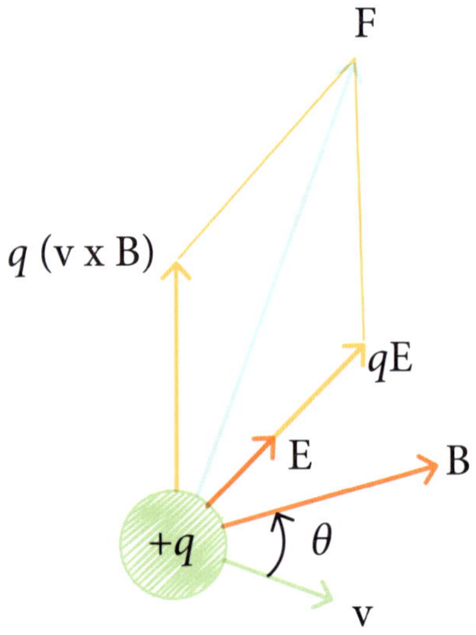

Lorentz force

The Lorentz force is the vector addition of forces experienced by an electric charge as it passes through both electric and magnetic fields.

Maxwell's equations pull together the combined knowledge of many experiments on electricity and magnetism to fully describe all links between the two. It is a set of four equations that are special versions of Gauss's two theorems, **Ampere's law** and Faraday's law. Along with the Lorentz equation, they describe all of electromagnetism. In combining these four laws, the British physicist James Clerk Maxwell showed that electric fields and magnetic fields are part of the same thing. He also showed that waves travel through these fields at a fixed speed. It was not long before experiments demonstrated that this speed was the same as the speed that light traveled through empty space. Maxwell had showed that light was nothing but traveling electromagnetic fields—**electromagnetic waves**.

The **electromagnetic spectrum** is the collection of electromagnetic waves spanning all frequencies and wavelengths. It divides all possible electromagnetic waves into eight distinct regions, each with different ranges in frequency and wavelength. These include: radio waves, microwaves, infrared light, visible light, ultraviolet light, X-rays, and gamma rays.

Without understanding the electromagnetic spectrum we would not know so much about the universe that we live in, or have developed the technologies we have come to rely upon. Electromagnetism underpins our entire modern world.

Maxwell's equations

Maxwell's equations brought together the forces of electrostatics and magnetism into one electromagnetic force. In doing so, Maxwell also proved that light was an electromagnetic wave. The equations shown below are in vector form (orange) and pictorial form.

Coulomb's law

$$\nabla \cdot E = \rho$$

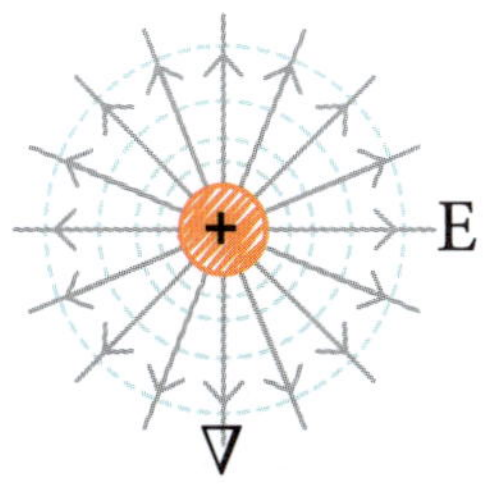

Gauss's theorem

$$\nabla \cdot B = 0$$

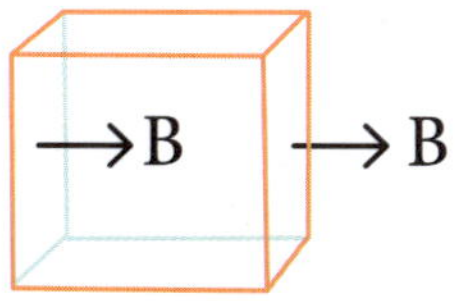

Ampere's law

$$\nabla \times B - \frac{1}{c}\frac{\partial E}{\partial t} = \frac{J}{c}$$

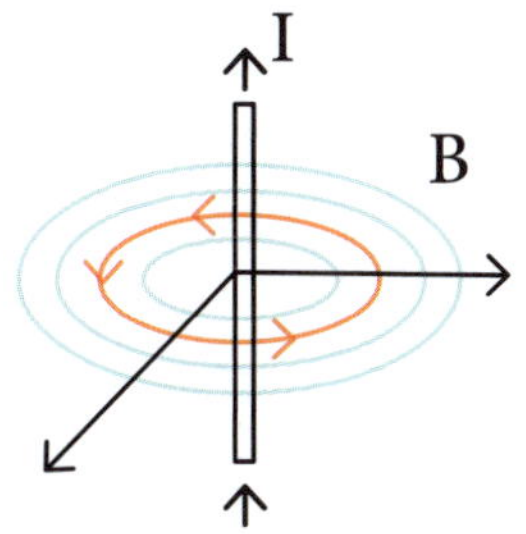

Faraday's law

$$\nabla \times E + \frac{1}{c}\frac{\partial B}{\partial t} = 0$$

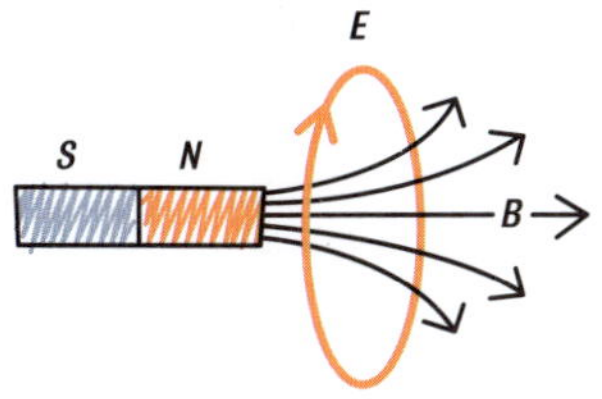

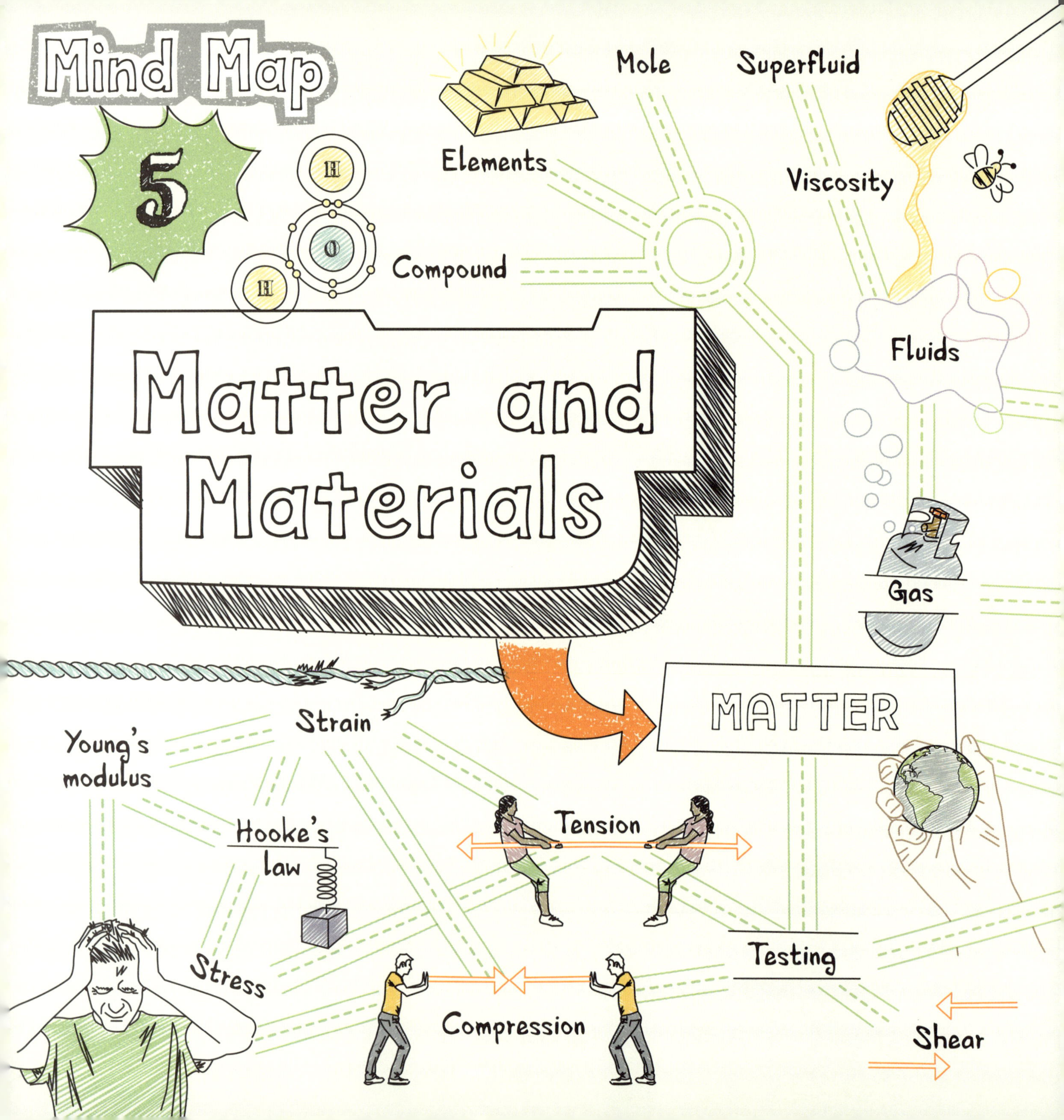
Mind Map
5
Matter and Materials
Elements
Mole
Superfluid
Viscosity
Compound
Fluids
Gas
MATTER
Strain
Young's modulus
Hooke's law
Tension
Testing
Stress
Compression
Shear

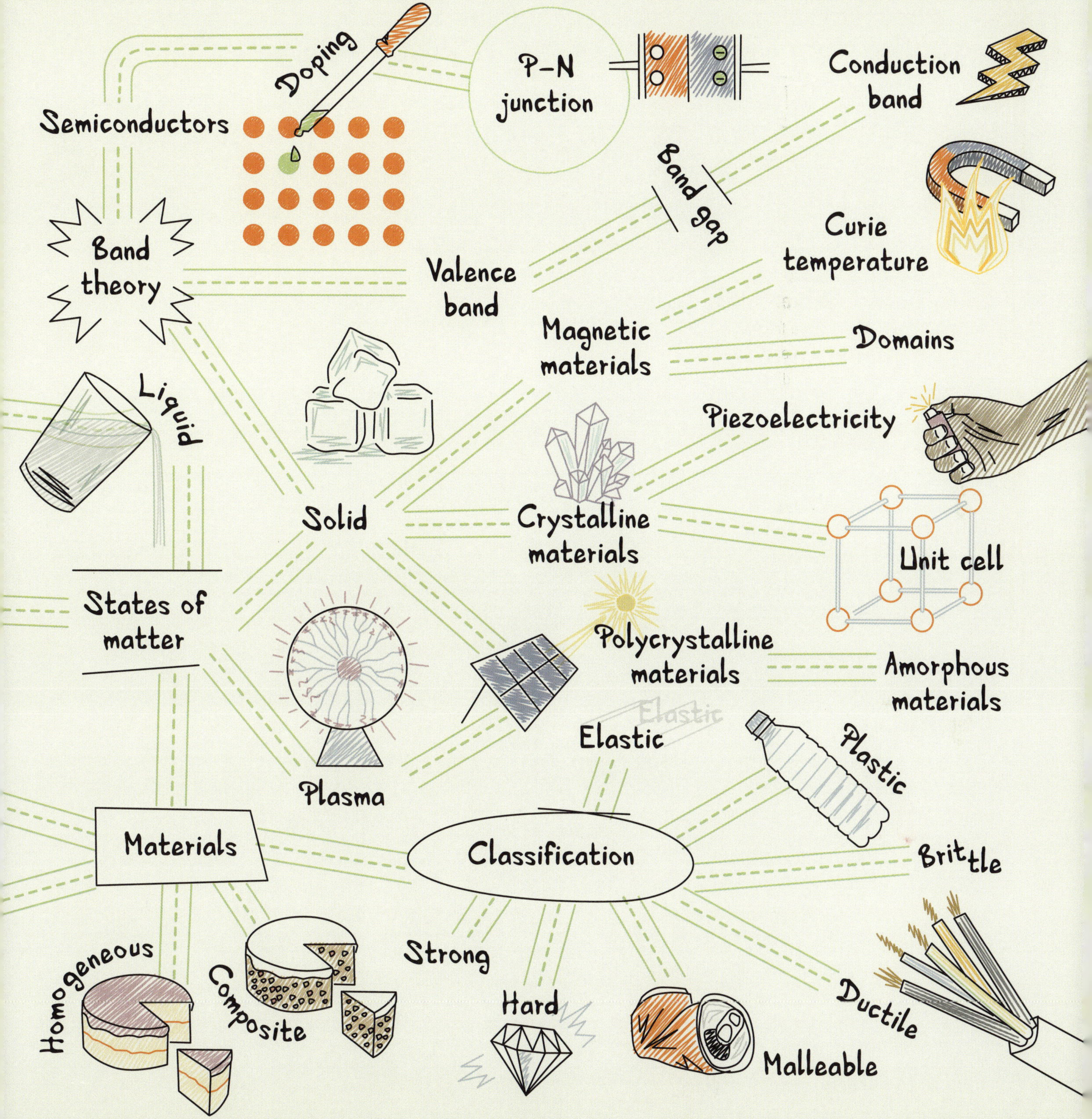

Semiconductors
Doping
P–N junction
Conduction band
Band gap
Band theory
Valence band
Curie temperature
Magnetic materials
Domains
Liquid
Piezoelectricity
Solid
Crystalline materials
Unit cell
States of matter
Polycrystalline materials
Amorphous materials
Elastic
Plastic
Plasma
Materials
Classification
Brittle
Strong
Homogeneous
Composite
Hard
Ductile
Malleable

What Is Matter?

Anything that is part of the physical world is **matter**. A **material** is an object made from matter that is employed for a particular purpose. Materials exist with different levels of complexity and many different properties.

The most basic building block of a material is an atom. Materials that consist of collections of just a single type of atom, or element, are the simplest type of material. Some **elements**, for example metals such as copper and noble gases such as argon, tend to exist together as collections of many individual atoms. But other elements prefer to exist as molecules comprising one or more atoms of a single type joined by a chemical bond. Oxygen (O) atoms, for example, naturally pair up to form molecular oxygen (O_2), while much larger numbers of carbon atoms can join together to form graphite or diamond. Given half a chance, though, most elements will readily form **compound** materials by combining with other elements through chemical bonds.

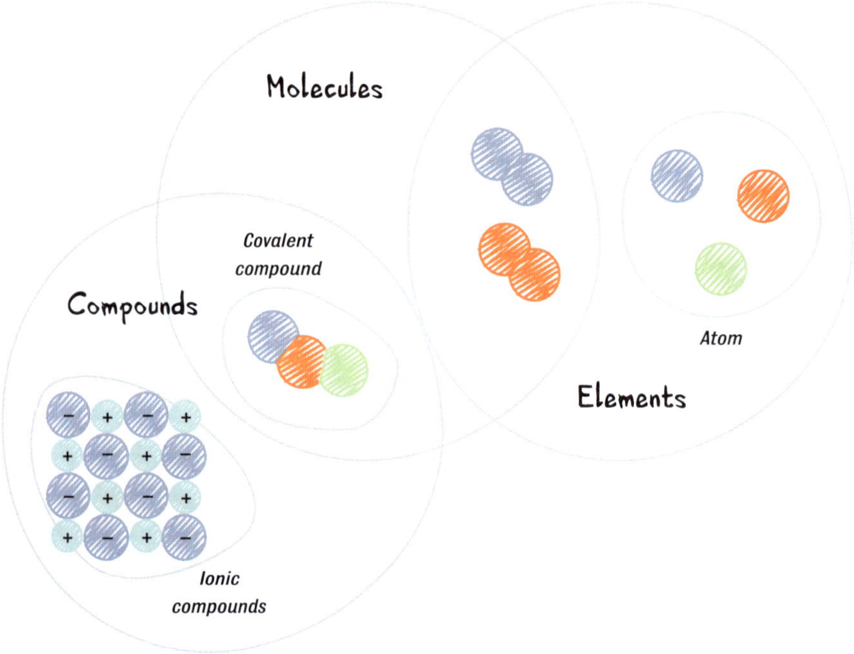

Elements and substances

An element is a substance made from one type of atom. Molecules are made from two or more atoms chemically bound together. A compound is a substance made from two or more different atoms bound together.

Materials can exist in different states of matter. A **solid** has a structure and shape held together by rigid chemical bonds. Atoms are not free to move over each other in a solid; they cannot flow. Atoms can flow in liquids, gases, and plasmas, and these three **states of matter** are referred to collectively as **fluids**. Particles in a **liquid** are bound to one another by weak forces between atoms or molecules. Particles in a

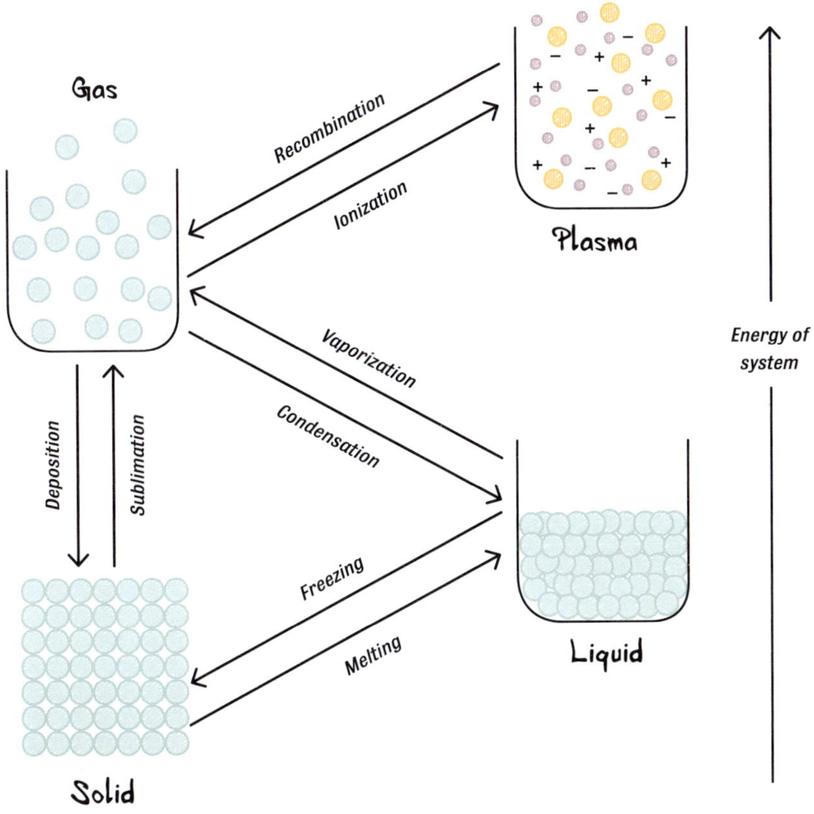

States of matter

Matter exists in four different states, each with their own properties: solids, liquids, gases, and plasma.

gas have very little interaction with each other and are spaced apart by large tracts of empty space. A **plasma** is similar to a gas in that the particles are spaced out, but it is comprised of a collection of ions and electrons rather than electrically neutral atoms or molecules.

To determine the behavior of a material we need some measure of the amount of a substance we have. We need to know how many separate particles of a substance are contained within a sample of a material. The particles can be atoms, molecules, ions, or electrons. The volume of a gas is dependent upon pressure and temperature, and so we cannot define the amount of such fluids by their volume. Different particles would each have a different mass and so just measuring the mass of a solid or fluid would not tell us the amount of a substance we have.

The unit of a **mole** tells us how many individual particles of a substance there are in any given sample. In 2018, one mole was defined as the amount of a substance that contains exactly 6.02214076 x10^{23} particles. This might seem like an arbitrary number, but it is a historical artefact from the previous definition of a mole. Previously, the mole was defined as the number of carbon-12 atoms in a 12-gram sample of carbon-12. In an elemental material like iron, one mole would contain exactly 6.02214076 x10^{23} iron atoms. In a compound such as water, it would mean that there were exactly 6.02214076 x10^{23} H_2O molecules in one mole of water. Although both samples contain one mole, they have very different masses. One atom of iron is more massive than an H_2O molecule of water, and so one mole of iron will have a greater mass than one mole of water. Of course, this is just one of many properties that are different between the samples because they are made of different materials.

Materials

Materials can be tested by applying force to stretch, squash, or twist them. A solid object is said to deform if it changes shape in any way when a force is applied. Through **testing**, engineers can choose the right materials for whatever job they have in mind. If they cannot find the right materials for the job, then materials can be combined in different ways to create something that fits the need. There are commonly three different forces used to test materials.

A **tension** force is any mechanical force that pulls away from the surface of a material in opposite directions at exactly opposite locations on opposite sides of a material. Materials are tested under tension to determine their ability to resist breaking or deformation when being pulled apart.

A **compression** force is any mechanical force that pushes into the surface of a material in opposite directions at exactly opposite locations on opposite sides of a material. Materials are tested under compression to determine their ability to resist breaking or deformation when being squashed by a force.

A **shear** force is a pair of pushes or pulls applied to the surface of a material at different locations on different sides of a material. Tension or compression are often coupled by some amount of shear force as pairs of applied forces are rarely exactly opposite each other. **Testing** of a material under shear force determines their ability to resist breaking or deformation under twisting.

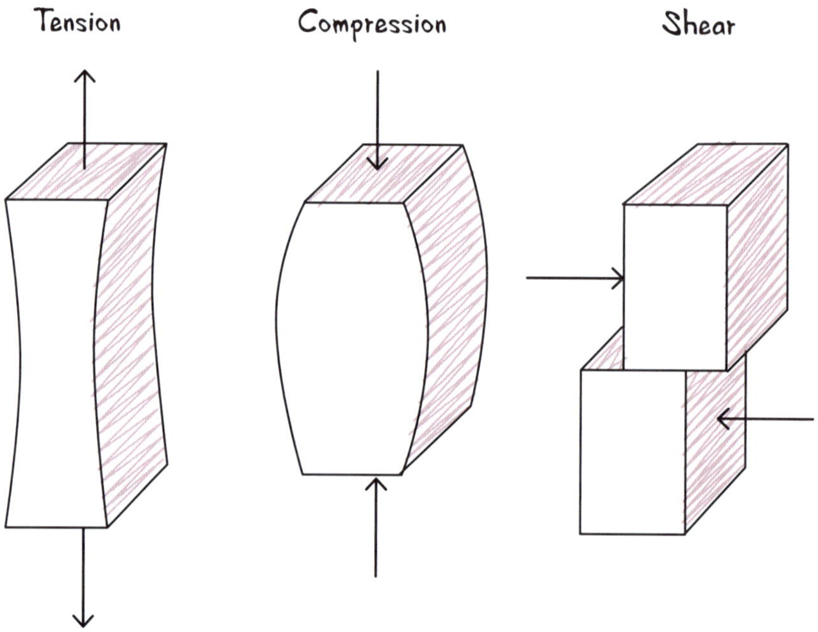

Tension, compression, and shear forces

These forces are very different and so are dealt with in different ways by different materials.

Elastic objects

Elastic objects deform when a force is applied but return to their original shape when the force is removed. Springs are a good example of elastic objects that deform under tension by stretching but return to their original length when the force is removed.

Extension of many elastic objects change in direct proportion to the applied force; if the force is doubled the extension (x) is doubled, quadruple the force and you quadruple the extension. This relationship is known as **Hooke's law**, as the British physicist, Robert Hooke, first noted it. Springs obey Hooke's law, which is why the constant number relating applied force to extension is called the spring constant (k). The value of the spring constant depends only upon the material being put under tension. A stiff material such as a car's shock absorbers has a large spring constant value because a large amount of force needs to be applied to extend it. A soft material requires less force to extend and so takes smaller values of spring constant. The point at which a material no longer extends in proportion to the applied force, and so no longer follows Hooke's law, is known as the limit of proportionality. Beyond this point, most materials can take on a little more force and still return to their original length but here they do not extend in proportion to the force.

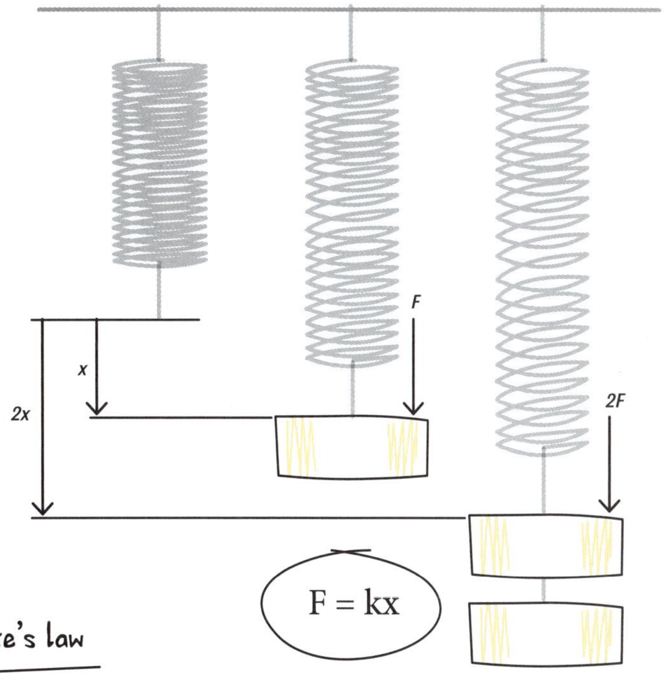

Hooke's law

Hooke's law states that if the tension force (F) on an elastic object doubles then so will the extension of the object (x) from its original length. The extent it extends for each unit of force is defined by the spring constant (k).

Although elastic, elastic bands do not follow Hooke's law; they change their stiffness. They are initially tough to stretch, as the long polymer molecules they are made from unfurl from each other. After this, they become much easier to extend as the molecules straighten themselves out. An elastic band becomes tough to stretch once again when all of the molecules are extended.

Two measurables allow the determination of a material's properties: stress and strain. **Stress** is the applied force acting on each unit area of a material. The forces can be compressive, tensile or shear, and each has its own stress associated with it. **Strain** is the length a material is deformed in the direction of an applied force per each unit of the object's original length in that direction. Again, each type of applied force has its own stress associated with it; tensile stress, for example, is the amount each meter of material is extended as it is pulled apart by a tension force.

Materials under stress

Measuring and then plotting a graph of a material's strain under an applied stress tells us a lot about a material's properties. The gradient, or steepness of the plotted line, of such a graph is known as the modulus of the material, sometimes referred to as the **Young's modulus** after the British physicist, Thomas Young. Materials that have a large modulus are said to be stiff, as they require a large stress to be applied before there is any deformation. Soft materials require little stress before changing shape.

Plastic objects deform under tension or compression but do not return to their original shape. Most materials exhibit plastic behavior when put under enough stress to pass a point known as the elastic limit. After this point, a material will never return to its previous shape.

Brittle materials, however, do not demonstrate any plastic behavior; instead, they break at a given stress without permanently deforming at all. The point at which a material breaks is known as the breaking stress.

Ductile materials demonstrate plastic behavior over a wide range of strains when under tension. This property allows metals such as copper to be drawn out into long thin wires when pulled in one direction. Ductile materials easily plastically deform past a certain stress and strain known as the yield point. Materials that deform plastically are usually able to take a far greater stress than the stress that causes them to yield, known as the ultimate tensile strength. But, they will break when they experience an insurmountable strain.

Malleable objects allow themselves to be plastically deformed over a large range of strains by compression, tension, and shear forces. Gold is a highly malleable metal, which can be beaten to a thickness of just a few atoms.

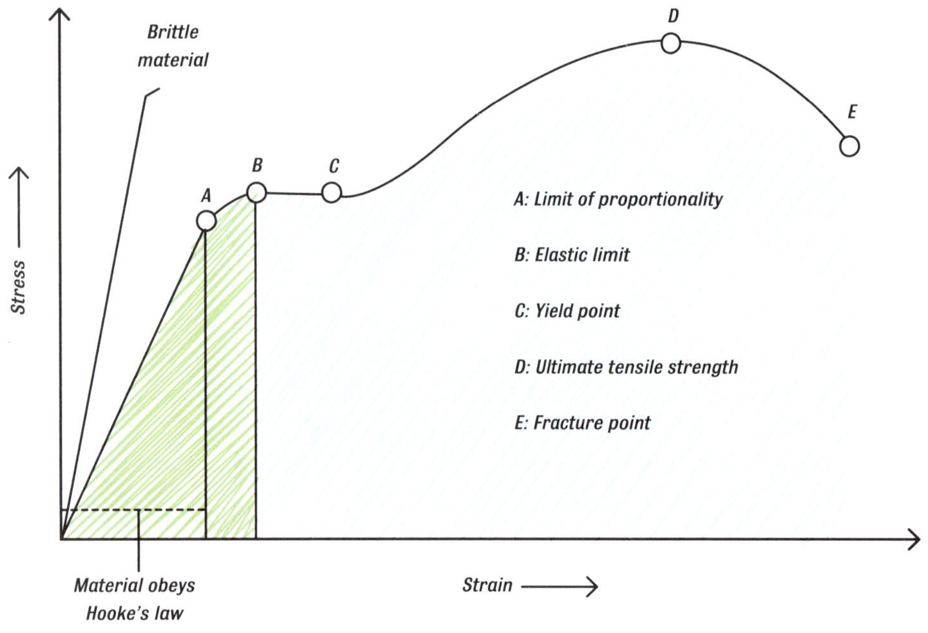

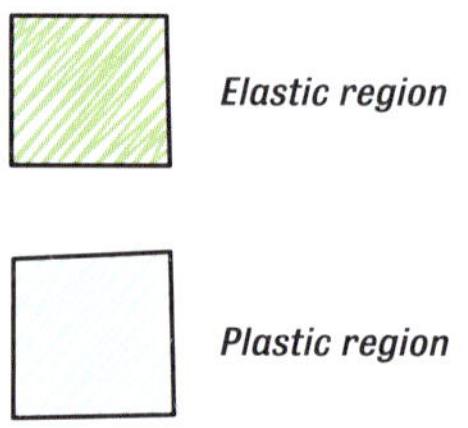

Young's modulus

Plotting the stress and strain of forces acting on an object reveals what type of material it is made from.

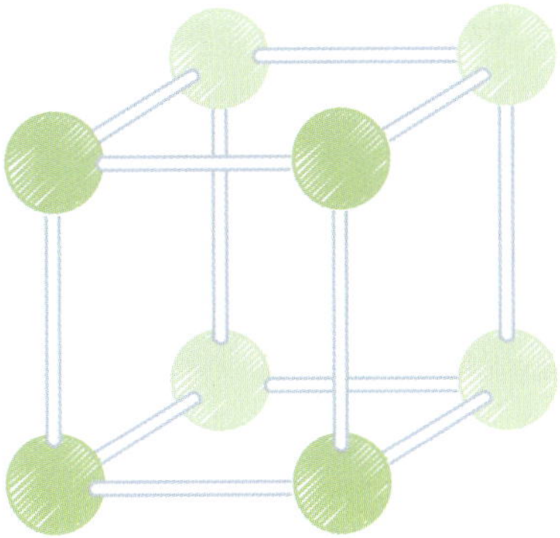

Simple

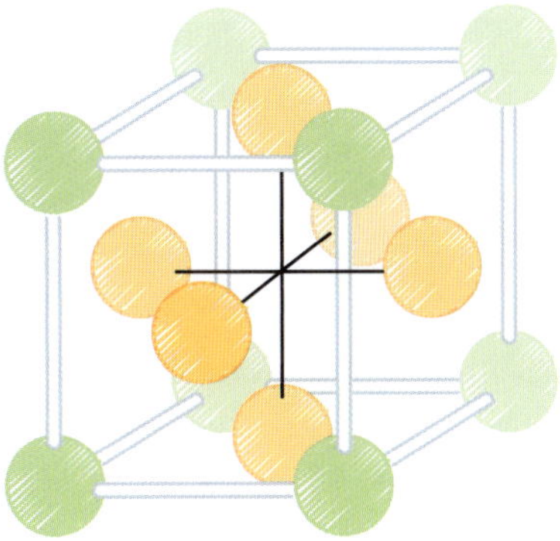

Face-centered

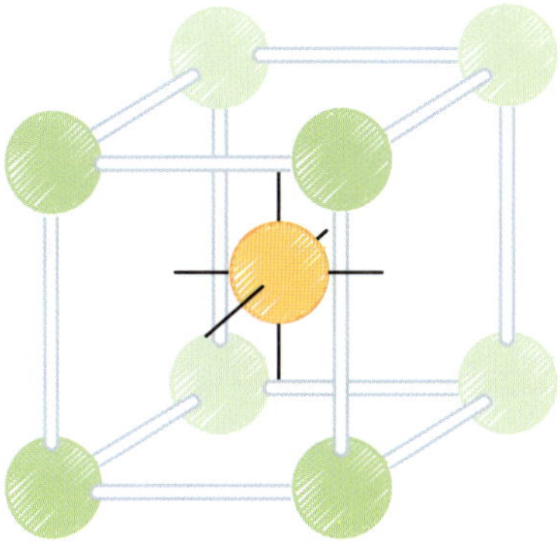

Body-centered

Unit cell

A unit cell is the smallest pattern of atoms that can be repeated to build up a larger lattice of a crystal. These are the three most common unit cells. Simple has atoms at the corner of the cell only, face-centered is so called as it has additional atoms in the center of the surfaces of the cube, and body-centered has an additional atom in the center of the unit cell.

Hard materials are able to withstand frictional wear; they are scratch resistant. Hardness can be measured using the Vickers hardness test, in which a certain shape of diamond is rammed into the surface of the material at different applied forces until it creates an indentation. Diamond is chosen because it is the hardest material known, which means that it will not deform during the test and so transfers all of the applied force to the surface of the material.

If a large force is required to deform a material, then we say that the material is **strong**. Strong materials can withstand a large amount of stress before they yield.

Crystalline materials

Crystalline materials have highly ordered microscopic structures with atoms arranged in regular and repeating patterns called a crystal lattice. Such an arrangement gives crystal materials large-scale structure and shapes that allude to the microscopic arrangement of atoms in the material. Naturally occurring crystal materials include table salt (sodium chloride), diamond, and snowflakes.

Crystalline materials can be classified by their microscopic structure, through identifying the most basic repeating group of atoms called a **unit cell**. Arrangements of atoms within the unit cell define the shape and properties of crystalline materials. The shape of a unit cell and how it fits together with the other unit cells is defined by its lattice system. Unit cells are all parallelepipeds—six-sided, 3-D-shapes—defined by the length of the sides, as well as the angles between them. Different types of lattice system arise because of the different ways that these shapes must be stacked together to form a crystal.

Crystalline materials

Polycrystalline materials

Amorphous materials

Crystalline materials have regular and repeating long-range structure. Polycrystalline materials have only short-range structure. Amorphous materials do not have any structure.

POLYCRYSTALLINE MATERIALS

Polycrystalline materials are composed of many microscopic crystals called crystallites or grains. These grains are irregular in shape and orientation, having grown from an initial center outward into the surrounding space until they push up against each other. Grain boundaries, where grains meet, represent weaknesses in the material, as there is less of a force connecting grains together. Many metals and semimetals are naturally polycrystalline in structure. Large, macroscopic, crystalline forms of a material can be grown from polycrystalline materials under the correct conditions. Single crystals of metals are grown under carefully controlled temperatures and pressures to be many meters in size. These single crystals of metal are then machined and used as turbine blades in jet engines among other things, as they are far more resistant to breaking compared with polycrystalline versions of a metal, which tend to break along grain boundaries.

Amorphous materials lack the long-range structure found in crystals; they do not have regularly repeating patterns but comprise a random orientation of molecules. Many different types of materials may have amorphous forms; the most common example is glass.

Electrons in materials can only take certain energies, defined by the atoms and molecules the material is made from. The spectrum of energies they can take is split into certain regions, which are referred to as bands in **band theory**.

Electrons associated with an atom are known as valence electrons. In chemistry, this term also refers to an atom's outermost electrons, as these are involved in chemical reactions. The range of energies electrons can take and still be bound to an atom is referred to as the **valence band**.

Electrons with energy in excess of the valence band, and thus able to free themselves of an atom to move freely within a material, are referred to as conduction electrons, as they are able to move and therefore conduct electric current. Electrons with these energies are said to be part of the **conduction band**. In metals, the outermost electrons in the atom have enough energy to roam free as part of the conduction band. This is why most metals are classed as electrical conductors. However, in most materials the conduction and valence bands are entirely separate. The two are separated into distinct regions of different energy.

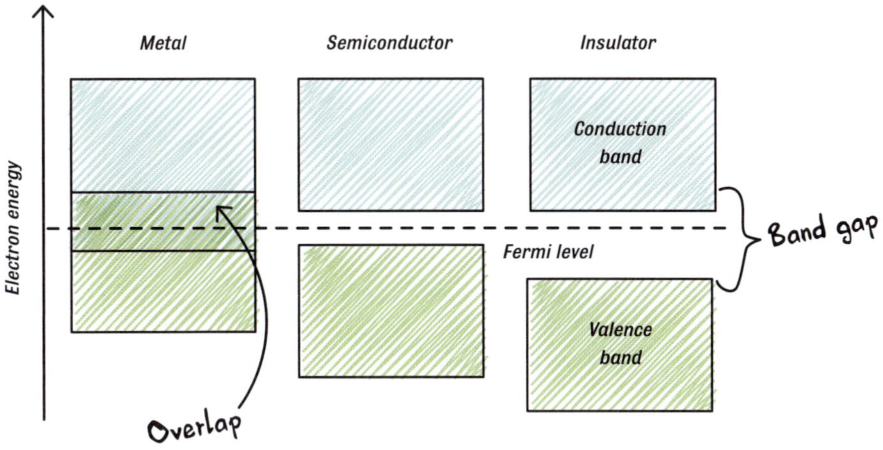

Band theory

Band theory allows for the description of different material types based upon the energies that electrons can take around atoms.

A **band gap** is a range in energies where no electrons can exist between the valence band and the conduction band within an atom. Most metals do not have a band gap, as their valence band and conduction band overlap. Electrical insulators have very large band gaps, where the energy required to promote an electron from valence to conduction is much larger than the onset of other processes such as catching fire, which is why paper burns before ever conducting electricity.

Semiconductors are materials in which the band gap is so small that a small change in electron energy can promote some valence electrons to the conduction band. As more energy is given to a semiconductor material, a greater number of electrons are promoted to the conduction band and the resistance of the material drops as its ability to conduct electricity increases. Many electronic components make use of the energy dependence of conductivity in semiconductors. For example, light-dependent resistors (LDRs) drop in resistance as light is absorbed by electrons in a semiconductor, promoting more electrons to the conduction band.

Semiconductor materials have revolutionized our modern world as our understanding of their behavior led to a vast range of uses. However, it is one particular use that has led us forward time and again into a technological revolution—the transistor. Transistors work in one of two ways: they can act as amplifiers or as switches. Early silicon transistors, invented in 1947, were used to amplify radio and TV signals in household devices. A small change in input voltage produces a large change in output; transistors are still used in this way in any modern device requiring amplification.

It is their use as switches, however, that has truly revolutionized our world. Working in this way, a transistor can act as a logic gate, switching on or off when given a certain set of inputs. This allowed transistors to be used to process logic and, eventually, when they were connected together, to handle complex algorithms. Transistors like this are etched side by side on to wafers of silicon to produce microprocessors, which are the brains that process data in computers, cell phones and every smart device around today.

Doping

Properties of semiconductor materials can be tuned by adding small amounts of other semiconducting atoms, a process known as **doping**. Pure semiconductor materials are called intrinsic; any semiconductor that has been doped is said to be extrinsic. Doping an intrinsic semiconductor with an element one place to the right in the periodic table creates an n-type semiconductor. The "n" stands for negative, as negatively charged electrons are the main charge carriers when this material conducts electricity. Doping with an element that has a greater number of valence electrons than the intrinsic semiconductor, leaves one electron unbound by the other atoms in the surrounding crystal lattice. This unbound electron can then conduct electricity.

Adding atoms of an element one place to the left in the periodic table leaves an absence where an electron would otherwise be found. These are called holes and are places where electrons would have otherwise bonded to complete the lattice in the intrinsic semiconductor. If an electromotive force (emf) is applied then electricity is conducted in these p-type extrinsic semiconductors by movement of the holes; because electrons fill in the holes as they move through the semiconductor, it looks like the holes are moving in the opposite direction.

If p-type and n-type semiconductors are brought into contact to create a **p–n junction**, there is an initial exchange of electrons into the p-type semiconductor, creating holes in the n-type. Eventually the exchange stops when the separation of charge creates an electric field that prevents any other electrons from moving. The electric field increases the energy required for electrons to be promoted to the conduction band, but only in one direction; in the other direction, the electrons would have to gain potential energy to get over the electric field acting against them. Electric components that allow electric current to flow in just one direction like this are called diodes. As electrons cross this depleted layer, they fall down in potential energy. In some diodes, this decrease in energy is achieved by emitting light, producing a light-emitting diode (LED). Tuning the properties of the semiconductor by selecting different intrinsic semiconductors and doping them with different elements gives material engineers the ability to modify the properties of diodes for specific uses.

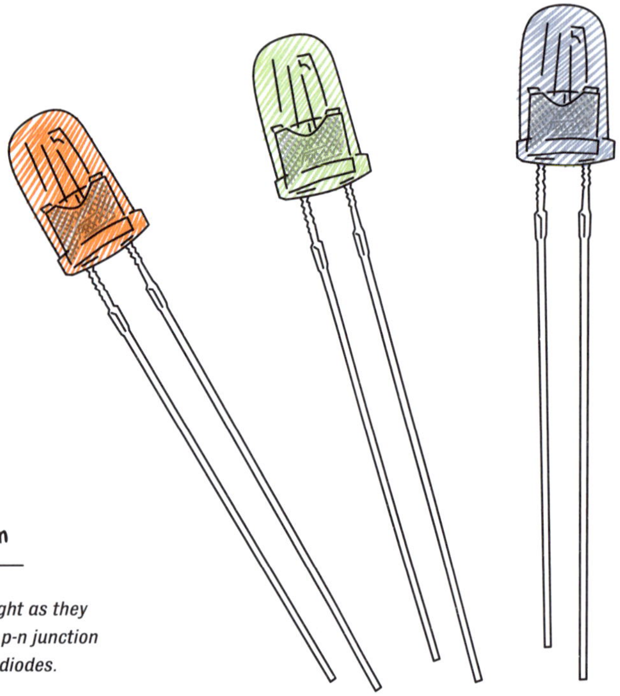

P-N junction

Electrons emit light as they jump across the p-n junction in light-emitting diodes.

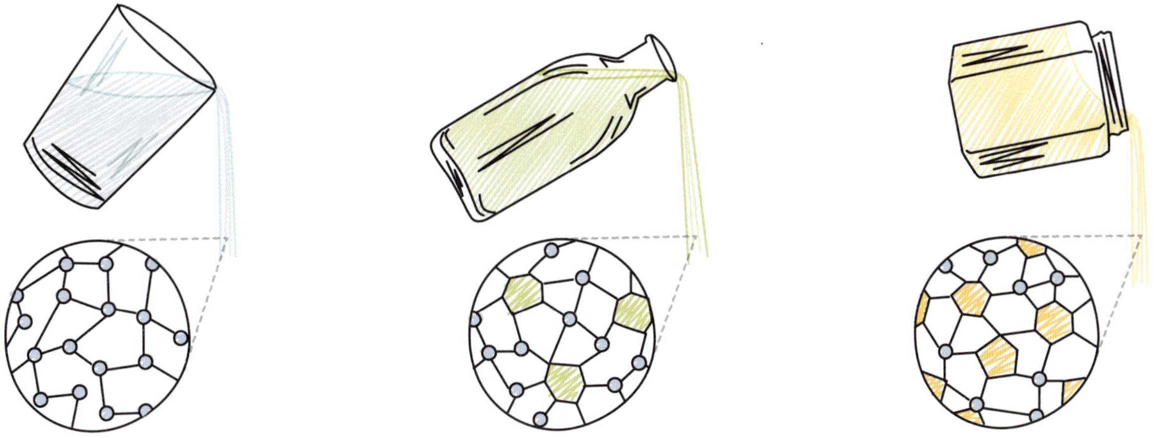

Water
Low viscosity

Olive oil
Medium viscosity

Honey
High viscosity

Fluids

Liquids, gases, and plasmas are all examples of a fluid. Particles in a fluid flow as they move past each other to take the shape of any container they are forced into. Fluids do not resist permanent deformation but have different rates at which they allow themselves to be deformed.

Fluid is a phase of matter, which is a region of space, temperature, and pressure where all physical properties of a material are the same. The one major difference between fluids is that liquids can form a free surface, a surface not defined by a container holding the fluid, but gases and plasmas cannot and expand to fill the container they are in.

The resistance that a fluid provides to the rate of deformation is known as **viscosity**. Liquids such as honey are viscous, as they take a long time to deform when a force is applied, while liquids such as water are not very viscous as they deform rapidly when a force is applied. Viscosity can be thought of as the frictional force between the fluid and another surface. When a fluid is relaxing into a container, the viscosity arises from frictional forces between the particles making up the fluid. These frictional forces arise from collisions between the particles as they move around thermally in random directions.

Viscosity

Different fluids deform at different rates when a force is applied; this is defined by their viscosity.

Close to absolute zero, some fluids reach zero viscosity and become a **superfluid**. Supercooled helium-4 was the first superfluid to be discovered. When helium-4 atoms are cooled, they occupy the same lowest energy level, which removes collisions between them and effectively gives the fluid zero viscosity.

Domains

Magnetic materials exhibit an overall magnetic field, which arises from the orientation of atoms that the material is made up of (see page 60). These materials are usually not described at the atomic level, but at scale sizes a little larger called domains. A domain is a region of a material in which the magnetic field is aligned in a uniform direction—all the atoms have their magnetic field pointing the same way. In unmagnetized materials, the fields of all the domains point in random directions, canceling each other out and giving the material a zero overall magnetic field. Applying an external magnetic field or working the material with heat and pressure can align the domains so that each of their magnetic fields adds together to produce a large overall magnetic field. Lodestones are naturally occurring magnets that form when iron ores are heated and crushed under huge pressure deep in the Earth, causing their domains to align.

Magnetic domains

Domains in iron align with an external magnetic field, creating an opposite pole to the one it is near. This results in iron being attracted to a magnet.

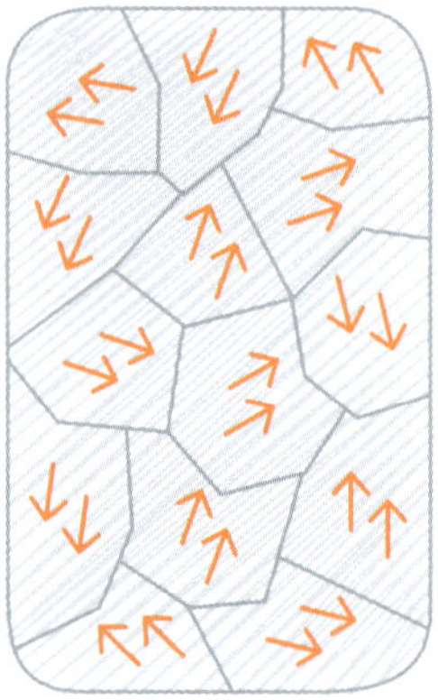

Usually magnetic domains are random in direction and cancel when added together

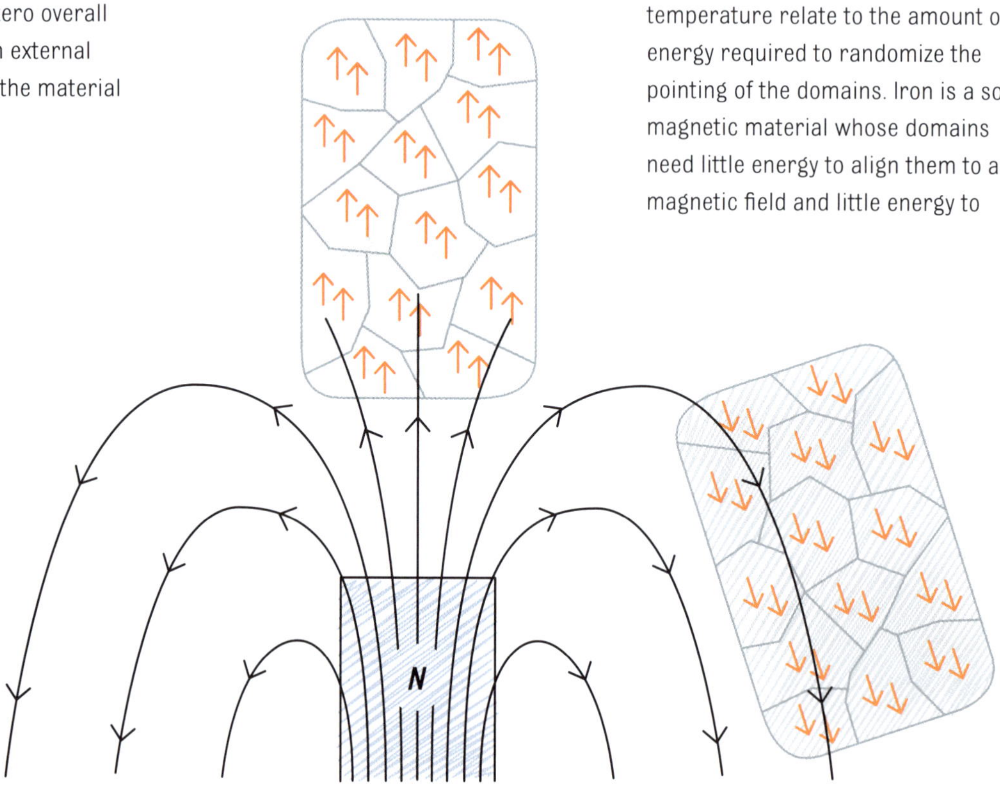

Aligned domains in magnetic materials can randomize and form a nonmagnetic material. Randomization can come from mechanical shock, by hitting the material hard to shake the domain orientation, or by heating the material so that the faster vibrating atoms shake the orientation of the domains. The temperature at which a magnetic material loses its magnetism through heating is called the **Curie temperature**. It tells us how hard or soft a magnetic material is—a hard magnetic material can withstand high Curie temperatures but a soft magnetic material will demagnetize at much lower temperatures. The hardness and Curie temperature relate to the amount of energy required to randomize the pointing of the domains. Iron is a soft magnetic material whose domains need little energy to align them to a magnetic field and little energy to randomize them once again. If you add a small amount of carbon to the iron to form steel, then it requires more energy to align the domains but also much more energy to randomize them again afterward. Steel is a hard magnetic material, while iron is soft.

Classification of material

A **homogeneous** material is uniform in composition. Uniformity at its most extreme is an elemental material made entirely of the same atoms, such as iron or diamond. Homogeneity may also refer to materials composed of one type of compound, such as the H_2O molecules that form liquid water. Materials that are formed from a microscopic mixture of different compounds may also be regarded as homogeneous; but if the mingling of different materials is not microscopic, then the material is not deemed homogeneous.

A **composite** material is composed of two or more materials with very different chemical or physical properties. Composite materials are designed to utilize the strengths of different materials to create a singular, strong composite material. For example, concrete reinforced with steel. Concrete is strong under compression and steel strong under tension. When combined they form a material stronger under both tension and compression.

Piezoelectricity is a behavior exhibited by crystals that have an asymmetric unit cell. While each unit cell is electrically neutral, the distribution of charge within the cell may not be symmetric. When the material is put under stress by a tension, compression, or shear force, this causes the shape of its unit cell to change, which alters the distribution of charge within every unit cell and creates an imbalance of electric charge across the whole material. This imbalance leads to a potential difference (voltage) across the material from one side to the other. If connected to a circuit, this potential difference can drive an electric current that can be measured. Therefore, piezoelectric crystals transfer mechanical energy into electrical energy at the microscopic scale.

A device that transfers one energy store to another is often called a transducer. Piezoelectric transducers are used in microphones, where pressure waves of sound periodically compress a piezoelectric crystal, causing it to produce a potential difference. The shape of this potential difference changing in time and the current it can produce in a circuit, becomes a map of the pressure waves hitting the crystal; when amplified, such a signal can be used to drive a loudspeaker.

Physics of materials allows us to define the bulk properties of different things in our lives and has also taken us to the edge of quantum physics. Our knowledge of materials has revolutionized the modern world and the way we are building our future.

Piezoelectric crystals

Piezoelectric crystals produce an electric potential difference when deformed by a force, such as compression or tension.

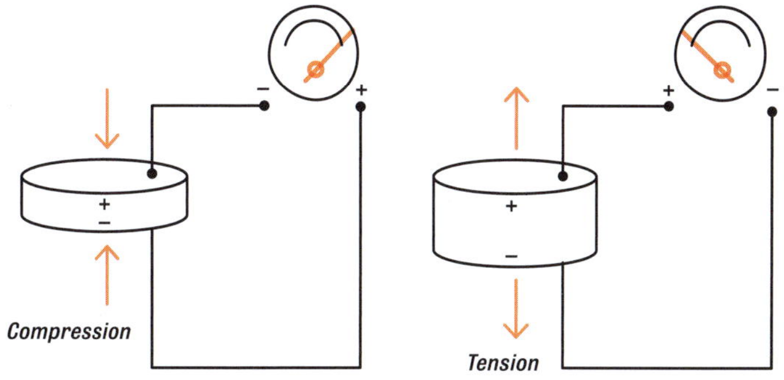

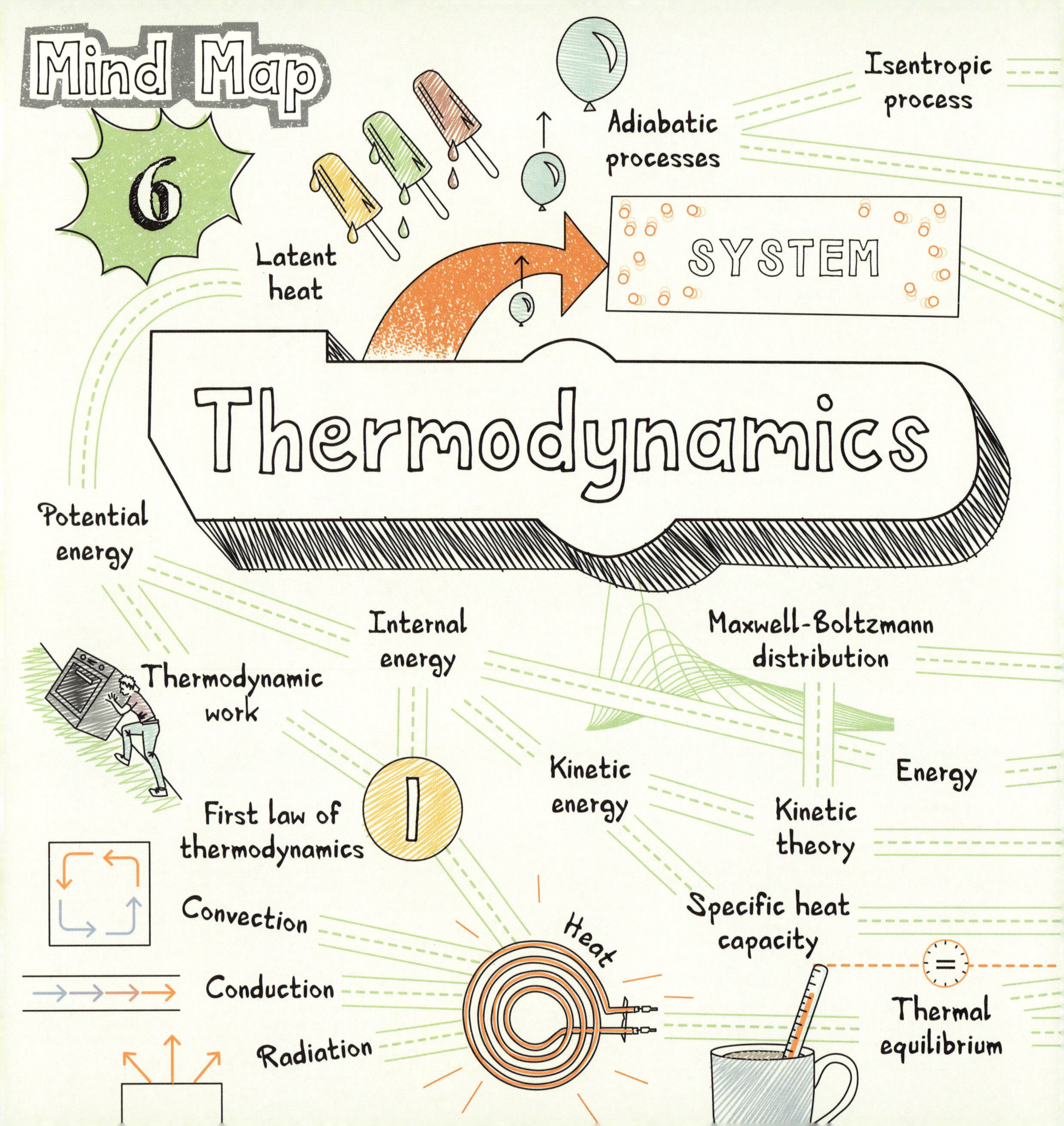
Mind Map
6
Thermodynamics
SYSTEM
Latent heat
Adiabatic processes
Isentropic process
Potential energy
Internal energy
Maxwell-Boltzmann distribution
Thermodynamic work
First law of thermodynamics
Kinetic energy
Kinetic theory
Energy
Convection
Conduction
Radiation
Heat
Specific heat capacity
Thermal equilibrium

Carnot cycle
Isothermal change
Isobaric change
Isochoric change
P
PV diagrams
V
Refrigerator
Heat engine
2
Second law of thermodynamics
Arrow of time
Entropy
N
Particle number
Multiplicity
Mass
3
Third law of thermodynamics
State variables
V
Volume
Statistical thermodynamics
Pressure
P
200
300
400
100
500
0
600
Absolute zero
Kinetic temperature
Boyle's law
Temperature
Charles's law
0
Zeroth law
Gay-Lussac's law
Ideal gas

Describing Systems

Thermodynamics does exactly as it says in Greek; it is the study of heat (*therme*) power (*dynamis*). As a field of study, it began in the nineteenth century, after the advent of the steam engine to pump water from mines. Since then, the field has matured and expanded to become a truly fundamental branch of modern physics; no longer confined to engineering but free to describe all manner of weird and wonderful things in nature. The theory is summarized in four laws, which define the different physical quantities of temperature, energy, and entropy, and which govern the evolution of our universe.

A thermodynamic **system** is a group of matter and **energy** surrounded by an outer boundary. Systems that allow matter and gas to pass across the boundary are called open systems; a box with no lid could be considered an open system. Closed systems do not allow matter to pass across the surrounding boundary, but do allow the transfer of energy; for example, gas in a balloon is a closed system as no gas can enter or leave, but energy can still flow into or out of the balloon across its surface. Isolated systems are collections of mass and energy that do not allow the transfer of matter or energy across the surrounding boundary; a perfect thermos flask is an example of an isolated system, as it does not let any contents or thermal energy leave the inside of the flask.

A thermodynamic system in equilibrium, within which no amount of energy is being transferred, is fully described by a state function. This comprises a set of numbers known as **state variables** that cover all relevant properties of the system. Any two systems with the same value for each state variable are identical, no matter how they arrived at that particular state function. The same amount of hot water cooling to room temperature would eventually reach the same state as exactly the same amount of cold water warming to room temperature.

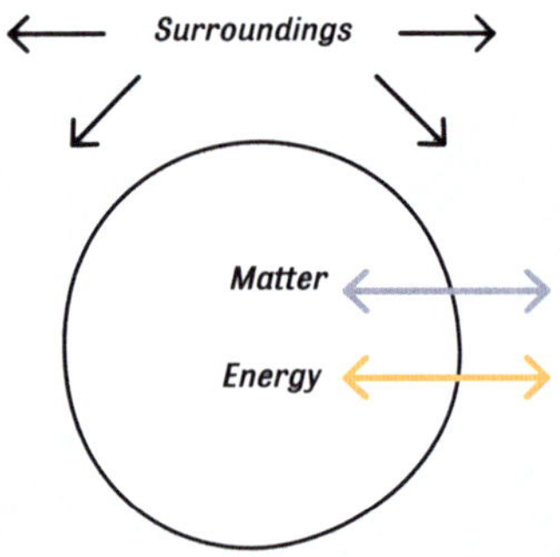

Open system

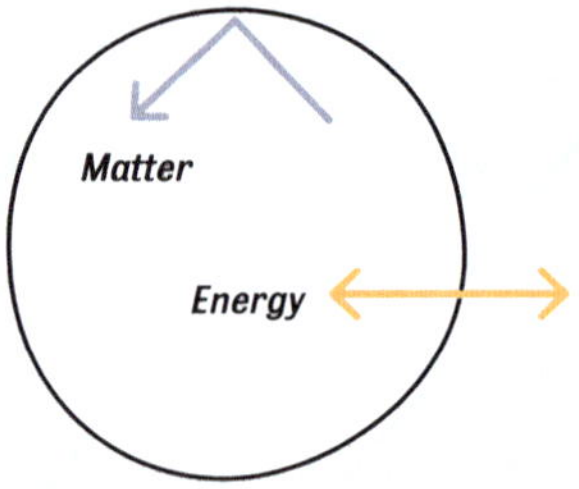

Closed system

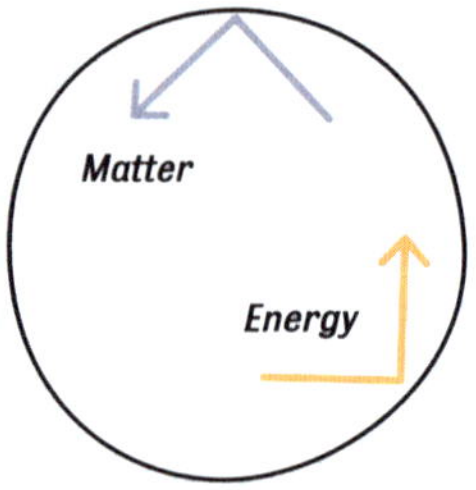

Isolated system

Systems

A system is defined as a particular grouping of particles in a region of space. Open systems allow matter and energy to be transferred between the system and its surroundings. Closed systems allow just energy to move in or out, and isolated systems do not allow energy or matter to be transferred.

The inertial **mass** of matter in a system is a state variable. Any two things with different masses will have very different kinematic properties (see page 18).

The number of unique parts to a system, such as particles making up a material, will alter a system's properties, so **particle number** is another important state variable. As particle numbers can be large and unwieldy, the amount of a substance in a system is often measured in moles (see page 69).

The **volume** of a system is the space that the system occupies. For solids and liquids, this is usually bound by their own surface, whereas a container usually defines gas volumes.

The **pressure** of a system is the force it exerts on each square meter of the surrounding boundary; for gases, this is the force exerted on the confining container.

Temperature can be defined in a number of different, but fundamentally related, ways. Temperature, like length and mass, is measured using a number of scales designed for different requirements, but all are measuring temperature. The Fahrenheit scale was originally defined based on zero equaling a cold day in Danzig in Poland and 96 degrees being the temperature for a healthy human.

Today, the Fahrenheit scale is defined by 32 degrees as the freezing point of water and 212 degrees as the boiling point of water, both at standard atmospheric pressure. The Celsius scale, previously referred to as centigrade, sets 0 degrees to equal the freezing point of water and 100 degrees the boiling point, again at standard atmospheric pressure. The international standard unit of temperature is the kelvin, whose zero is set to the coldest known temperature, termed absolute zero, where atoms and molecules stop moving. Each kelvin unit is the same size as a degree Celsius, 1/100th of the temperature difference between freezing and boiling water.

Temperature scales

There are many different scales with which temperature is measured, each based upon a different physical phenomenon (numbers have been rounded up or down in the chart for simplicity).

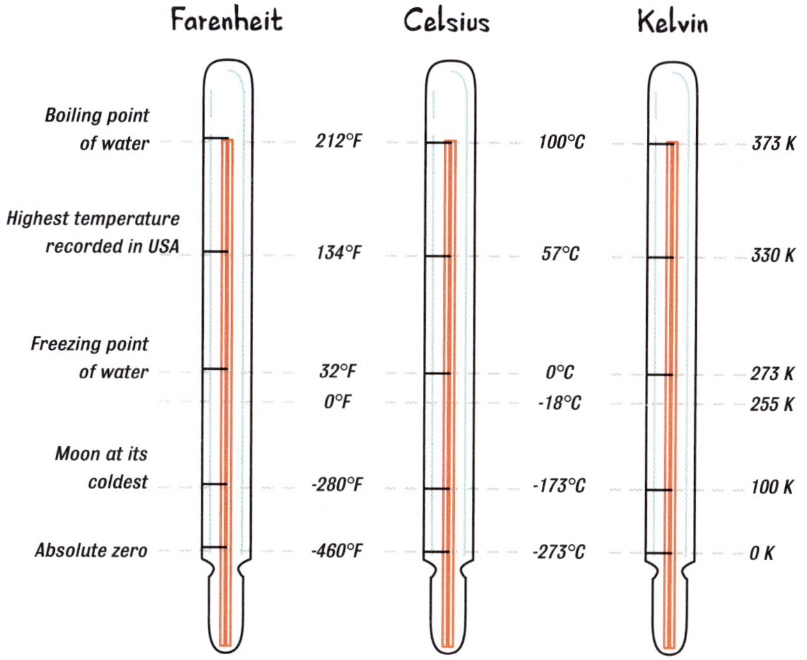

The Life of Gases

In 1662, **Boyle's law** was published; this work by the Anglo-Irish scientist Robert Boyle showed the mathematical relationship between the pressure of a gas and the volume it occupies. When the pressure and volume of a fixed amount of gas at constant temperature are measured and multiplied together, they always give the same number. The product of pressure and volume is a constant for a certain amount of gas at a certain temperature.

In 1787, French physicist Jacques Charles investigated the relationship between the temperature and volume of a gas. **Charles's law** tells us that if a fixed amount of gas is kept at constant pressure then the volume changes proportionally to temperature. Raising the temperature of a gas increases its volume, and decreasing the temperature reduces its volume. They are directly proportional to each other.

In 1802, French physicist Louis Gay-Lussac rediscovered Charles's law and also revealed his own. **Gay-Lussac's law**, or the pressure law, links the pressure of a gas with the temperature. For a fixed amount of gas in a constant-volume container, the pressure and temperature are directly related. Increasing the temperature increases the pressure, and decreasing the pressure decreases the temperature. This allowed people to develop

Boyle's law

Boyle's law informs us of the relationship between the pressure and volume of a gas.

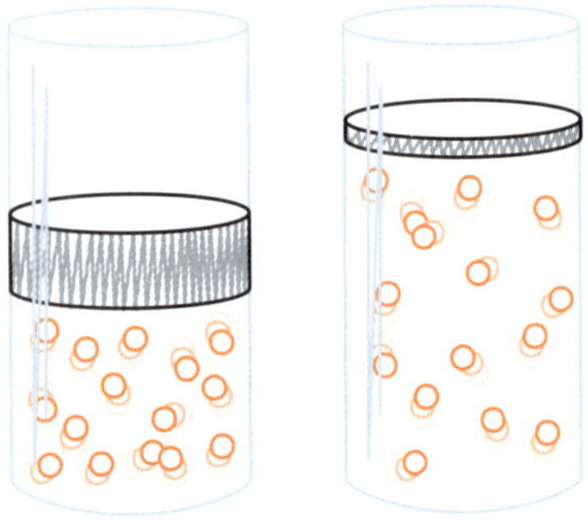

This shows the relationship between the pressure and volume of a gas kept at constant temperature.

They are inversely proportional: doubling the pressure halves the volume of the gas; halving the pressure doubles the volume.

Charles's law

Charles's law gives the relationship between the volume and temperature of a gas.

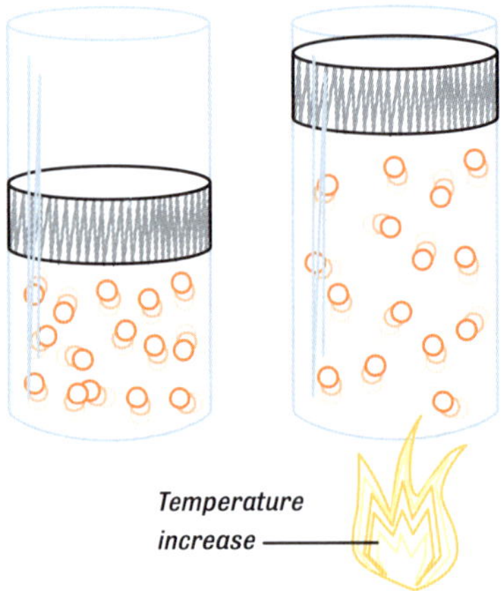

This shows the relationship between the temperature and volume of a gas kept at constant pressure.

They are directly proportional: doubling the temperature of a gas doubles its volume.

refrigerators. Expanding gases growing lower in pressure will grow colder as their pressure drops. Heat can then be exchanged to this cold gas from some other object to cool the object down. These laws signaled the birth of experimental thermodynamics.

Treatment of a gas as ideal allows the three gas laws to be simplified and combined into the ideal gas equation. An ideal gas has zero interparticle forces, with particles modeled as solid points colliding elastically. The only thing that then links the temperature, pressure, and volume is the amount of gas present multiplied by a constant scaling factor. The amount of gas is measured in moles, which is a count of the number of particles, and the scaling constant is the molar gas constant. This constant can only be measured through experimentation.

Absolute zero is the lowest possible thermodynamic temperature: zero on the Kelvin scale (-273.15°C and -459.67°F). Its value can be estimated when charting the relationship between pressure and temperature of an ideal gas. Tracing the relationship between these two until the gas has theoretically zero pressure, you reach absolute zero. Zero pressure suggests that at absolute zero all particles in a system cease to move. If this is the case, the state of a system is entirely defined by the position of the particles in it.

Ideal gas equation

This equation combines the three gas laws into a single equation relating the pressure, temperature, and volume of an idealized gas.

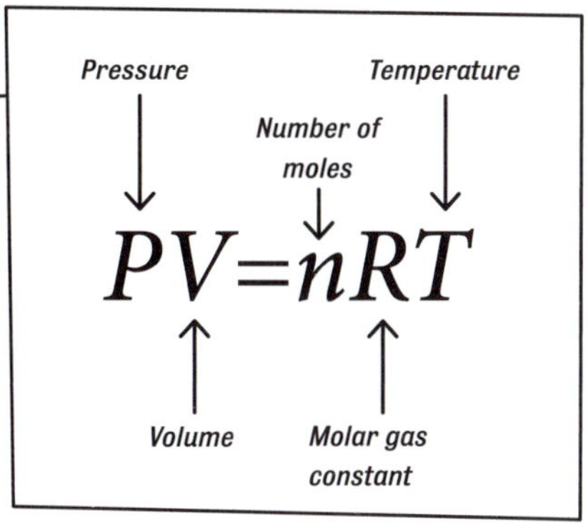

Gay-Lussac's law

Gay-Lussac's law states the relationship between the temperature and pressure of a gas.

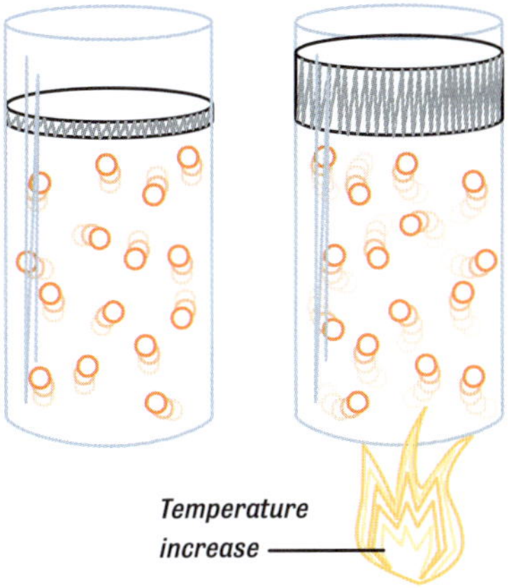

This shows the relationship between the temperature and pressure of a gas kept at constant volume.

They are directly proportional: doubling the temperature of a gas doubles its pressure.

Heat and the zeroth law

Thermodynamic temperature is related to the transfer of energy between thermodynamic systems. If two closed systems are left in contact, energy will be transferred between them until a balance is reached and the exchange of energy either way becomes equal. These two systems have reached **thermal equilibrium** and have reached the same thermodynamic temperature. A hot cup of coffee will cool down as it transfers more energy to its surroundings than it receives. The rate at which energy is transferred to the surroundings reduces as the coffee loses energy, but the rate that the surroundings supply heat to the coffee remains constant. Eventually, the coffee is emitting the same amount of energy as it is receiving from the surroundings. With zero net movement of energy, the coffee and surroundings have reached thermal equilibrium.

THE ZEROTH LAW OF THERMODYNAMICS

The zeroth law of thermodynamics tells us that if any two systems are in thermal equilibrium with a third system, then they are also in thermal equilibrium with each other. A cup of coffee and a cup of tea in a room are isolated from each other, as they are not in direct contact, but both are in contact with the room. Eventually, both the coffee and tea will reach thermal equilibrium with the room. The zeroth law tells us that when both the tea and coffee have reached thermal equilibrium with the room, then they are also in thermal equilibrium with each other. Bringing the tea and coffee into contact now means there would be no net heat transfer between them because they are at the same temperature.

Thermodynamic work is the energy transferred when a force acts through a distance in the direction of the force. For a gas of pressure (P) to expand a little by a change in volume (ΔV), then the gas must apply a force to its surroundings to push outward. In this case, we say that the gas is doing work and that work is equal to $P\Delta V$. Work is not a state variable because it is not a property of the system itself, but only of energy transfers to and from a system.

Heat is the name given to all energy transfers to or from a system that are not work. When heat is stored, it is locked up in the random kinetic energy of the particles and any radiation in a system. Heat is not a state variable because it is not a measurable property of a system; it only exists when energy is being transferred.

Conduction transfers heat energy through direct collisions between particles. The overall effect over many collisions is that the energy spreads out throughout the material.

Convection is the transfer of particles with energy from one place to another. Convection can only occur in fluid materials where the particles are free to move, such as liquids or gases. Energy is transferred because of differences in density; colder, denser material pushing less dense hot material upward against gravity and setting the energy it possesses in motion.

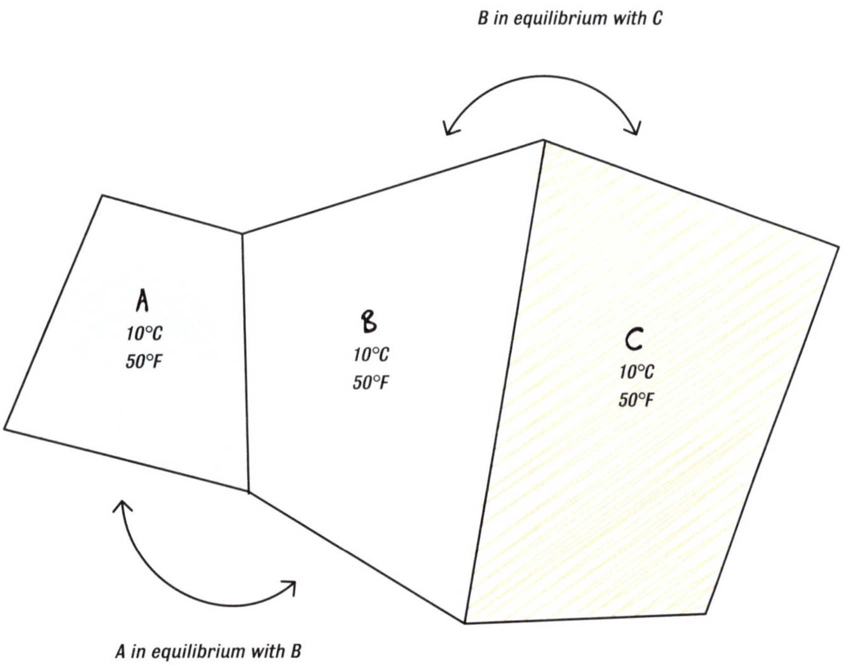

Zeroth law

If object B is in thermal equilibrium with object A and object C, then objects A and C must also be in thermal equilibrium with each other. All three would be at the same thermodynamic temperature.

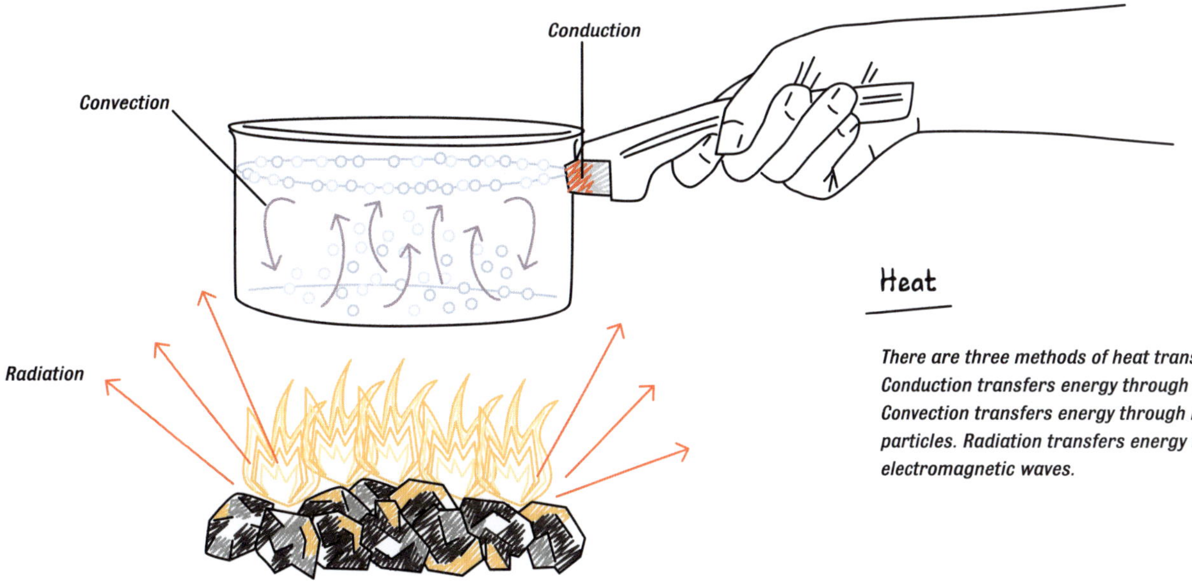

Heat

There are three methods of heat transfer. Conduction transfers energy through collisions. Convection transfers energy through moving particles. Radiation transfers energy through electromagnetic waves.

Radiation is heat transfer through the exchange of electromagnetic waves. Oscillating electrons inside matter generate electromagnetic waves: the hotter an object is, the more vigorously an electron oscillates and the higher the frequency of the electromagnetic wave. On Earth, most objects are low enough in energy that they predominantly emit infrared radiation.

Energy

The **first law of thermodynamics** is a restatement of the law of conservation of energy (see page 33). It applies to an isolated system that must contain the same energy before and after any physical change to the system. The first law tells us that any change in the internal energy of a system (ΔU) is equal to the heat energy supplied to the system (Q) minus any work the system has done to its environment (W): $\Delta U = Q - W$. Sometimes, the first law is also stated as plus the work done to the isolated system: $\Delta U = Q + W$.

$$\Delta U = Q - W$$

Change in internal energy of a system equals the heat supplied to the system minus the work done by the system.

If quoted with a "+W" then the "W" represents work being done to the system. If minus is indicated, then it is work being done by the system on its environment.

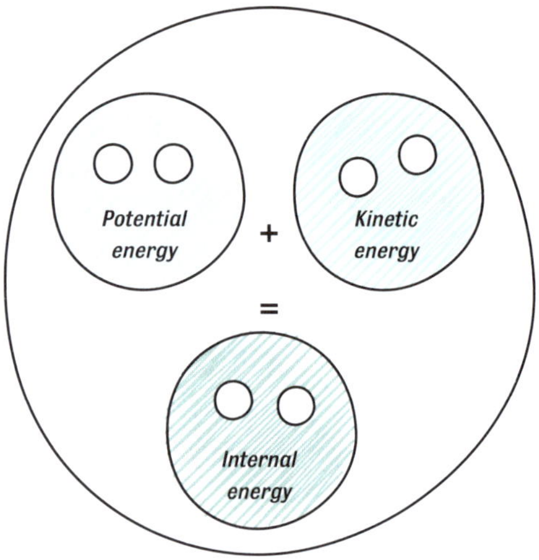

The **internal energy** of a system of particles is the sum of the energy stored by all particles in the system. This is the sum of the kinetic and potential energies of every particle.

Potential energy of a material changes when the positioning of particles in a material are changed; this is demonstrated most dramatically when materials change states of matter. Dramatic changes in positions and interparticle forces when changing state produce huge changes in the potential energy of the system. The heat energy required to cause the change in state is called **latent heat**. The latent heat of fusion is the energy released when changing from liquid to solid, or the energy that is required to go from solid to liquid. The energy required to go from liquid to gas, or released when gas becomes liquid, is known as the latent heat of vaporization.

If heat is transferred to a system, then the random motion of particles in the system increases, which is experienced as an increase in temperature. The heat energy required to raise 1 kilogram of a material by 1°C (1 K) is determined by the material's **specific heat capacity**. Different materials have different specific heat capacities, dependent upon their microstructure.

Latent heat

Latent heat is the energy required to change the potential energy of particles when they change between different states of matter.

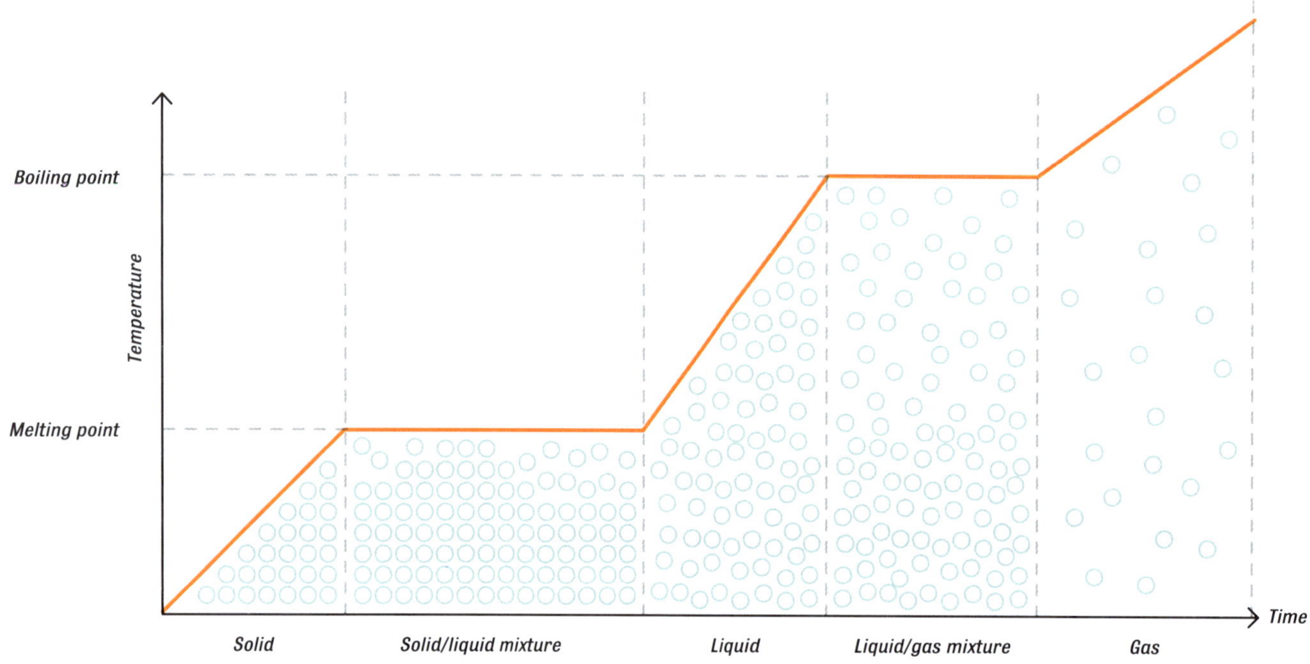

Kinetic disorder

Entropy is a state variable of thermodynamics, like pressure, temperature, or volume. While heat is not a measurable property of a system, it turns out that the amount of heat transferred for each kelvin of temperature is: this is entropy. Entropy is a measure of the order of a system. A perfectly ordered system, where everything exists with the same energy and location, is very low in entropy. A system that is randomly filled with various energies is high in entropy.

The **third law of thermodynamics** states that the entropy of a system approaches a constant value as a system approaches absolute zero in temperature. This is logical given the definition of absolute zero, because the only option available to particles is a position that becomes fixed when they stop moving.

In **statistical thermodynamics**, entropy is related to the multiplicity of a system. **Multiplicity** is a measure of all of the different ways a state can exist microscopically but still have the same set of measurable state variables. States that can be formed in many different ways microscopically are said to have a high multiplicity and are far more likely to form than states with a lower multiplicity that have fewer ways to exist.

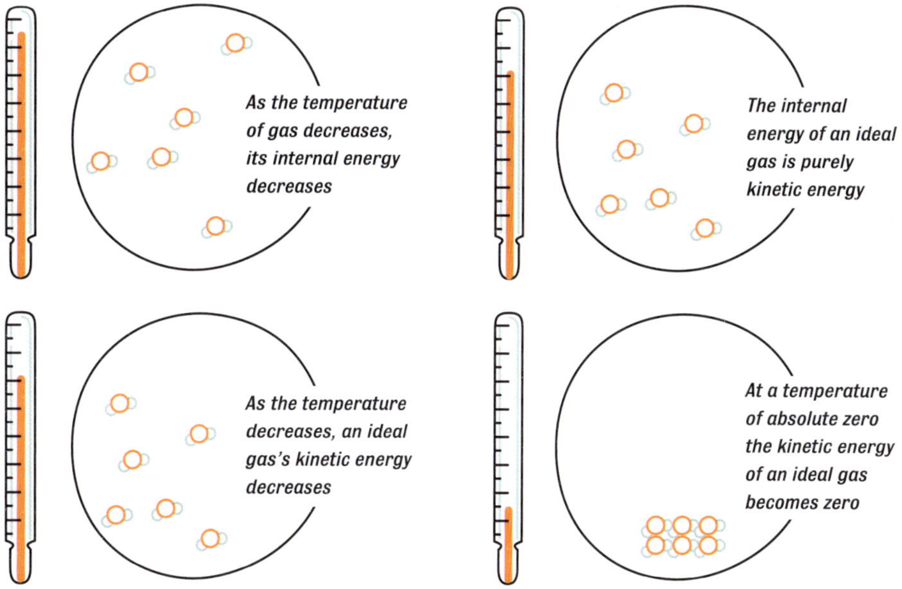

Third law of thermodynamics

As an object approaches absolute zero it stops moving. This leaves the object with constant entropy defined only by its arrangement, no longer by energy.

Therefore, high multiplicity states have higher entropy than lower multiplicity states. A simple example can be found when considering a pair of headphones. Why, when headphones are put in a bag and jumbled up, do the wires always get tangled? If we think about it, there is only one way in which the headphones exist untangled but many ways they can exist as tangled. We can calculate the probability that as the system changes there are far more ways for it to be disordered (tangled) than ordered (untangled). The tangled state has a much higher multiplicity than the untangled state. It is this reason why entropy increases in most real-world processes, because a state with less order is simply far more likely to occur.

Heating a gas allows for a greater range of energies than particles in the gas can take, which increases the multiplicity of the system. This leads to hotter systems usually possessing higher entropy than cooler ones. Gases occupying a larger volume or comprising a larger number of particles also tend to have larger multiplicity, as there are more positions that more particles can be in, which is a higher multiplicity.

Kinetic theory

Thermodynamics is most commonly demonstrated by imagining an **ideal gas**, a material in which there are no interparticle forces, which means that the internal energy is purely **kinetic energy**. Newton's laws of motion can then be used to derive the observed laws of thermodynamics from the particle level. This **kinetic theory** simplifies the idea of matter as being made from particles that are much smaller than the distances between them, each with identical mass. Pressure in kinetic theory arises from the force applied by particles bouncing off the container in which the gas is being kept. Kinetic theory results in an equation linking the pressure and volume of a gas with the average kinetic energy of particles in the gas.

Connecting the kinetic equation for pressure with the ideal gas equation demonstrates the fundamental link between the average kinetic energy of particles in an ideal gas and its temperature. It demonstrates that the average kinetic energy of particles in a gas is directly related to what we measure as the temperature of the gas. This derivation of temperature is often referred to as **kinetic temperature**.

In 1860, using the principles of kinetic theory, Scottish physicist James Clerk Maxwell derived an equation that gave the probability of any given particle in an ideal gas having a certain velocity. The distribution of velocities depended upon the temperature of the ideal gas only. Twelve years later, German physicist Stefan Boltzmann derived exactly the same distribution using Newton's mechanics alone and showed that over time any system will evolve toward this distribution. The distribution became known as the Maxwell-Boltzmann distribution. For a gas of a given temperature, the **Maxwell-Boltzmann distribution** gives the spread in velocities, and therefore energies, of the particles it is made from.

Maxwell-Boltzmann graph

The Maxwell-Boltzmann distribution charts the variety of energies of the particles in a gas when a gas is said to be of a particular temperature.

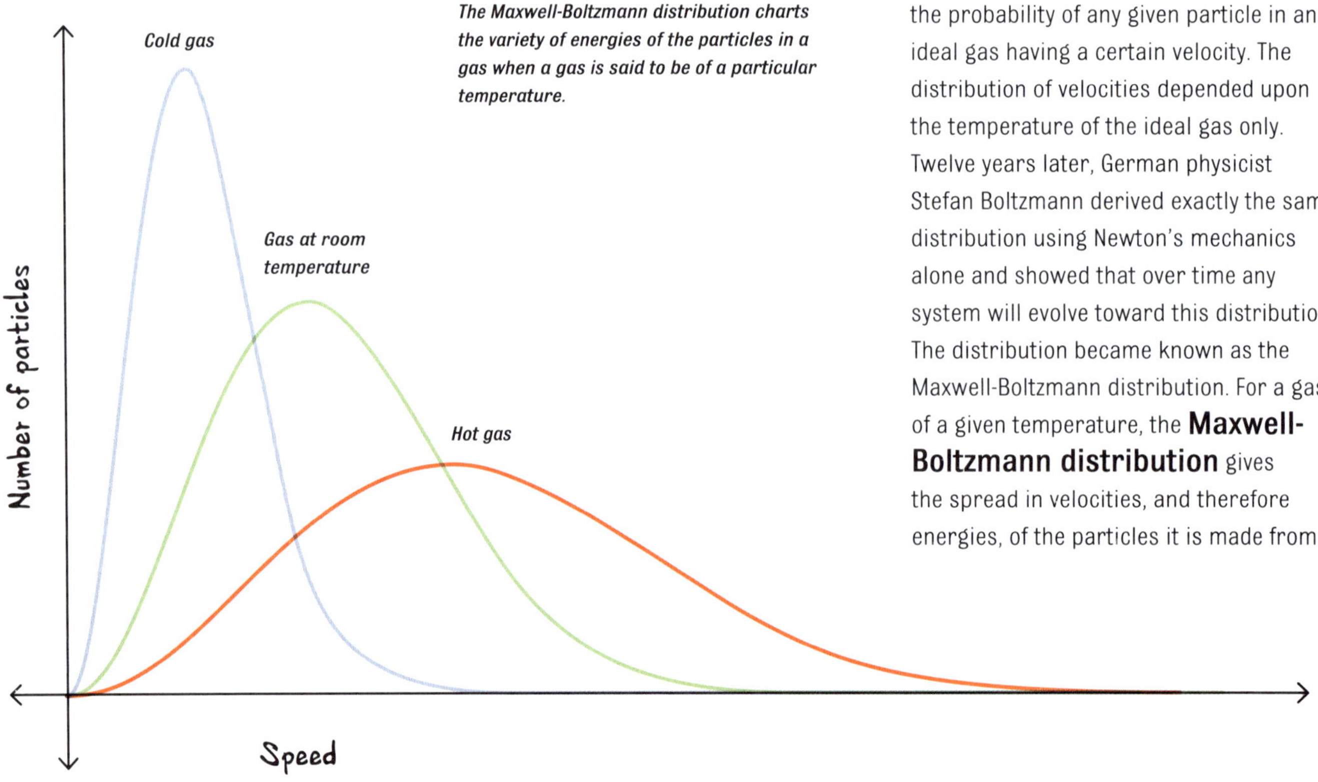

The second law and heat engines

The **second law of thermodynamics** started life from the observed behavior of heat in experiments: it stated that heat will spontaneously flow from hot to cold but not in the opposite direction. From this early definition, we can see that the second law is a statement about order in our universe and its relationship with time; by defining just one direction of spontaneous heat flow, it provides a definite direction for time. Looking at the direction heat flows defines the direction time travels: the **arrow of time**.

Today, the second law is stated in terms of entropy rather than heat; entropy of any isolated system can never decrease over time.

If a system described by a set of state variables changes in a way that returns it to the same state later, it has undergone a cyclic change. A **heat engine** is a thermodynamic system that performs work on its environment while transferring energy between a hot reservoir and a cold reservoir.

The amount of work a heat engine can do is determined by the first and second law of thermodynamics. The first law applies the conservation of energy, while the second law determines the efficiency of the transfer from heat to work that is made by the engine. Many heat engines follow cyclic routes in which certain state variables repeat.

Heat engine

A heat engine transfers heat from a hot reservoir to a cold reservoir while doing mechanical work in the process.

Q = heat (Joule, J)
W = work (Joule, J)
h = hot
c = cold

Work is done when heat is transferred from a hot to a cold reservoir by a heat engine

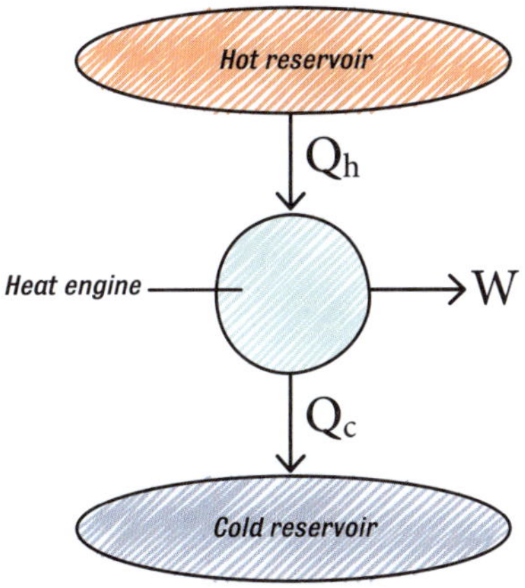

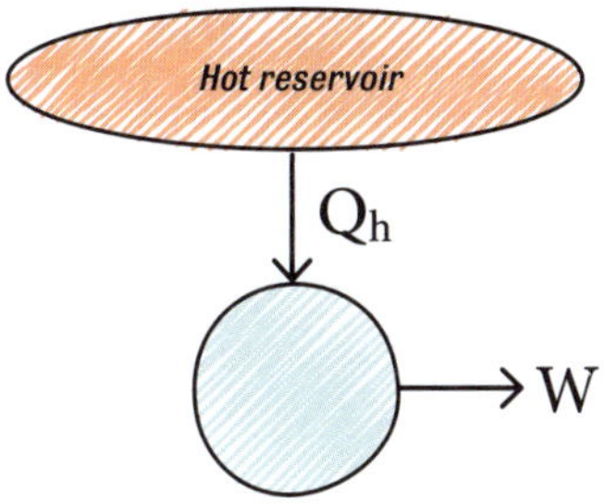

The second law forbids all heat being converted to energy as there is no flow to a cold reservoir

$$\text{Efficiency} = \frac{W}{Q_h} = \frac{Q_h - Q_c}{Q_h}$$

The fraction of work done to heat flow from the hot reservoir gives the efficiency of a heat engine

A **refrigerator** is simply a heat engine in reverse, where work is used to transfer energy from a cold reservoir into a hot reservoir. This principle is used in domestic refrigeration, where work is supplied by an expanding gas to transfer heat from the inside of a refrigerator to the environment. An electric pump is then used to compress this gas (called a refrigerant) once more, so that it can be used for another cycle of expansion and heat transfer.

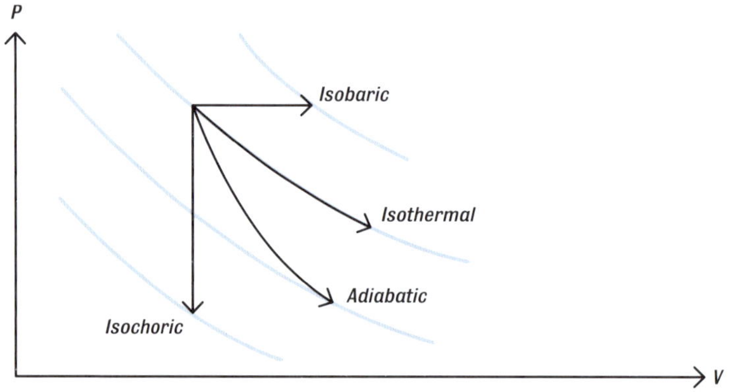

Refrigerator

A refrigerator is a heat engine working in reverse, performing work to pump heat against the usual gradient from a cold reservoir to a hot reservoir, like pushing a rock up a hill.

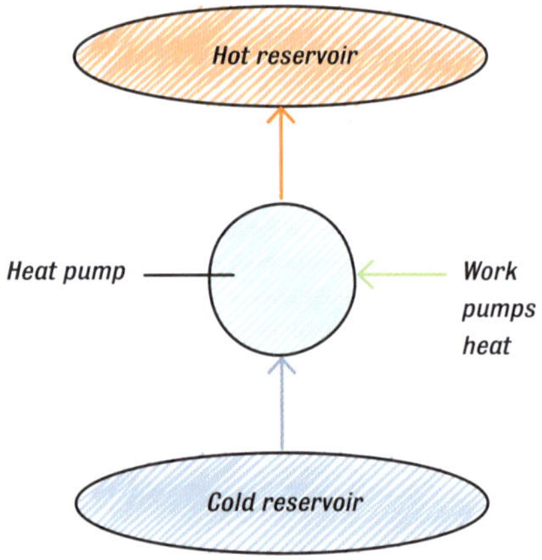

PV DIAGRAMS

Most heat engines use a gas as the working substance and so their behavior is governed by pressure, temperature, and volume, as indicated by the ideal gas equation. Processes that occur in such heat engines are visualized using **PV diagrams**, which plot the pressure (P) and volume (V) of gases at different stages in an engine's cycle. Using a PV diagram, we can plot different examples of heat engines and explore the second law further.

Changes in a gas can happen in many different ways, each type of change has its own name and shape on a PV diagram. An **isobaric change** modifies the volume and temperature of a gas, but keeps the pressure in the gas constant. This is shown as a horizontal line on a PV diagram. An **isochoric change** fixes the volume of a gas but allows the temperature and pressure to change, which is a vertical line on a PV diagram. An **isothermal change** fixes the temperature of the gas but allows the volume and pressure to change. This is shown as a curve on the PV diagram because of the inverse relationship between P and V.

Adiabatic processes do not transfer any heat (or matter) into or out of the system. Any change in internal energy is entirely due to work being done by the system, if internal energy is reducing, or to the system, if the internal energy is increasing. Adiabatic changes form curves on a PV diagram.

Constant changes

Some changes in a state have unique names. Changes of constant pressure, volume, or temperature are named isobaric, isochoric, and isothermal respectively. Adiabatic changes occur without a transfer of heat.

An **isentropic process** is one in which the entropy of a system does not change from start to end. It is an adiabatic change that is fully reversible, because any work being done to or by the system is done so without transfer of energy into other forms through frictional forces. Isentropic changes are shown on a PV diagram as a curve. Because entropy is a function of heat and temperature, the evolution of entropy around the cycle of a heat engine is usually plotted against temperature.

Carnot cycle

State variables are used to construct diagrams of a system undergoing changes. The most common diagram is a PV diagram, which plots pressure of a system against volume. The T-S diagram is another common state diagram, this plots the temperature (T) of a system against the entropy (S). These diagrams show the changes in a Carnot cycle.

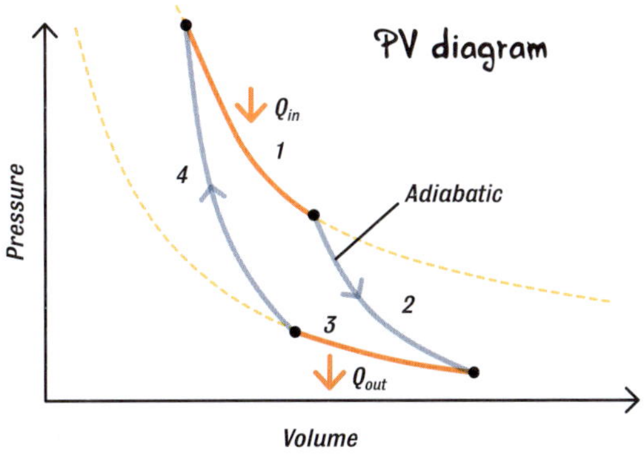

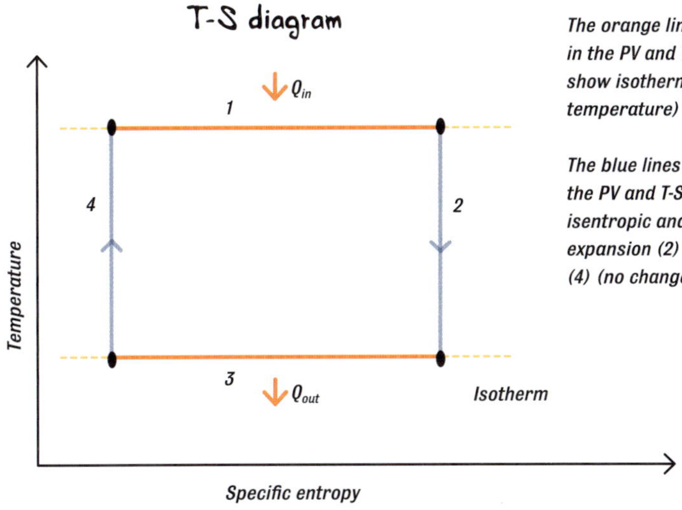

The orange lines (1 and 3) in the PV and T-S diagrams show isothermal (no change in temperature) exchange of heat.

The blue lines (2 and 4) in the PV and T-S diagrams show isentropic and adiabatic expansion (2) and compression (4) (no change in entropy).

CARNOT CYCLE

The most efficient heat engine possible was discovered in 1824 by French physicist Sadi Carnot and is named after him. A **Carnot cycle** starts with an isothermal expansion as heat is added to the system from some hot reservoir (1), followed by an adiabatic expansion to a lower temperature (2). An isothermal compression of the gas then transfers the heat energy out of the gas into the cold reservoir (3), before an adiabatic compression reduces the volume and increases the pressure back to the system's original value (4). The cycle returns the system to the same pressure, volume, temperature, and entropy. The efficiency of the Carnot engine's transfer of heat to work done is determined only by the temperature of the reservoirs that the engine is transferring heat between; it is the difference in temperature between the hot and cold reservoir as a percentage of the hot reservoir temperature.

Carnot engines are not practically useful because isothermal expansions are slow processes where heat is added a little at a time. Instead, most engines, such as the internal-combustion engine, have a large deposition of heat over a short time frame and are therefore much lower in efficiency than a Carnot engine.

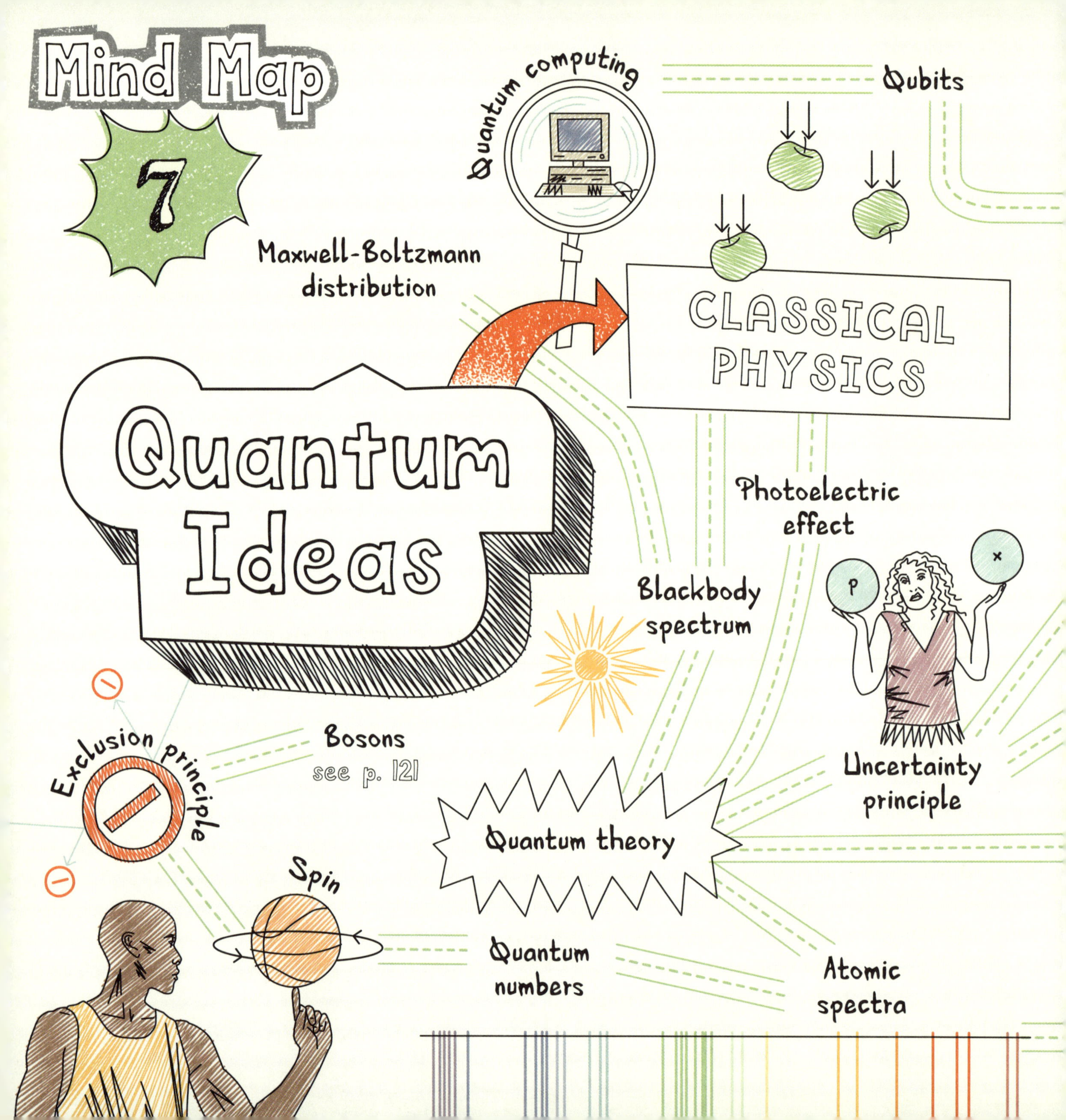

Mind Map
7
Quantum Ideas
Quantum computing
Qubits
Maxwell-Boltzmann distribution
CLASSICAL PHYSICS
Photoelectric effect
Blackbody spectrum
p
x
Uncertainty principle
Bosons
see p. 121
Exclusion principle
Quantum theory
Spin
Quantum numbers
Atomic spectra

Quantum teleportation
Quantum entanglement
Many-worlds interpretation
Decoherence
heads?
tails?
EPR paradox
Hidden variables
Schrödinger's cat
Wave-function collapse
Copenhagen interpretation
Bell's inequality
Matrix mechanics
Wave function
Born rule
Double-slit experiment
Wave-particle duality
Schrödinger's wave equation
de Broglie wavelength
Newton's laws
see p. 34

From Classical to Quantized

In this book we have been discussing theories that are classified as classical physics. **Classical physics** is deterministic, which means that if we know everything about a system at a point in time then we can predict how the system will evolve and, therefore, what it will look like at some later time. Classical physics is also continuous; when considering properties such as energy, all values from zero to infinity are a possibility.

At the turn of the twentieth century, physicists were puzzling over why hot objects emitted the different energies of light they did, in particular objects called black bodies. These objects absorbed all the radiation that hit them and radiated energy out to its environment with maximum efficiency. The collection of energies of light they emitted was called the **blackbody spectrum**. Attempts to explain the shape of this spectrum using a wave theory of light worked at long wavelengths but failed totally at short wavelengths, something known as the ultraviolet catastrophe.

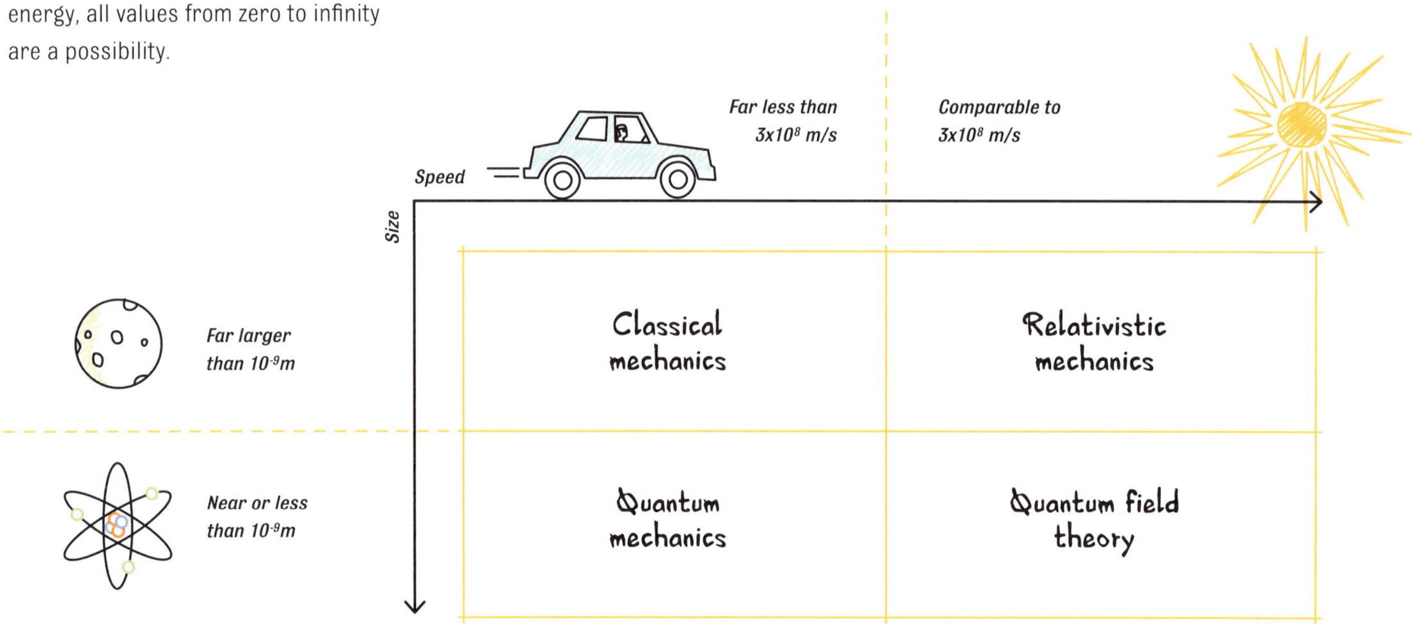

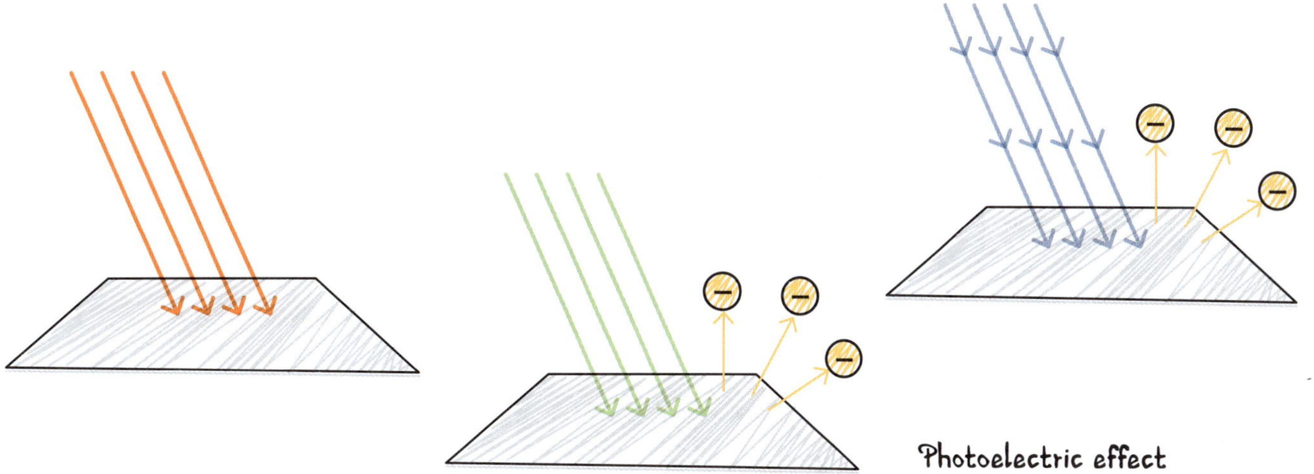

Photoelectric effect

Red light does not have enough energy, no matter how bright, to liberate electrons from the surface of a metal. This is because single photons of light interact with individual electrons, so if the energy is not high enough they will never free electrons.

It was not until 1900 that the German physicist Max Planck noticed that the shape of the spectrum was similar to the **Maxwell-Boltzmann distribution** (see page 90) for particles in an ideal gas. He imagined that light was not emitted as a wave but instead as discrete lumps, like the discrete particles in a gas. Just as Boltzmann's constant defined the relationship between temperature and the energy of a particle, a new constant referred to as the Planck constant related the frequency of light to its energy.

Toward the end of the nineteenth century, the electron particle was discovered by Englishman J. J. Thomson. In a later experiment, Thomson noticed that these same electrons are emitted when light was shone onto plates of metal. The light was providing electrons moving freely in the metal with enough kinetic energy to escape. This process is called the **photoelectric effect**, because the light (photo-) produced measurable electricity (-electric) in the form of free-moving electrons. It was thought that shining higher-energy, bluer light would provide more electrons with energy to break free, but it didn't. In 1905, a Swiss patent clerk called Albert Einstein explained these unexpected results by suggesting that light was lumpy. Each lump of light would interact with just one electron. Increasing the energy of each lump would only increase the energy that each electron received. Only increasing the brightness, and therefore increasing the number of lumps of light that could interact, would free more electrons.

Both Planck and Einstein had discovered something fundamental about the world smaller than an atom. While on the scale of atoms, larger things may seem continuous and smooth, when looking at smaller things the universe becomes discrete and lumpy. The step from continuous to discrete is known as quantization and the theory is known as **quantum theory**.

Classical physics

Classical physics concerns itself with things that move relatively slowly and are a nanometer or larger in size. Small, slow things are dealt with by quantum mechanics, large, fast things by relativity, and small, fast things by a combination of the two called quantum field theory.

From particle to wave

The quantum nature of light and other particles is best shown in the **double-slit experiment**. In 1801, British scientist Thomas Young passed sunlight through two slits and observed a pattern on a screen that could only be explained if light were a wave. Light waves coming through each slit interfered with each other as they traveled to the screen. With a wave you expect the bright patches on the film screen to slowly grow brighter and brighter, as it is exposed over time to the dim light coming through the slits. Instead, the bright patches were filled up like a pointillist painting, a dot at a time. These dots are light arriving as lumps. This experiment has also been performed with electrons, with exactly the same results; electrons arrive as lumps but over time build up a picture, which suggests that waves had passed through the two slits and interfered.

The double-slit experiment demonstrates the dual nature of light, electrons, and all tiny things. When traveling between places they act like waves but when interacting with the world they behave as particles, something known as **wave-particle duality**. Truly these things are not a wave or a particle but quanta, the plural of quantum. The photon is the special name given to quanta of light, its wave-particle duality.

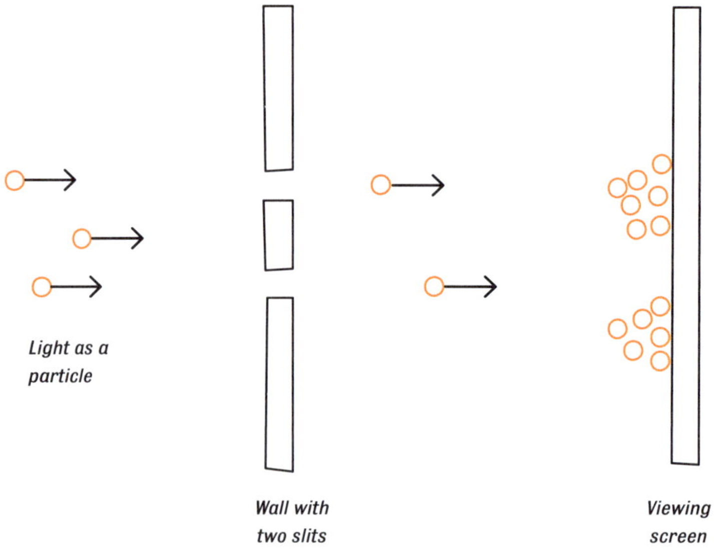

Double-slit experiment

When light or electrons pass through two gaps in a barrier they interfere, behaving like waves not particles.

Light is emitted as particles but travels through space as a wave before being detected as individual lumps at some later time.

Another route to quantum physics was found in explaining **atomic spectra**, the range of light emitted by atoms. Since the mid-nineteenth century, chemists have noticed that atoms did not emit light of all colors, but instead emitted light of just certain wavelengths. This was explained by Danish physicist Niels Bohr. Instead of a continuous range of energies, Bohr said that electrons' orbits around the nucleus in an atom could only take certain quantized values of energy. Light was emitted when electrons move from higher energy orbitals to lower energy orbitals. Because the orbitals had well-defined energies, the light could therefore also only have certain energies.

Defined by numbers

Bohr defined the discrete energy levels that electrons could take using **quantum numbers**. These numbers were integers that defined the level of each successive electron orbit. The lowest energy level closest to the nucleus, defined as the ground state, was assigned number 1. Higher energy levels further from the nucleus had numbers

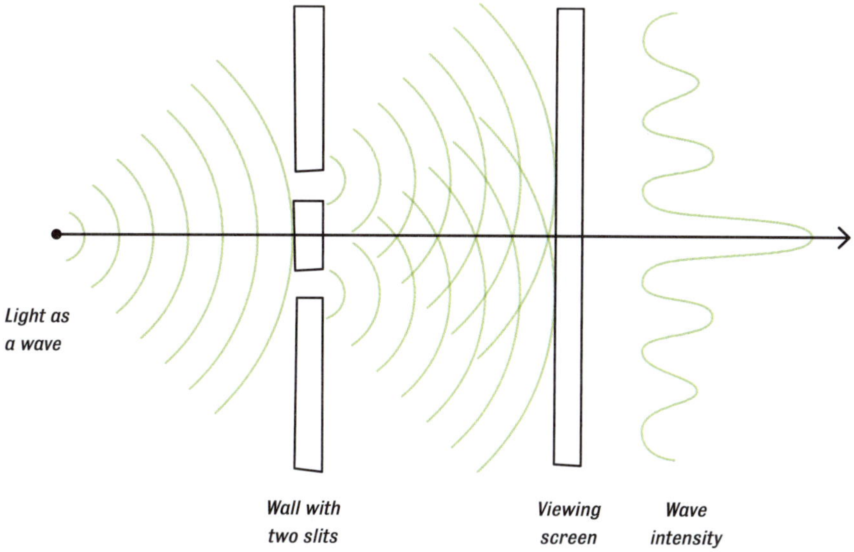

In his PhD thesis, French physicist Louis de Broglie provided the world with the equation linking particle momentum with its **de Broglie wavelength**, marrying particle and wave behavior. Particles with high momentum have a tiny de Broglie wavelength, low momentum particles a larger wavelength. Modeling electrons as standing waves around a proton, de Broglie calculated the allowed energies of electrons in a hydrogen atom. From his calculations, he accurately predicted the same energy of light as Niels Bohr.

increasing by one whole number each time. Electrons orbiting in a 3-D atom are defined by three numbers, one for each dimension, given the letters n, l, and m.

In 1921, German physicists Otto Stern and Walter Gerlach looked at the movement of silver atoms passing through a strong magnetic field. They were electrically neutral, but had a number of unpaired electrons orbiting the atom. Interaction between the magnetic field and the tiny magnetic fields of the unpaired electrons guided the motion of the silver atoms. Atoms were expected to be deflected at a range of angles if the orientation of the electrons' magnetic field was random. Instead the silver atoms emerged at just two angles. This suggested that the orientation of an electron's magnetic field is quantized, allowed only certain values. This quantum property was named **spin**.

Wave-particle duality

Quantum objects act as both wave and particle at different times. Various behavior of light can be described by treating them as either wavelike or particle-like.

Phenomenon	*Can be explained in terms of waves*	*Can be explained in terms of particles*
Reflection		
Refraction		
Interference		
Diffraction		
Polarization		
Photoelectric effect		

Exclusion principle

Noting that elements with even numbers of electrons are less chemically reactive than those with odd numbers, Italian physicist Wolfgang Pauli deduced that electrons filled energy levels in pairs. This meant every electron had an exclusive set of quantum numbers defining it, which became known as the Pauli exclusion principle. The fact that no two electrons can occupy the same quantum number's position in space, energy, and spin, leads to some very interesting things. Electrons are not all allowed to occupy the lowest energy level nearest the nucleus, hence electrons fill different energy shells. Electrons in metals are high enough in energy that they are free to move through the material, allowing them to conduct electricity. It is also the reason you do not fall through the floor. You might think that electrons in your feet repelling the electrons in the floor do this job, but this force is not enough to hold you up. Additional force comes from electrons pushing apart because they cannot occupy the same location in space and spin.

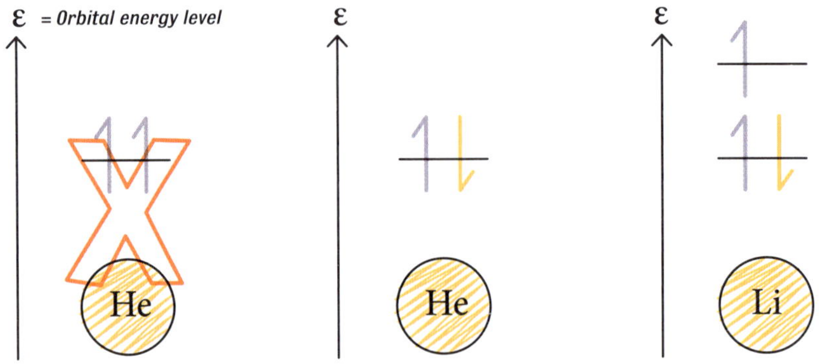

Exclusion principle

No two fermion particles (e.g. electrons) may exist with the same properties. Two electrons must have opposite spin to exist at the same energy in an atom. The third electron in a Lithium atom must occupy a different energy level to possess unique quantum numbers.

Building quantum mechanics

Physicists describe a wave with a mathematical function called a **wave function**. A wave function in quantum physics contains all of the measurable information about a particle. For a freely moving particle, the function is a simple sine wave, such as simple harmonic motion. Wave functions of trapped particles can be described using standing waves.

Wave function

A wave function of a quantum object contains information about the particle's position, linked to its momentum, and its energy, linked to its frequency.

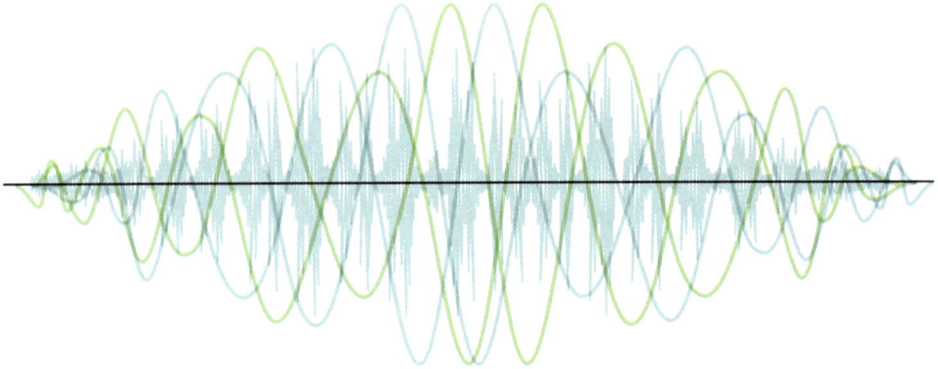

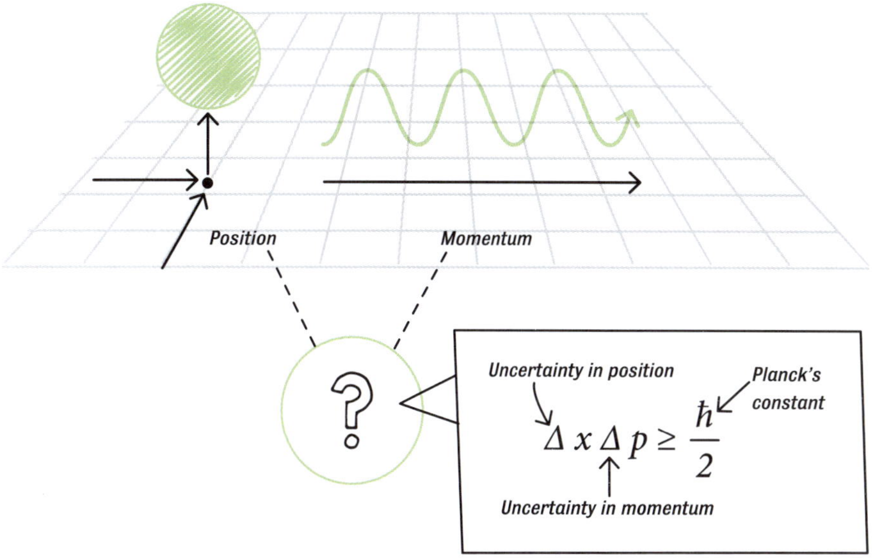

Austrian physicist Werner Heisenberg tried to piece together all of the quantum ideas known in 1925 into one theory to explain the intensity of the bright lines in the spectra of light emitted by hydrogen atoms. He searched for a function of amplitude that was quantum in nature and accounted for the fact that atoms only emit light of certain frequencies. He found that to get the correct intensity, he needed to multiply together his amplitudes in a special way. Heisenberg's boss, Pascual Jordan, noticed that the equation Heisenberg had found was equivalent to multiplying together two mathematical objects called matrices. This **matrix mechanics** approach to quantum physics did not take off initially because of the difficulty in understanding the derivation.

It doesn't matter in what order you multiply two numbers you will always get the same answer.

Two numbers, e.g. 3 and 4, do commute:

$$3 \times 4 = 4 \times 3$$

Two matrices, e.g. M and N, do not commute:

$$N \times M \neq M \times N$$

Multiplication of numbers is commutative, you can commute (change the position) of each number and you get the same answer. Matrices are different, they are noncommutative. You get two different answers when multiplying two matrices one way around or the other. Heisenberg noticed that the answers differed by a constant number when multiplying matrices representing particular pairs of properties in his matrix mechanics: momentum and position, or energy and time. This mirrors experiments where we can only measure one property at a time, and by measuring one you affect the other. The math was telling Heisenberg that it is impossible to accurately measure certain pairs of properties to better than some small constant difference; you always have at least that amount of uncertainty. This uncertainty is a factor of the tiny Planck constant, so in our large-scale day-to-day we wouldn't notice the tiny effect of this. This **uncertainty principle** is a cornerstone of quantum physics. It is a further departure from the idea of determinism, stating quite clearly that there is literally no way that certain properties of a particle may be known exactly, meaning there can never be a way of exactly determining the future of that particle.

Uncertainty principle

Nature does not allow us to measure pairs of properties to exact accuracy. If we know the position of a quantum object we have less of an idea of its momentum and vice versa.

Schrödinger's wave equation

Another way of describing quantum objects came a year later in the wave equation of Austrian physicist Erwin Schrödinger. **Schrödinger's wave equation** developed from the idea that if a wave function describes the properties of a wave at some time then there must exist an equation that can predict how this wave equation evolves in time. Schrödinger used his wave equation to calculate the energy of electron waves trapped around a proton, as de Broglie had done before him. His results agreed brilliantly with the different energies of light emitted by hydrogen gas, and is equivalent to Heisenberg and Jordan's matrix mechanics.

Despite the development of wave equations nobody initially understood what the wave function of a particle meant physically. But in 1926, German physicist Max Born explained in his **Born rule** that the wave function was a function of probability. While the amplitude of the wave function does not represent anything physical, when you square it by multiplying it by itself, then it represents a probability. If you wanted to discover how likely it would be to find a particle in some region of space or time, all you need do is square the wave function and sum up the probabilities over all the space or time you are interested in.

From wave to particle

One of the biggest questions in quantum physics is how the immeasurable wave function becomes a real-world measurable particle, a process known as **wave-function collapse**. Wave functions contain probabilities of every possible outcome seen when interacting with the world around it. When interacting, all but one of the possible outcomes disappear to leave a single set of properties defining the particle it has become. The process of going from an infinite number of possibilities with different probabilities to one single definite result is one of great debate even today. How is the final state selected? What happens to all of the information about the other possibilities?

Born rule

Squaring a wave function and plotting it against a position provides a plot of probability as to where a particle is most likely to be found.

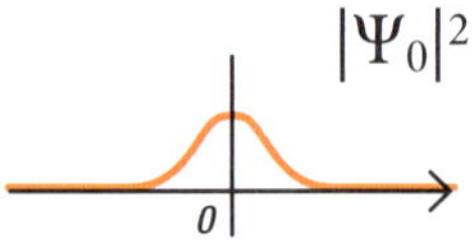

This squared wave function shows that the particle is most likely to be found around the zero position

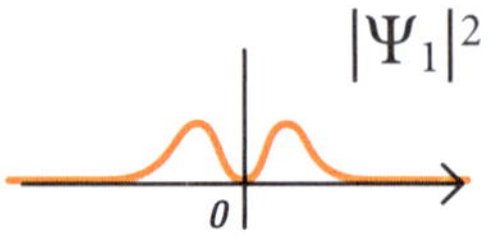

This particle is equally likely to be found in a positive or negative location in space, away from zero

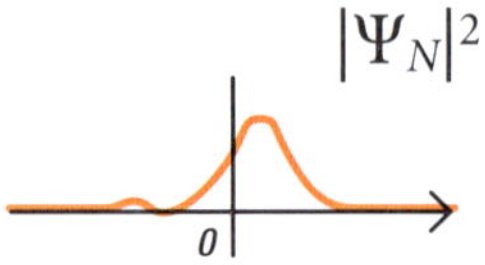

This particle is most likely to be found in a positive location in space, just a little away from zero

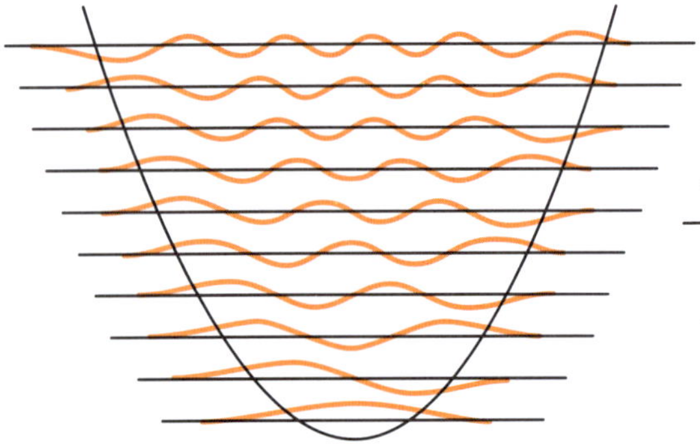

Schrödinger's equation

The time independent version of Schrödinger's equation describes standing waves of electrons trapped in an atom. It is this form Schrödinger used to calculate the energies of electrons in hydrogen atoms.

The simplest way to approach wave-function collapse is the **Copenhagen interpretation**, defined by Niels Bohr and Werner Heisenberg. It suggests that the act of measurement by a piece of lab equipment triggers the collapse of the wave function. Once a real-world measurement has been made, all other outcomes that were a possibility now cease to exist. It is similar to rolling a die. During the roll there are a number of different possibilities, which, just like the wave function, we are unable to see. When the die lands, it is forevermore observed as that number. Some feel this makes the wave function just a theoretical instrument with which the possible outcomes of an experiment can be calculated.

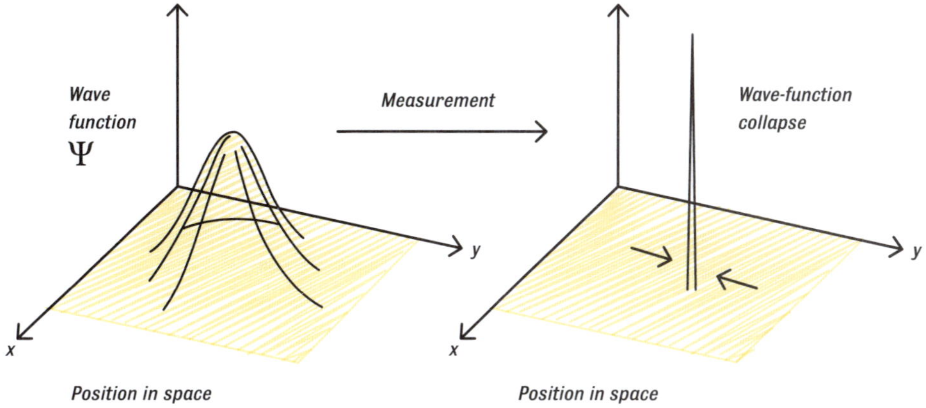

Erwin Schrödinger wrote to Albert Einstein to share an interesting thought experiment, in an attempt to show how absurd he thought the Copenhagen interpretation was. He suggested that the life of a cat placed inside a sealed box depended upon the quantum fate of a single radioactive atom. If the radioactive atom decayed, then poison would be released to kill the cat; if it did not, then the cat remained alive. He noted that after some time, thanks to his wave equation, you would determine that the wave function of the unobserved radioactive atom would be in some mixed state of both decayed and undecayed. This would in effect also mean the fate of the cat was also in some mixture of both dead and alive! Although it was originally designed to show how absurd the Copenhagen interpretation was, the **Schrödinger's cat** thought experiment has stood as a test of all other interpretations of quantum physics.

The Copenhagen interpretation

The Copenhagen interpretation of quantum physics simply states that the wavelike nature of a quantum object collapses and ceases to exist as soon as the object is measured.

Schrödinger's cat

Schrödinger developed a thought experiment to demonstrate how silly the Copenhagen Interpretation would be. In it the life of a cat is determined by whether or not a single radioactive atom decays or not, leaving the cat in limbo.

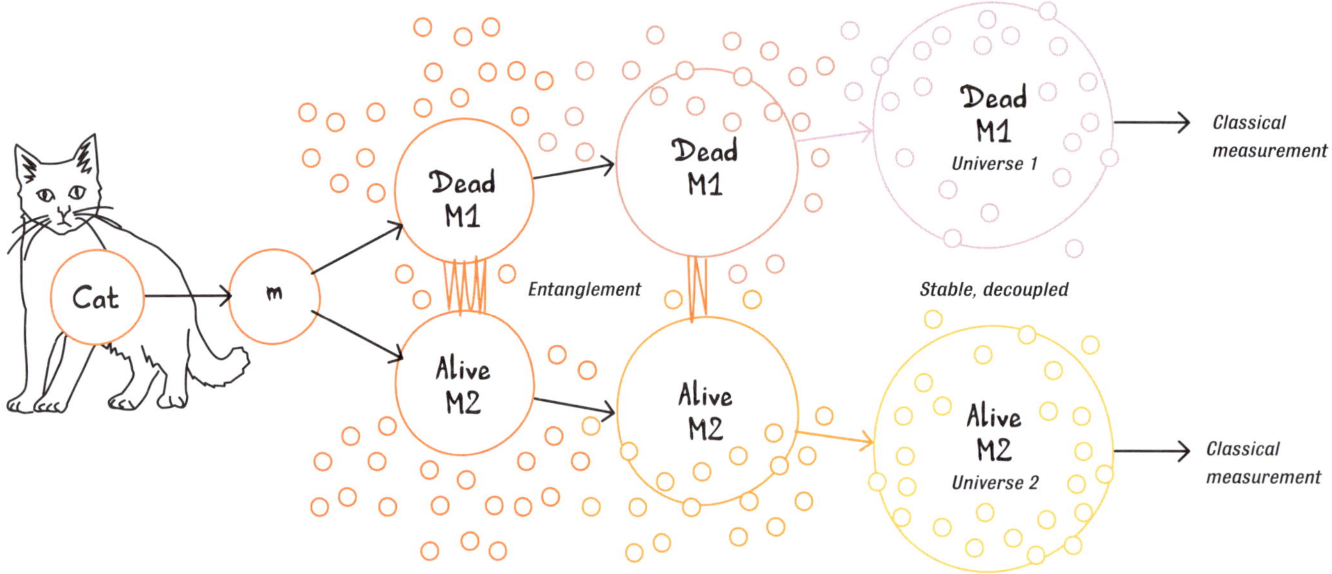

Decoherence

Decoherence of a wave is different to wave-function collapse: an observer only perceives the collapse of the wavelike nature of a quantum object, it does not completely collapse. Decoherence tells us that we cannot ignore the role of the observer in the outcome that is observed. Any observer or experimental equipment will itself have a wave function because it too is made from quantum objects. Decoherence is the apparent collapse of the wavelike nature of a quantum object as it interacts with the wave of the observer. Continued interaction eventually renders the probability of most outcomes to zero apart from just one. An observer would perceive such a quantum thing to be not wavelike but particle-like with definite properties. This idea of decoherence takes away the unknowns in the transition between wave and particle behavior. It might seem that if we know the wave function of both the observer and the quantum particle we could effectively predict the outcome, making quantum physics deterministic again. There's just one problem: observers are large and made of trillions upon trillions of atoms each contributing an influence on the total wave function. We could never hope to understand this observer wave function. Decoherence offered a way forward as an explanation, but experimentally it poses difficulties.

Decoherence of a wave function

Decoherence of a wave function is the gradual entangling of the quantum object's wave function with that of the thing measuring it until only one outcome remains possible.

In 1957, American physicist Hugh Everett published a new interpretation of quantum physics, which he called the Universal State Formulation. Wave function became particle through decoherence as some Universal State wave function merged with the wave function of the quantum object. This merging, Everett said, would result in all possible outcomes of the quantum object's observation becoming true but each outcome would be played out in different, alternative universes. As observers we only see one outcome, not because the others do not exist, but because we live in just one of these many universes. This idea was named the **many-worlds interpretation** by American physicist Bryce DeWitt, who popularized the idea.

Action at a distance

Ripples on a pond from two stones will eventually meet. When they cross, each wave continues on in the direction they were traveling but will have been forever changed from their encounter. In a similar way, quantum objects sharing a common origin are born with knowledge of each other's wave function. As they then travel out into the world and evolve, the two wave functions remain inextricably linked—this is known as **quantum entanglement**. Decoherence is the gradual entanglement of an object's wave function with that of an observer.

Schrödinger was not the only one to highlight paradoxes of the Copenhagen interpretations with thought experiments. Albert **E**instein, Boris **P**odolsky (Russian-American physicist), and Nathan **R**osen (American-Israeli physicist) also developed one, known as the **EPR paradox**. If two particles A and B are born in the same process, then their wave functions are entangled. The uncertainty principle states that accurately measuring particle A's momentum leaves us uncertain of its position. However, the momentum of particle A and B must be conserved, so we could calculate the momentum of the as-yet-untouched particle B. If we now measure the position of particle B, we should have an accurate idea of both its position and momentum. EPR argued that this contradicts both the uncertainty principle and the Copenhagen interpretation.

The paper continued to discuss how particle B would somehow "know" about the measurement of particle A. According to the Copenhagen interpretation, the information would have to be shared between the two particles instantaneously at the exact moment the wave function collapses. This suggests the information travels faster than light, which contradicts special relativity, itself a pillar of modern quantum physics. Some suggested there was some secret pact based on hidden knowledge that the waves carried with them, implying that there was more to the wave function than first thought.

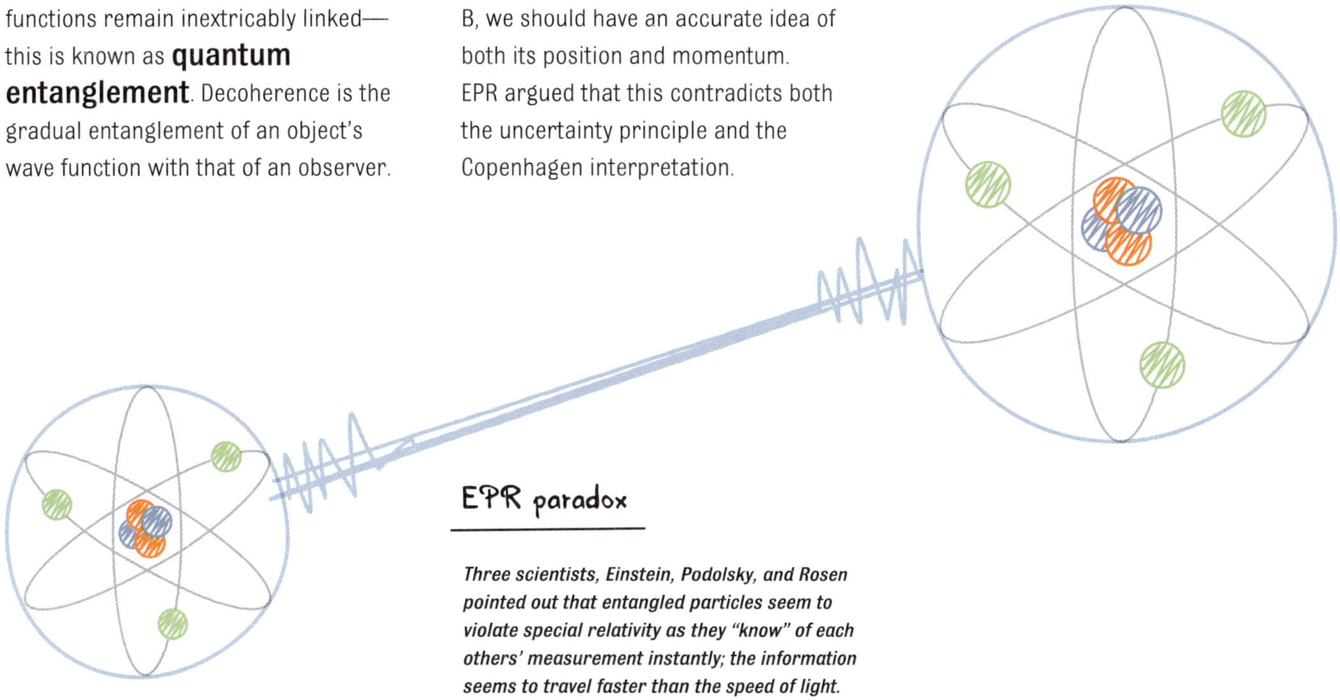

EPR paradox

Three scientists, Einstein, Podolsky, and Rosen pointed out that entangled particles seem to violate special relativity as they "know" of each others' measurement instantly; the information seems to travel faster than the speed of light.

Hidden variables

In 1964, Irish physicist John Bell suggested a number of experiments to see if wave functions were carrying hidden knowledge, which he called hidden variables. Particles had to carry this information with them locally. If one particle in a pair of entangled particles were to be measured, these hidden variables would inform the other particle of the result.

Entangled wave functions would each be time-sharing the same hidden variable knowledge. Measuring the properties of pairs of these entangled objects in different scenarios should demonstrate a correlation in behavior determined by the time-share. A good analogy of measuring entangled particles is police interviewing a gang of criminals. Police ask questions relating to different aspects of each member of the group's past activities. Perfect correlation would lead police to think they are getting all of the information. Any inconsistencies in the answers between pairs of gang members may point toward some hidden knowledge. Differences between questioning of pairs of entangled particles is known as **Bell's inequality**. When experiments investigating this problem were conducted, they seemed to prove that particles do not possess hidden knowledge, suggesting that information was exchanged faster than light.

Quantum teleportation uses quantum entanglement to transfer information. Particles A and B are entangled; particle A is then kept while particle B is transported somewhere else. At a later time, particle A is entangled with some third message particle M through an interaction, collapsing particle A's wave function. Entanglement tells us that this instantaneously changes the wave function of particle B. If A and M are entangled and A and B are entangled, then it makes sense to think that B and M are also entangled. Information about the messenger particle M has been teleported instantaneously to particle B.

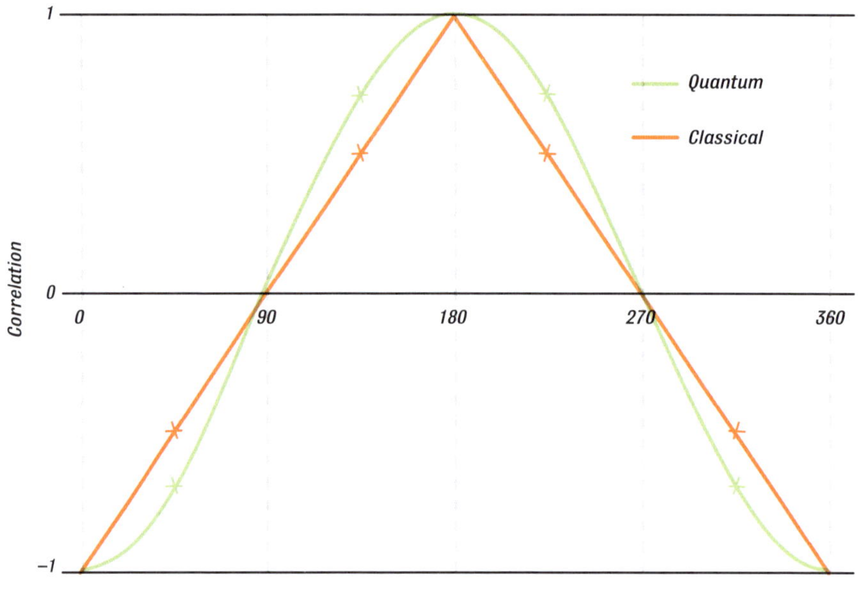

Angle between detectors (in degrees)

Bell's inequality

Irish physicist John Bell suggested an experiment to test if the Copenhagen interpretation or the idea of "hidden variables" was the way quantum objects behaved. It showed that hidden variables did not seem to be the answer.

Quantum computing

Classical information flows through optical fibers and copper cables to bring the internet to our homes as a string of 1s and 0s called bits. Quantum bits, or **qubits**, are quantum versions of this classical bit. Quantum bits are not limited to 1 or 0, they can be some mixture of both 1 and 0 at the same time. Measuring a qubit collapses its wave function to give a classical 1 or 0. Qubits are far more powerful than classical bits when their values are all set using the same process because their wave functions will be entangled. As each qubit evolves and changes through some calculation each qubit knows what every other qubit is doing. This connection allows qubits to perform mathematical calculations that could never be done with classical bits.

Quantum computers are machines that can physically create and manipulate qubits. They come in many shapes and sizes and use very different things as a qubit. Some use the spin of atoms or electrons to encode information. The particles are trapped in specialized materials, between other atoms or in the lattice of crystals; strong magnets are then used to encode, manipulate, and read the atoms. Other technologies use the polarization of light trapped between cavities in materials, like bouncing the light between two mirrors. The polarization of the light is encoded and manipulated by special lasers and read out using filters similar to the ones used in 3-D movie glasses.

At the turn of the twentieth century, some scientists thought physics all wrapped up, but the quantum physics that was to come proved them incorrect. Today, quantum physics has presented us with as many questions about our universe as it has offered answers to. We know now we live in uncertain times and that this is the way nature has chosen it. Yet we are still no closer today to understanding why nature behaves in this bizarre probabilistic way.

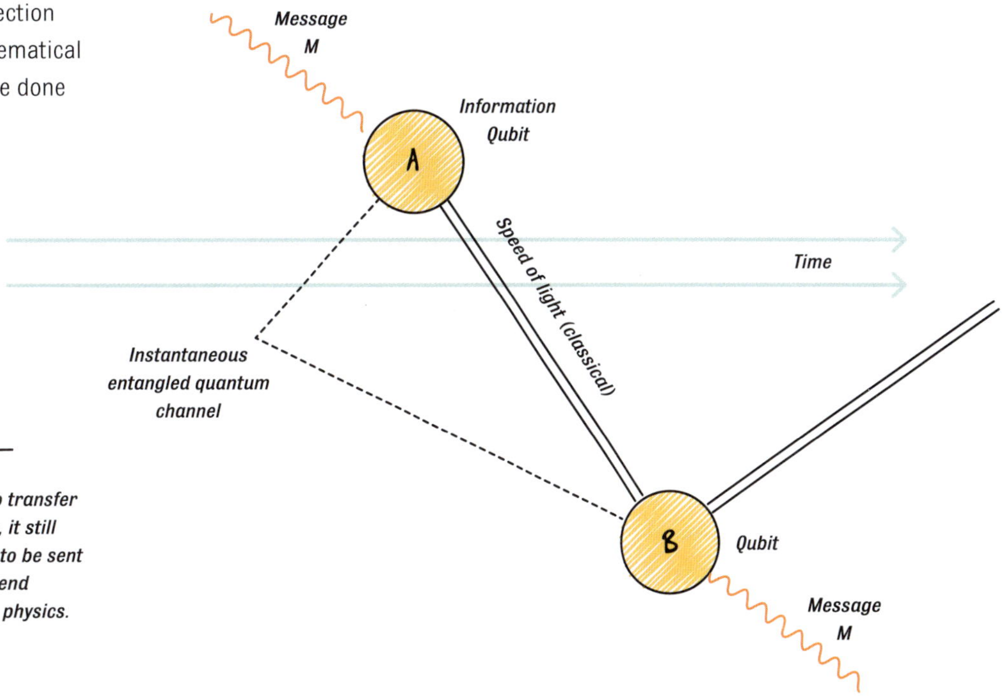

Entangled communication

Two entangled quanta can be used to transfer data through their hidden link. Sadly, it still requires some classical information to be sent as well, which means that we can't send information instantly using quantum physics.

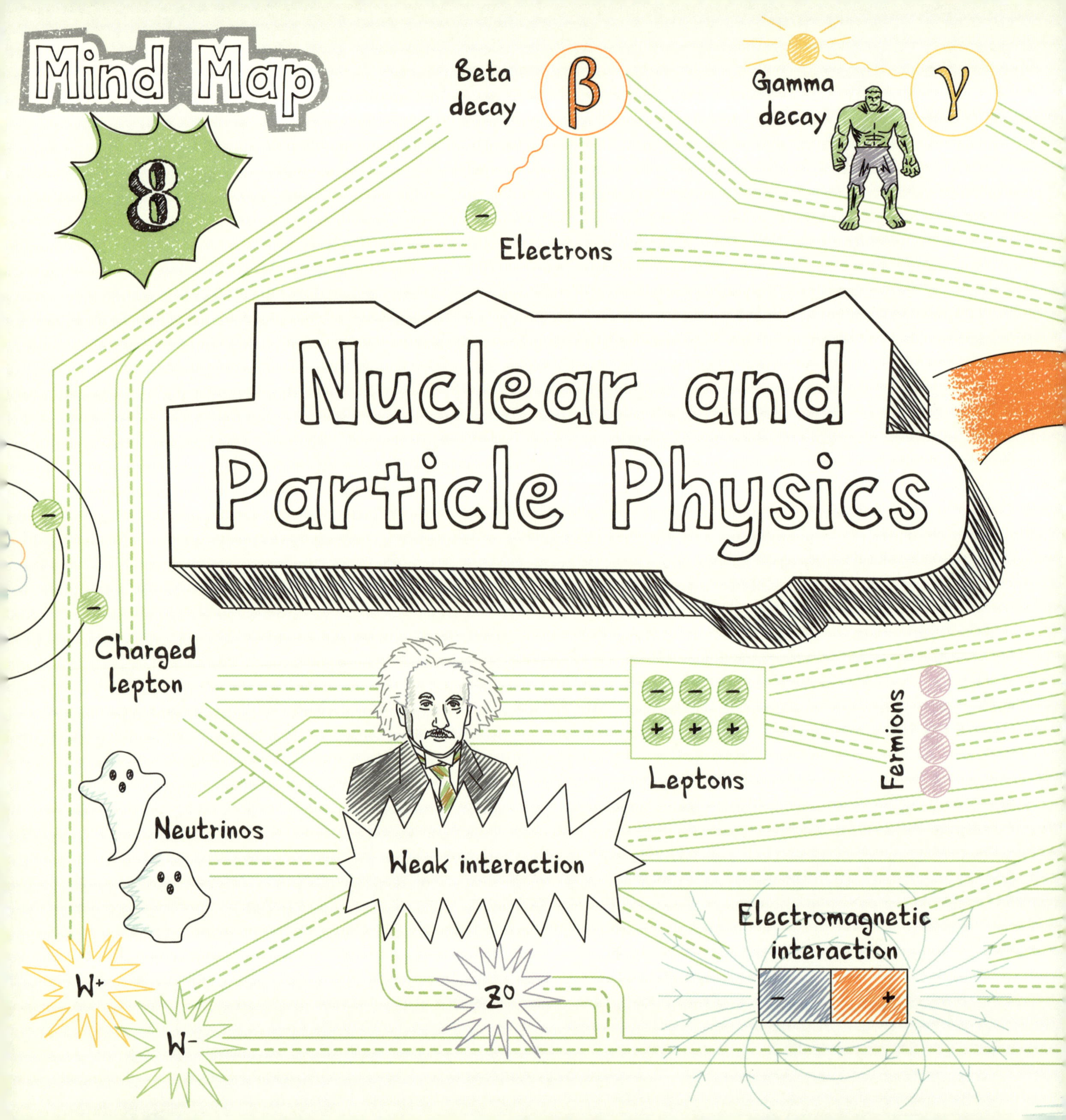

Mind Map
8
Nuclear and Particle Physics
Beta decay
β
Gamma decay
γ
Electrons
Charged lepton
Leptons
Fermions
Neutrinos
Weak interaction
Electromagnetic interaction
W+
W-
Z0

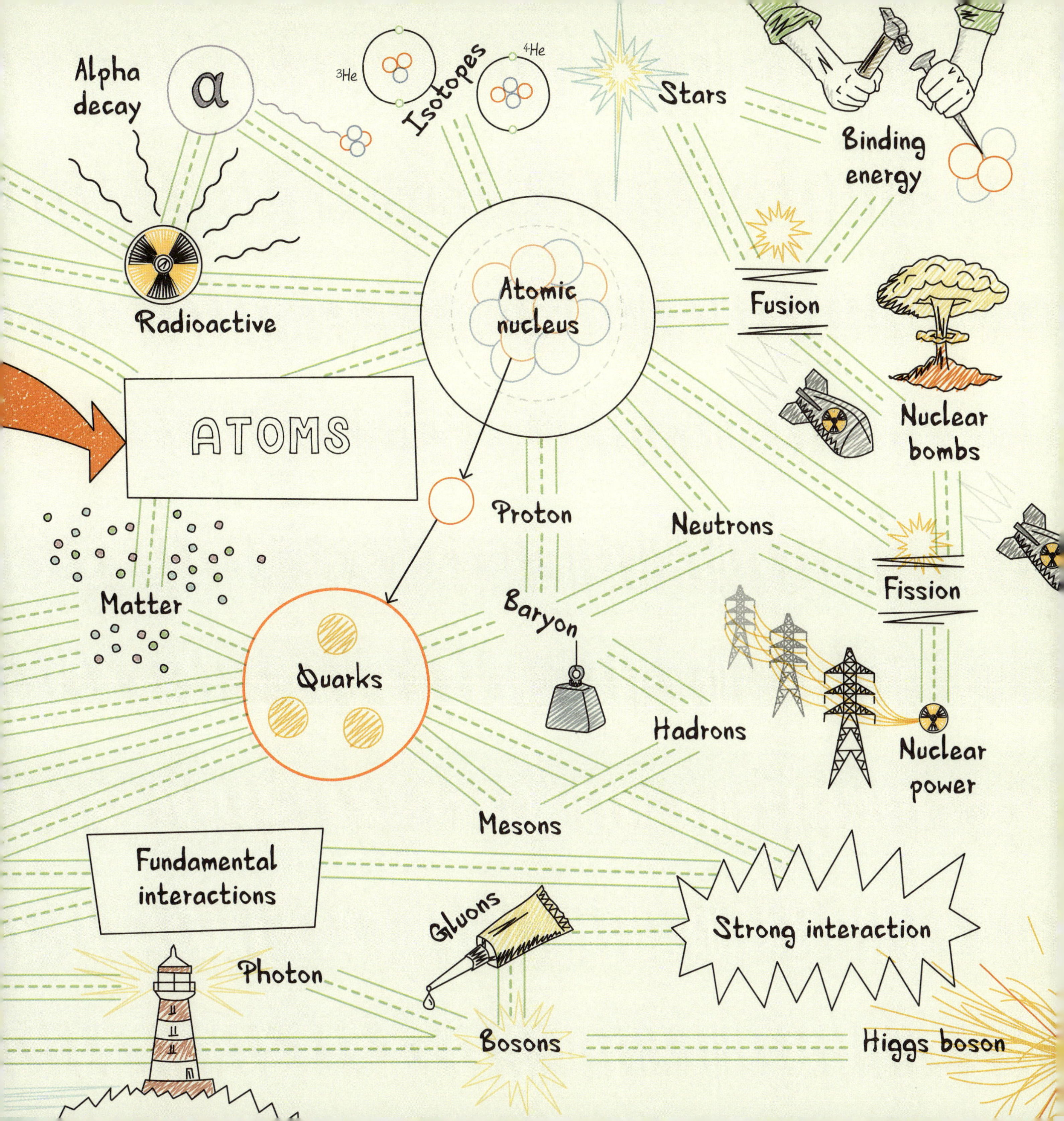
Alpha decay
3He
Isotopes
4He
Stars
Binding energy
Radioactive
Atomic nucleus
Fusion
ATOMS
Nuclear bombs
Proton
Neutrons
Fission
Matter
Baryon
Quarks
Hadrons
Nuclear power
Mesons
Fundamental interactions
Gluons
Strong interaction
Photon
Bosons
Higgs boson

Atomism and Strange Rays

Everything physical in our visible universe is made up of stuff we call **matter**. The ancients Greeks thought this matter was made from small unbreakable building blocks called atoms, which take their name from the Greek **atmos** meaning "uncuttable." These atomists believed that if you could understand these atoms and the forces that governed them, then you could understand all of nature. The atomist view was lost to antiquity but reemerged during the scientific revolution. With the advent of chemistry, British chemist John Dalton revived atomism for a modern world by stating that each of the chemical elements is made from unique and indivisible atoms.

The atomist view remained until the end of the nineteenth century, when things smaller than the smallest known atom of hydrogen were discovered. Strange rays were observed being emitted from highly electrically charged plates of metal. Experiments showed these rays to be made of negatively charged particles called **electrons**, which are the basic unit of electricity.

Electrons are much lighter in mass than the lightest known atom, hydrogen, showing that atoms have smaller things inside them and might therefore be breakable after all.

Different strange rays were also discovered coming from inside atoms. These atoms were **radioactive**, which means anything that actively emits radiation spontaneously. Three types of rays were discovered coming spontaneously from within atoms. Some of these rays were released when an atom changed into another atom of a different type, a process called decay. These rays were very different in their properties and were given their names after the first letters of the Greek alphabet: alpha, beta, and gamma.

Atoms to quarks

From thinking the world was made of atoms in the nineteenth century, we have since discovered that there are many smaller things. An atom is made from a central nucleus filled with particles called protons and neutrons, which are made from smaller things called quarks. Surrounding the atomic nucleus are electrons.

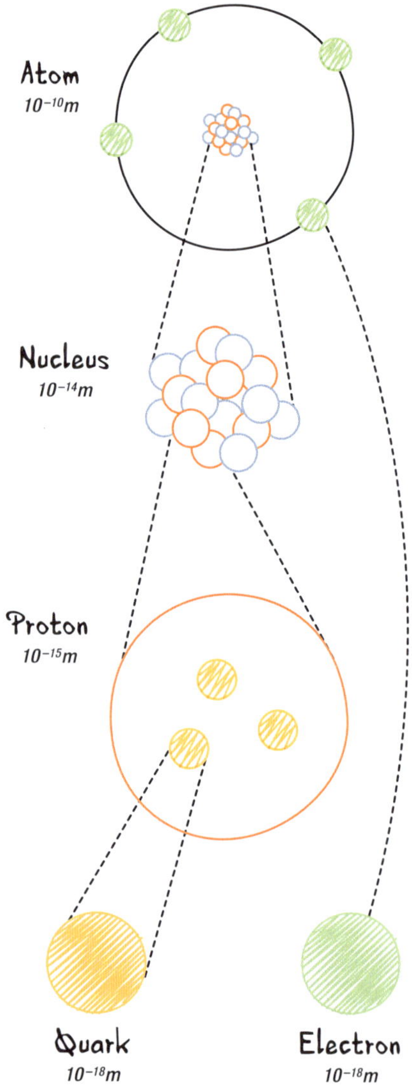

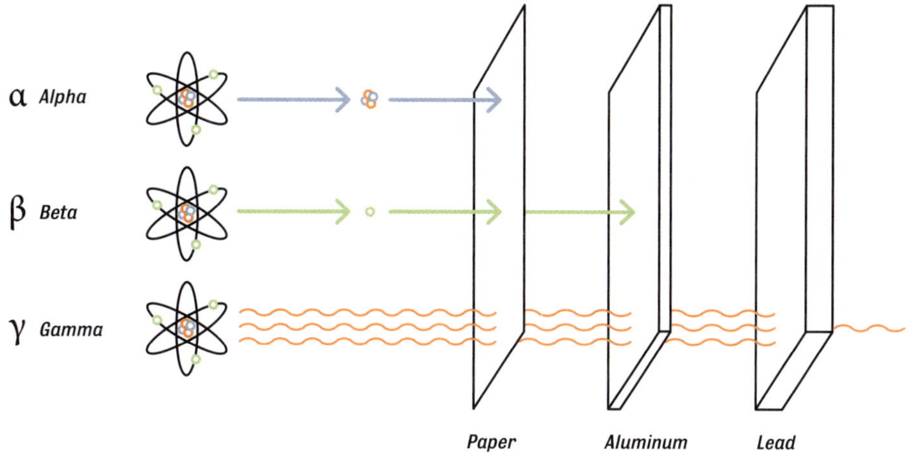

Penetrating power

The three different radiations are each able to pass through different amounts of material. Alpha is the least penetrating while gamma is the most.

Alpha decay produces alpha radiation that can travel around a centimeter through the air and is easily stopped by a sheet of paper. Alpha radiation is deflected by an electric field, suggesting it possesses an electric charge, but it does not curve greatly, suggesting it is also quite massive. We know today that these alpha particles, which are emitted during alpha decay, are electrically charged nuclei of helium.

Beta radiation from **beta decay** packs more punch and travels much further in air, stopped only by a thin sheet of aluminum. Beta radiation is deflected by electric and magnetic fields. It is made up of fast moving electrons.

The third and most penetrating of the radiations is gamma, which is emitted in **gamma decay** and can pass through air almost entirely unhindered. Gamma radiation is not deflected by electric and magnetic fields such as alpha and beta.

It was identified as very high-energy light with a frequency higher than the X-rays discovered by Wilhelm Röntgen in 1895.

The activity of a sample of radioactive atoms is defined as the number of decays that occur each second. Activity is given the unit Becquerels with symbol Bq after Henri Becquerel, the French physicist who first discovered radioactivity in 1898. Activity is related to the number of radioactive atoms in a sample by a decay constant, a number that essentially represents the probability of any atom in the sample decaying each second. Highly active radioactive samples will have many radioactive atoms and a large decay constant. Each decay reduces the number of radioactive atoms in a sample, and so will also reduce a sample's activity. Activity and number decay exponentially, and the decay constant is the determining factor as to how quickly a radioactive sample is depleted.

Deflection and charge

Both alpha and beta radiation are deflected as they move through an electric field because each has an electric charge. Gamma radiation is not deflected by an electric field as it does not have an electric charge, it is an electromagnetic wave.

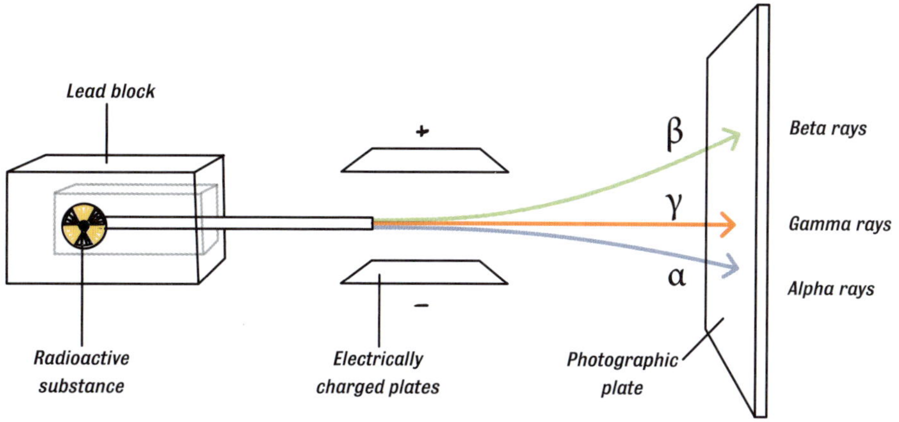

Half life

Half life is a way of describing the activity of a particular type of radioactive atom that is independent of sample size. It's the average time it would take for radioactive atoms to reduce in activity or number by half. It is directly related to the decay constant and therefore the probability that individual atoms will decay each second. The half lives of elements heavier than uranium in the periodic table are so short that, while they existed in the early years of Earth, the following 4.5 billion years of decay means they can no longer be found naturally on Earth.

The center of the atom

If alpha radiation is fired like a small bullet at a thin sheet of gold foil, about one in 8,000 will bounce right back. To explain this, scientists reimagined the atom as a miniature solar system. All of the mass and positive electric charge of an atom is packed tightly into a very small central region called the **atomic nucleus**. Electrons were then predicted to orbit like planets around this compact, positively charged nucleus.

The lightest known atom has the lightest possible nucleus. It is logical therefore to think that all other atomic nuclei are made from some multiple of hydrogen nuclei. This building block, which became known as the **proton** because of its positive charge, is the basic unit from which all other atomic nuclei are made.

Nucleus/gold leaf

When alpha particles were fired at a thin foil of gold most passed right through, as was expected given J. J. Thomson's plum-pudding model of the atom. However, a small handful bounced right back, which could only be explained if there were a central clump of positive electric charge.

When balancing the books between the number of protons in a nucleus, defined by its place on the periodic table, and an atom's mass, things don't add up. If the nucleus were solely made from protons, then every atom should be much lighter than it seems. To fix this, there must also be other particles in the nucleus alongside the proton. These particles must not change the charge of the nucleus and so must be electrically neutral, which led to the name **neutrons**. Because lighter elements seem twice as heavy as the

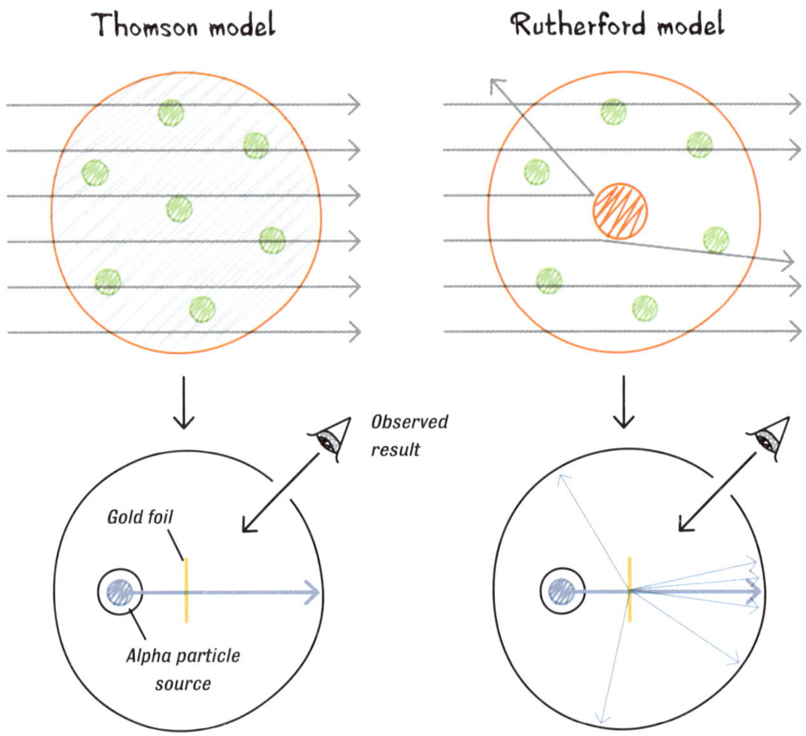

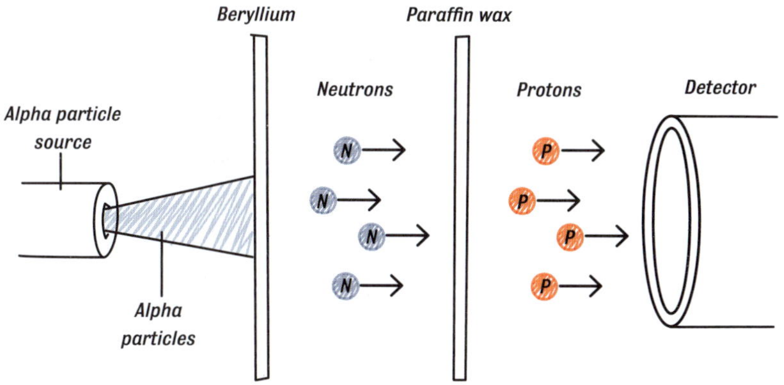

Neutrons

Neutrons were discovered when produced by alpha particles striking a beryllium target; they went on to knock protons out of a thin sheet of wax. The protons were struck from the wax by an unseen electrically neutral particle with a similar mass.

number of protons they possess, neutrons must have a similar mass to the proton. The atomic nucleus as we know it today was complete and packed full of nucleons, the collective name for protons and neutrons.

Isotopes

Most elements have different versions of themselves with the same number of protons in the nucleus but a different number of neutrons. These are called **isotopes** of an element. Protons provide positive electric charge and define how many electrons must orbit around a nucleus so that each atom is electrically neutral. It is the electrons that define the chemistry of an atom.

As neutrons have no electric charge, changing the number of neutrons does not change the chemical properties of an atom in any way. So, isotopes of an element will behave in the same way chemically, but may behave very differently in their nucleus.

Isotopes are distinguished from one another by their mass number, which is a sum of the number of protons plus neutrons. All carbon atoms have six protons in the nucleus, which defines the chemistry of the six electrons that orbit around it in an atom. Carbon-12 and carbon-14 are two isotopes of carbon, with six and eight neutrons in the nucleus respectively. Carbon-14 is an unstable isotope of carbon and decays via beta decay to form stable nitrogen-14.

Similar yet different

Isotopes are different atoms of the same element with the same number of protons and electrons, but a different number of neutrons in the nucleus.

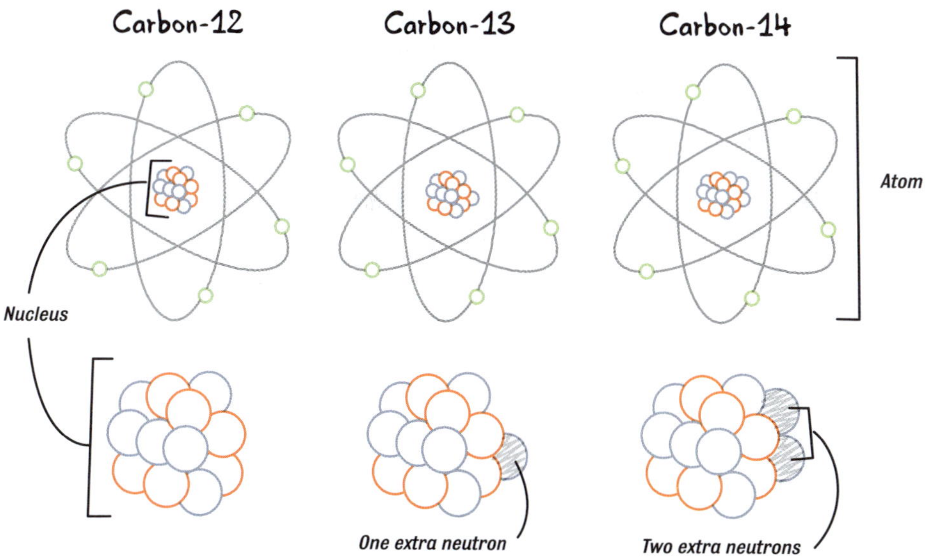

Binding energy

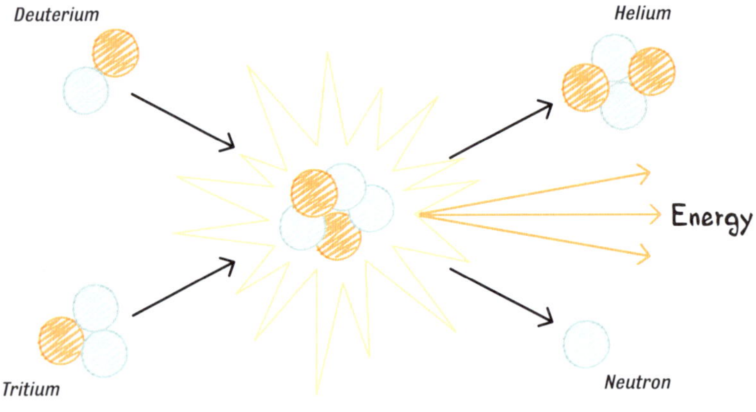

Most elements have at least one stable isotope, where the mix of protons and neutrons is just right, so that the nucleus does not want to spontaneously change. All elements have unstable isotopes, in which the mix of protons and neutrons could be made better, and so the nucleus decays radioactively. The stability of a nucleus is measured by the **binding energy** of each nucleon within it. A larger binding energy means that the nucleus is more stable. Plotting the binding energy for stable isotopes of all naturally occurring elements shows an interesting trend. Iron-56 has the highest binding energy for each nucleon of any common isotope, which makes its nucleus the envy of all other atoms. Low-mass and high-mass elements have much lower binding energies, making their nuclei less stable.

To attain a more stable nucleus, low-mass nuclei want to combine to form a single, heavier nucleus that brings them closer to stable iron-56. To achieve this, they must get incredibly close together, which means overcoming a large electromagnetic repulsion because both have positive electric charge. This shows that light nuclei only usually stick together when they are hot enough and therefore moving fast enough that they overcome this push apart. The **fusion** of light nuclei to produce heavier elements releases vast amounts of energy and is the source of power for **stars**. Light produced in these fusion reactions pushes back against gravity to form a stable star like our Sun. Fusion is the source of all of the light elements used in the chemistry of life on Earth. We are made from this star dust.

High-mass elements often decay via radioactivity to lower masses to gain a nucleus closer to that of the most stable iron-56 isotope. But some high-mass isotopes are quite stable and can resist decay. However, if neutrons are fired into some of these isotopes then the extra energy in the nucleus splits it apart in a process called induced **fission**. The nucleus, and therefore the atom, disintegrates to form at least two new atoms while releasing large amounts of energy.

Nuclear fusion

Nuclear fusion occurs when two light atomic nuclei strike each other with enough force that they become stuck together to form a heavier, more stable nucleus.

When some isotopes fission, they produce a spray of neutrons alongside these new atoms. These neutrons can then go on to trigger fission in other heavy nuclei, which will trigger fission in yet more nuclei. This is an example of a chain reaction, where the reaction of fission produces more of the things required to initiate the reaction in the first place. The result is a runaway increase in the amount of fission occurring, and therefore of energy being released. These chain reactions, as well as some fusion reactions, are used to release huge amounts of energy in **nuclear bombs**.

Nuclear fission

Nuclear fission occurs when a heavy atomic nucleus splits apart into two lighter atomic nuclei. This is usually induced through making the nucleus unstable by firing a neutron into it.

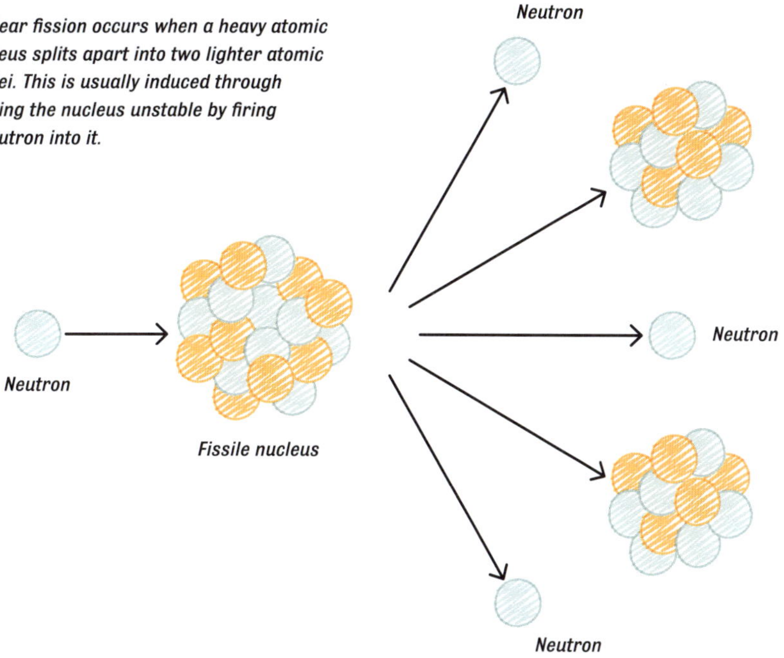

Fission chain reactions can be controlled by using different materials to absorb different amounts of the neutrons being produced. Getting the balance just right will allow the chain reaction to continue occurring, but not run away to produce huge amounts of energy in a flash. This is how chain fission reactions are used in **nuclear power** stations to produce controlled amounts of energy to generate electricity.

Nuclear power

Heat generated by the fission of uranium-235 or plutonium-239 in a nuclear reactor is used to boil water. The steam produced expands and spins a turbine before being cooled down to be used again. The turbine turns an electric generator to produce an electric current.

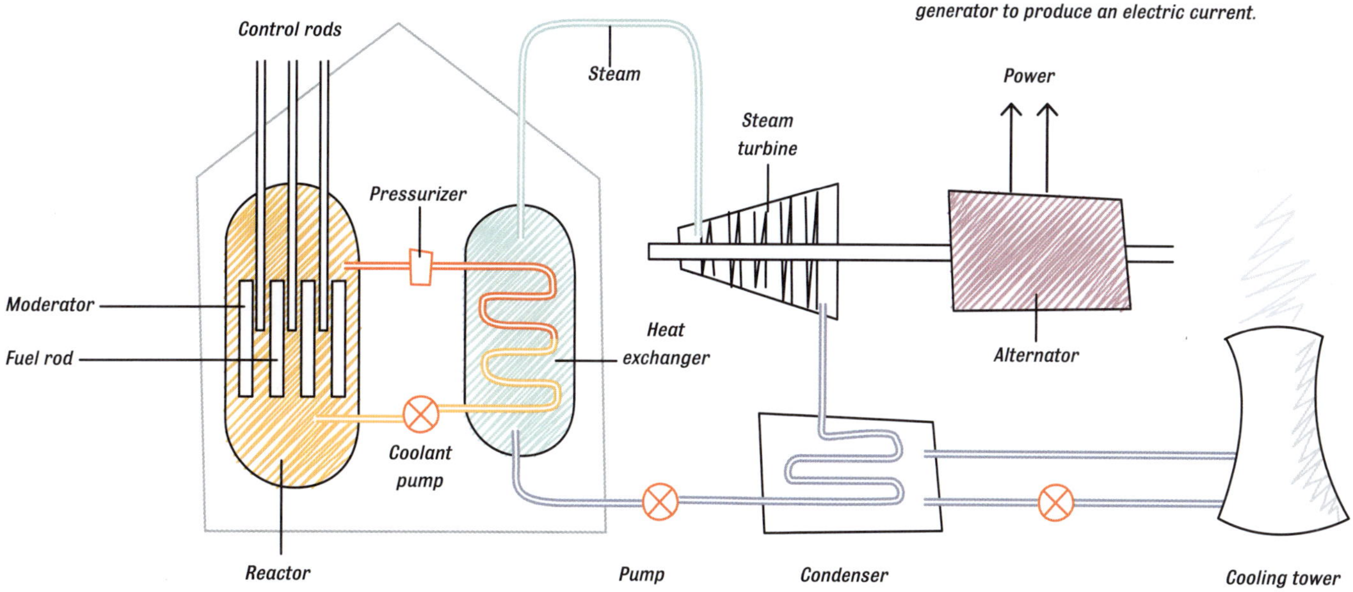

Classifying Particles

Particle is the name given to any tiny unit that has its own unique identity. Particles may be composite, made from a number of different smaller particles, or fundamental, made from nothing smaller at all. There are 12 known fundamental particles: six called quarks and six called leptons. These are the most basic building blocks from which every atom is made. Quarks are never found alone but always form composite particles: heavy baryons with three quarks or lighter mesons with two quarks. The leptons are light in mass and come in two distinct types: one with an electric charge and one without.

Hadrons

Protons and neutrons are part of a family of particles called baryons, named from the Greek *baryos* meaning "heavy," as they hugely outweigh electrons. As heavy as they might seem, though, the proton is the lightest-mass baryon we know of. In the 1960s and 1970s, there was an explosion in the number of particles discovered at particle-accelerator experiments all over the world. Lots of them behaved in some ways like protons and neutrons.

Quarks are small and light particles that group together to form heavier particles such as baryons. They are a fundamental particle with no further internal structure, so they cannot be broken apart.

Baryon is the name given to any particle that, like the proton and neutron, is composed of three quarks. Experiments show that there are six quarks in total, grouped into three pairs. The first pair of up quark and down quark combine to make the lightest baryons: a proton is made from two up quarks and one down quark, a neutron from one up quark and two down quarks. From this definition it can be shown that up quarks have a positive charge two-thirds that of a proton while a

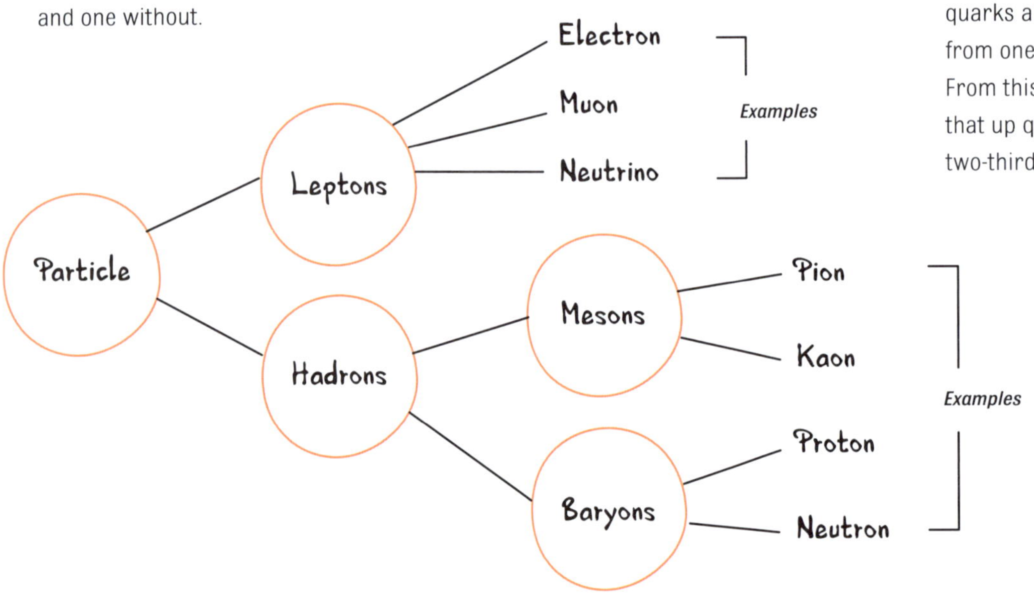

Particles

Particles have a hierarchy of different names, usually derived from ancient Greek. The meanings of the names have changed over time, but they chart the discovery of each type of particle.

down quark has a negative electric charge one-third that of the electron. These quark electric charges balance out in the neutron to give zero electric charge, but add to +1 in the proton to give the particle its electric charge.

The further two pairs of quarks act in the same way as the up and down quarks apart from one thing—they are much more massive. The heavier versions of the up quark are called the charm quark and top quark, the top being most massive. The heavier versions of the down quark are called the strange quark and the bottom quark. Baryons made from these heavier quarks have similar properties to the proton and neutron apart from their mass. Heavier particles are unstable, as they know that they can be lower in mass if they decay into combinations of other quarks. This is why we don't experience heavy particles every day and why atoms are made the way they are, because all particles want to be the lowest energy and least massive possible. All baryons want to be a proton.

Among the zoo of discovered particles were those that did not fit the pattern and had a lightest mass between that of electrons and protons, which led to them being called **mesons**, from the Greek *mesos* for middle. Like baryons, mesons are also made from quarks, but fewer of them, which is why they have a smaller mass.

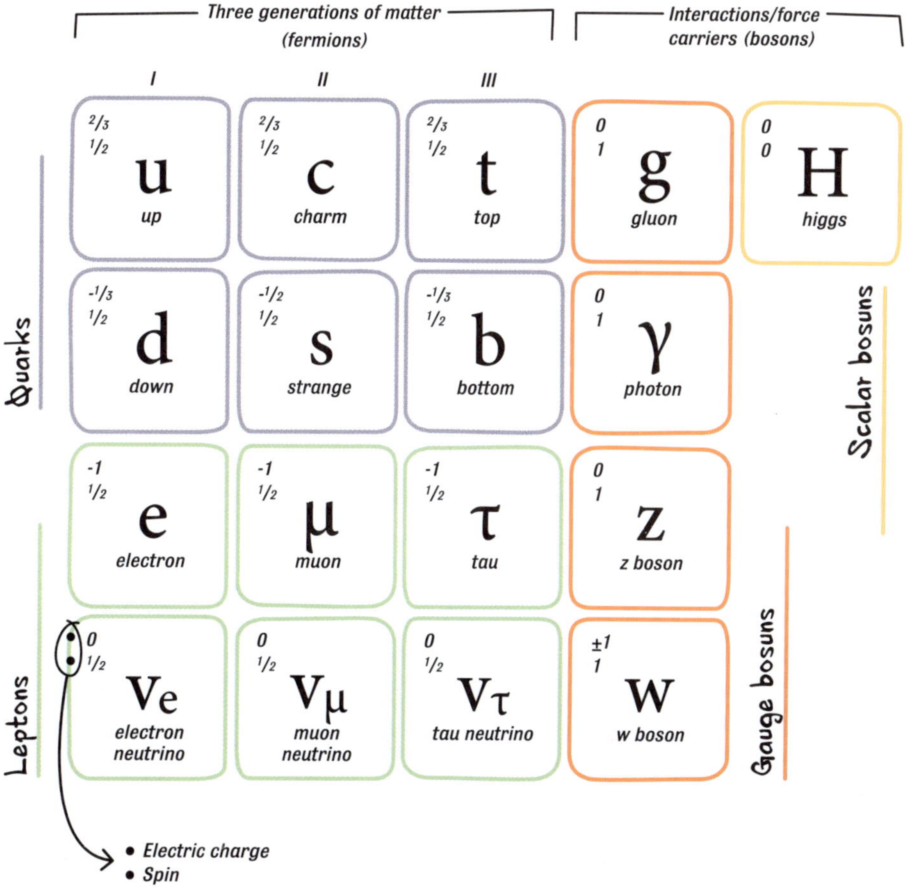

Baryons and mesons, all particles made from quarks, are collectively called **hadrons**. The name comes from the Greek *hadros* meaning "bulky," because of their generally large size.

Standard model of elementary particles

Our entire visible universe is made from just 12 building blocks, the fundamental particles: six quarks and six leptons. Alongside these are a group of particles that exchange interactions and energy between these 12, called bosons.

Leptons

Quarks are only half of the building blocks of matter; there are also six particles called leptons, three with and three without an electric charge. The most famous electrically **charged lepton** is the electron, which is responsible for all of chemistry and electricity, among many other things. The name lepton comes from the Greek *leptos* meaning "light," because the electron was so much lighter than the other particles in the atom. Just as there are heavier versions of the lightest quarks, two heavier cousins join the electron: the muon and the tau (sometimes referred to as the tauon). They are greater in mass but identical in all other respects, including having a negative electric charge. Electrons, muons, and taus therefore interact with other particles through the fundamental interactions in the same way. The tau betrays its lepton name a little, as it is heavier than a proton, but it is still lighter than particles made from the heaviest version of quarks. These three electrically charged leptons are paired, by weak interactions, to electrically neutral particles called **neutrinos**.

Fermions

All quarks and leptons are part of a family of particles called fermions. Fermions are the particles that build up to make the matter around us. All fermions have a quantum spin that is a half (or in special cases one-and-a-half), which means they must obey the Pauli Exclusion principle (see page 100). It is for this reason that fermions cannot all occupy the same energy, dictating that they must instead build on top of each other to form structures like the atomic nucleus and atoms.

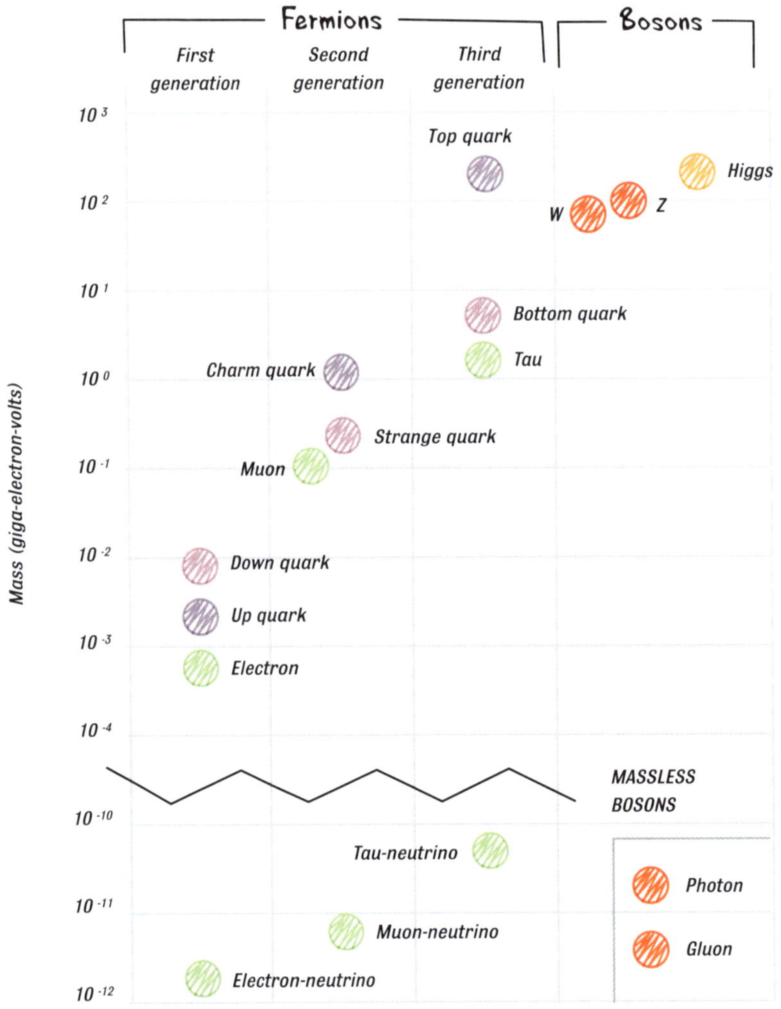

Mass of particles

Each of the 12 fundamental particles have very different masses. It is not known why they have the value of the masses that they do, but these values have been measured accurately in experiments.

Fundamental Interactions

The three **fundamental interactions** important to particles are strong interaction, electromagnetic interaction, and weak interaction (see page 27). They give rise to forces and transformations that dictate the way that fundamental particles behave. Each interaction has its own associated force-carrying particles that transfers information and energy between particles that experience that interaction.

Strong interaction

The strong interaction binds quarks together to form hadrons. It gets its name from its secondary role as a nuclear force that binds protons and neutrons together in the nucleus of an atom, where it must be stronger than the electromagnetic interaction pushing apart positively charged protons. The strong interaction is defined by three color charges: red, green, and blue. As the strong interaction acts only on quarks, it is only quarks that possess color charge. Particles with strong color charge attract other particles with color charge until they form color neutral particles. Mixing red, green, and blue light produces colorless white light, and this analogy is used in the strong interaction. Three quarks, each with a different color charge, would combine to form a white colorless particle, resulting in a baryon.

Nature's interactions

The different interactions of nature operate over very different scales and strengths. The strong interaction is strongest but only has a range that is smaller than a proton. The weak interaction can only influence things within an atomic nucleus. Electromagnetic interactions can occur on cosmic scales, as light is free to roam infinitely in space.

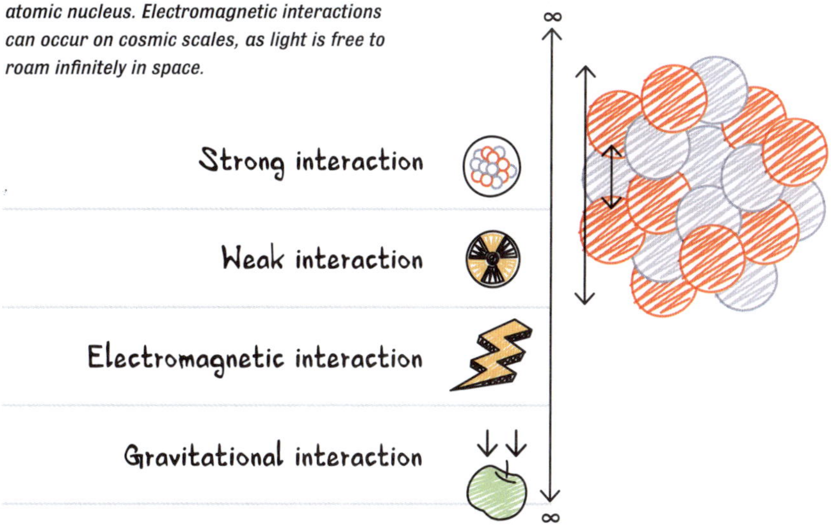

Gluons are the force-carrying particles of the strong interaction. They carry color charge between quarks. Gluons cannot travel far and do not make it out of the inside of a hadron. It is not gluons that are passed between nucleons to stick them together in a nucleus. Instead, pi-meson particles are exchanged and carry with them a watered-down, residual strong interaction to entice nucleons to stay together.

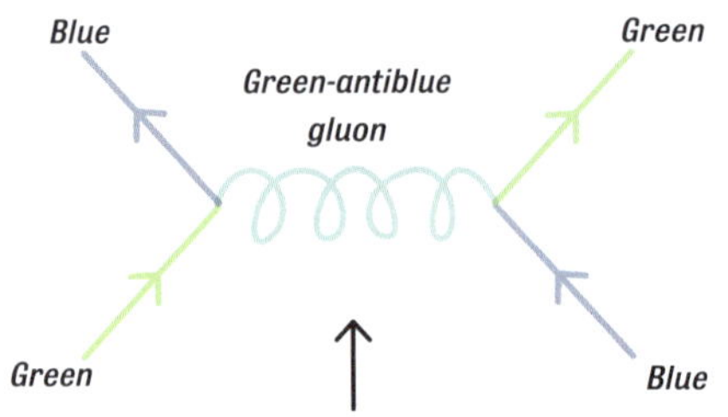

Strong interaction
between quarks

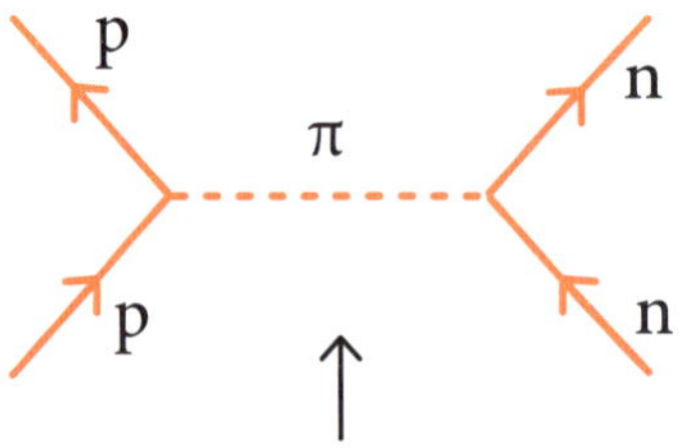

Nuclear force
between nucleons

Electromagnetic interaction

The electromagnetic interaction produces a force between any two particles with an electric charge or magnetic field. The **photon** is the force-carrying particle of the **electromagnetic interaction** and can be exchanged between particles that have electric charge. As mentioned previously, all subatomic particles not only behave like a particle but also like a wave. Photons are the quantum version of electromagnetic waves; they are tiny packets of light. Photons can travel well beyond the confines of the atom, as can be observed by looking deep into the night sky where light reaches us from vast distances across the cosmos.

It is light's ability to travel large distances that allows it to share the influence of the electromagnetic interaction between atoms, molecules, and much larger electrically charged things. We can only observe the presence of a subatomic particle using the electromagnetic interaction, as the other two fundamental interactions are limited to influencing things within the atom. Electromagnetic interactions that ionize or excite atoms produce measurable electric charge or light along the path taken by an electrically charged particle.

Weak interaction

The third fundamental interaction is called the weak interaction. This interaction is not felt as a force but brings about transformation of particles. In the early universe, weak interactions were as common as electromagnetic interactions, but as the universe cooled weak interactions died off. Photons have no mass of their own so little energy is required to create one, making it highly likely for an electromagnetic interaction to take place if it can.

The weak-interaction carriers, however, do have a mass and so lots of extra energy is required to make one, as Einstein's famous equation tells us: $E = mc^2$ (see page 143). In the hot, young universe after the Big Bang, this was not a problem as all the energy was squeezed into a smaller volume, and so there was lots to go around.

Weak →

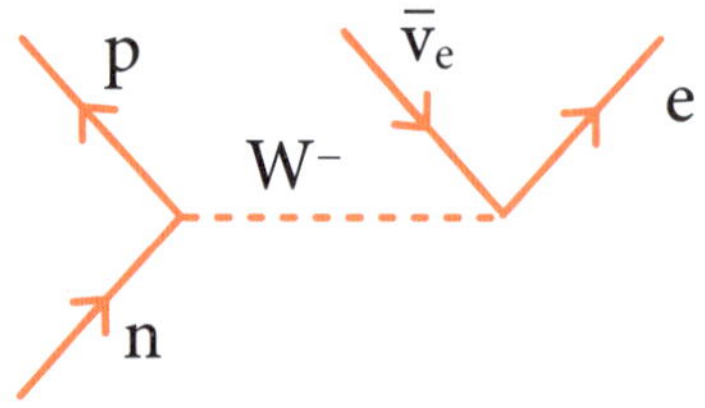

Electromagnetic →

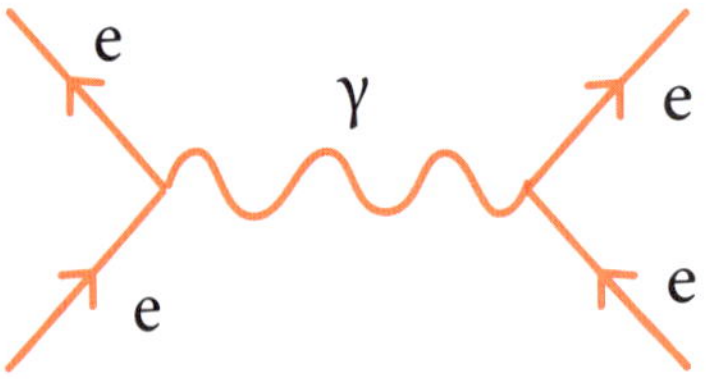

Feynman diagrams

Particle interactions can be drawn in Feynman diagrams. Time increases from bottom to top of the diagram; before interaction at the bottom and after at the top.

Today, the universe is much larger and energy is spread much more widely, so it is far less likely that there is enough energy around to make a weak-interaction carrier. It is possible to borrow this energy thanks to the uncertainty principle (see page 100), but such a large amount of energy could only be borrowed for an extremely short time. All of this means that the weak interaction appears weak because it is very unlikely in our cold universe that a weak-interaction carrier can be made to exchange the interaction between particles.

The **Z^0** particle is the electrically neutral weak-interaction carrier. It is not much more than a massive version of the photon, although it can interact with neutrinos and the photon cannot.

The **W^+** and **W^-** particles are electrically charged weak-interaction carriers. The W stands for weak while the Z is so-called because it is the final piece of the puzzle, having been discovered after the W particles. The charge they carry allows them to transform particles from one type to another. The W^+ can turn negatively charged down type quarks into positively charged up type quarks. It can also turn negatively charged leptons into electrically neutral neutrinos. The W^- is just as transformative but in reverse.

Bosons

All of the messenger particles of the fundamental interactions do not obey the Pauli exclusion principle like the other particles. Instead, they obey rules first noted by Indian physicist Satyendra Nath Bose, and so have been named **bosons** after him. Bosons can all occupy the same quantum numbers and energies; this is seen in lasers, where all photons of light occupy the same energy at the same time to produce intense light.

Bosons have quantum spin of integer value. The bosons that are responsible for the fundamental interactions all have a spin of one. Mesons are not carriers of the fundamental strong interaction, but because they are made from quarks, they do carry some strong-interaction influence between protons and neutrons in the atomic nucleus to keep them bound together.

Last, but not least, in our journey into the atom is the Higgs boson, named after the British physicist Peter Higgs, as he first predicted its existence. The **Higgs boson** is not a carrier of any fundamental interaction, but is still a boson, which is why it has a quantum spin of zero. It does, however, interact with fermion particles, but just to slow them down. The Higgs boson interacts different amounts with different fermions. Any interaction with a Higgs boson slows you down. Those fermions that interact strongly will find it difficult to move at all. Interactions like this are seen when measuring particles as an inertia, which is a measure of the force required to accelerate an object (see page 34). This inertia is what we measure as the mass of a particle.

The Higgs boson particle

The Higgs boson was discovered in 2012 at the Large Hadron Collider at CERN in Switzerland. It is the particle that provides the inertial mass for all other particles.

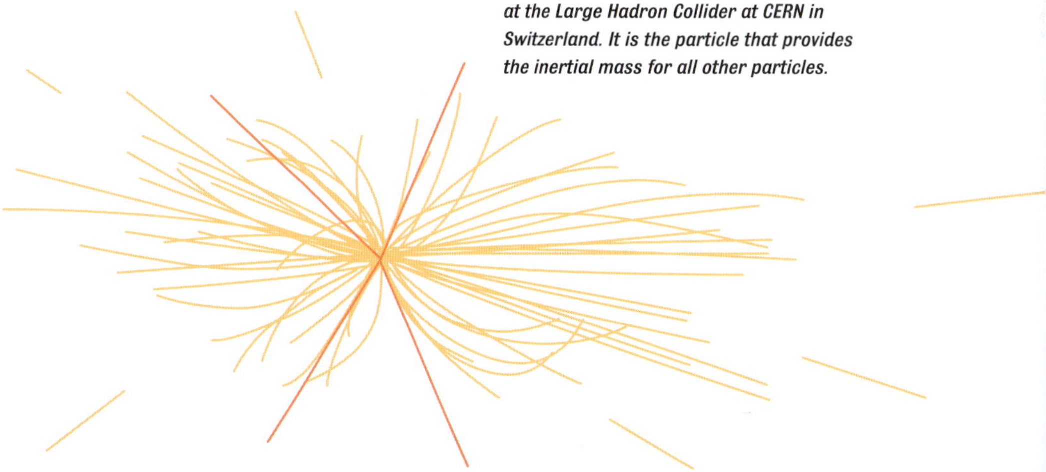

Mind Map
9
Astrophysics
Milky Way
The Sun
Spiral galaxy
Dark matter
Galaxies
Gas clouds
Cosmic microwave background radiation
Plasma
Expansion
He
H
Big Bang
Inflation

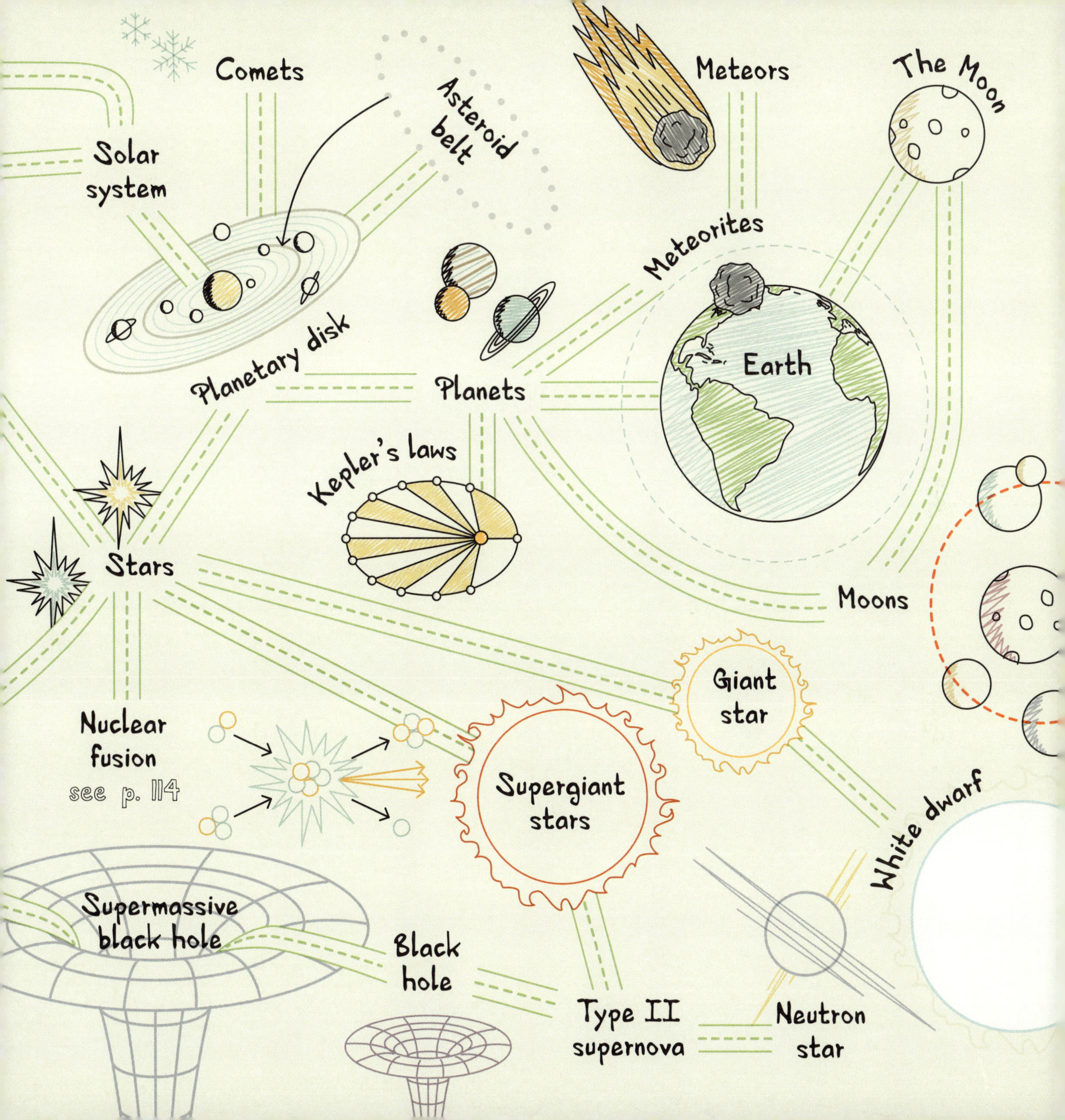

Comets
Asteroid belt
Meteors
The Moon
Solar system
Meteorites
Earth
Planetary disk
Planets
Kepler's laws
Stars
Moons
Giant star
Nuclear fusion
see p. 114
Supergiant stars
White dwarf
Supermassive black hole
Black hole
Type II supernova
Neutron star

Early Universe

It is thought our universe started with a **Big Bang**. Before this event, there was nothing, including no space for things to move in, or time to grow old by. At some point, some quantum fluctuation triggered energy, space, and time to be unleashed.

In the first moments, the universe expanded outward into the nothing faster than the speed of light, a tiny period of time known as **inflation**. Space and time unfurled like a carpet as the universe doubled in size many times over until it reached about the size of a golf ball. This young universe, much less than one second old, was very hot, as huge amounts of energy were confined to a very small space.

In the moments that followed, energy was converted into different forms, including the mass of many fundamental particles. Strong interactions almost immediately bound quarks into baryons and mesons, while electrons and other leptons stood by as spectators (see page 118). At just minutes old, the universe was a **plasma** of electrically charged particles, each sharing energy through the exchange of light. Light remained trapped in this dense fog of plasma for around 380,000 years, a time known as the dark period.

Big Bang

It is though that our universe began around 13.8 billion years ago in a dramatic explosion of energy, space, and time called the Big Bang. Ever since then, the universe has been expanding in size and cooling in temperature.

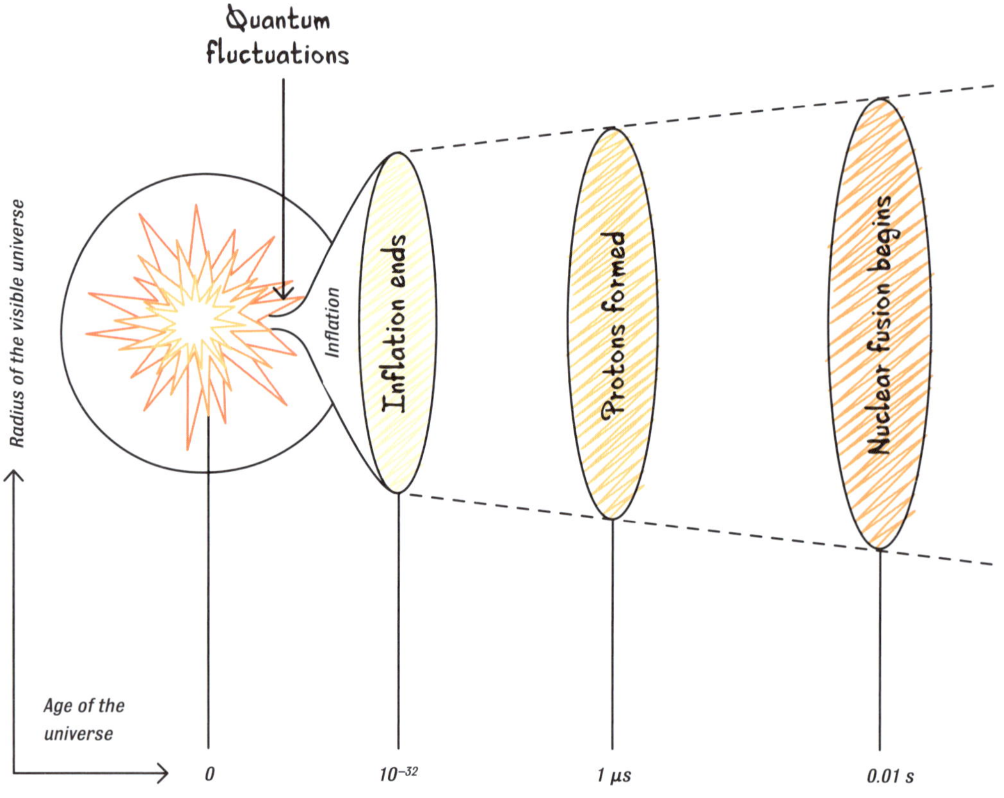

Expansion spread energy thinner, which cooled the universe down. This meant oppositely electrically charged particles were no longer moving fast enough to escape their electromagnetic attraction to each other. Negative electric charges canceled positive across the entire universe as they combined to form electrically neutral atoms and molecules. These molecules and atoms, which were mainly hydrogen and helium, then collected into **gas clouds** hundreds of thousands of light years in size.

Light previously trapped inside a plasma in the early years became free, streaming outward into the wider universe. When first emitted, this light was in the microwave region of the electromagnetic spectrum, which earned it the name **cosmic microwave background radiation** (CMBR). Billions of years of expansion stretched space and radiation with it until the CMBR today is found at longer radio wavelengths.

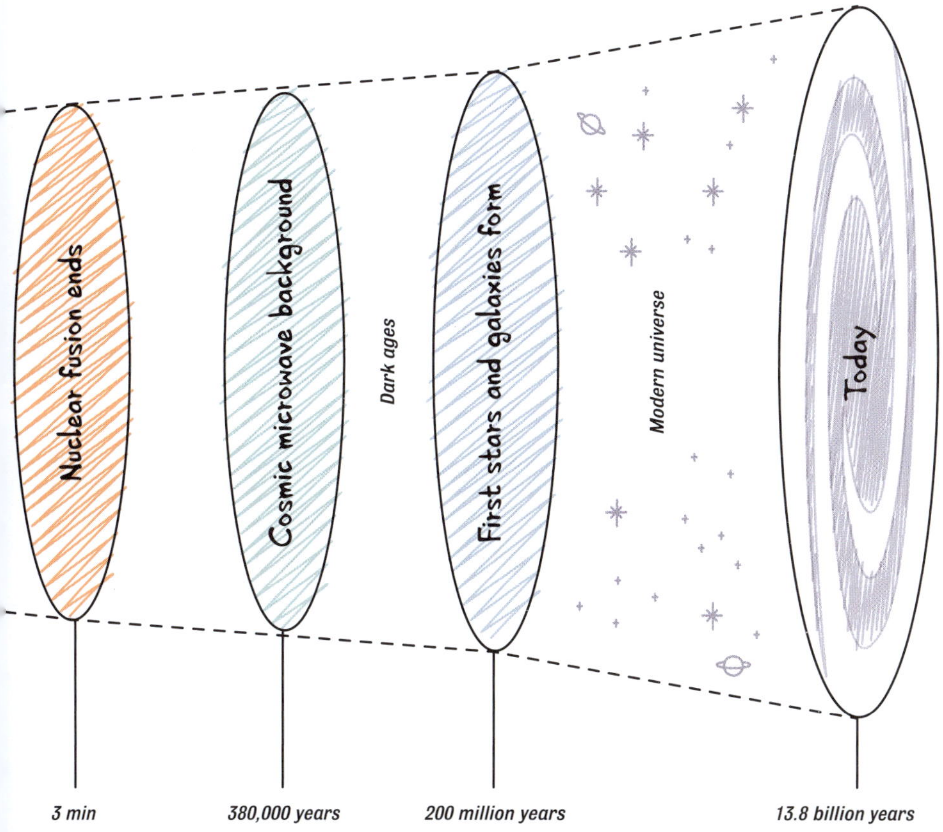

Structure emerges

The vast clouds of gas in the electrically neutral universe cooled down for hundreds of millions of years until gravity, the weakest force known, was finally able to pull them together. Smooth, giant clouds of gas started to become lumpy as clumps formed. As gas fell inward to the center of these clumps, and the clumps toward the center of the cloud, everything started to spin, like water draining down a plughole. A galaxy was forming, and it was soon to be host to millions of stars with many more planets and other strange celestial bodies.

Summing up the total amount of mass we see, from shining stars to the leftover gas between them, allows us to predict how stars will move in a galaxy using our knowledge of gravity. The problem is that it does not work. Stars that are further away from the center of a galaxy should be moving slower than those closer to the center, similar to the way spinning ice skaters slow down if they stretch their arms out. Instead, stars further out seem to still move as fast as those closer to the center, which requires something dragging the stars around at that speed, like a vinyl record on a turntable. As we cannot see this thing and because it must interact with the stars via gravity, we call this curious stuff **dark matter**.

Dark matter

Dark matter may have governed the positions in which galaxies were first formed. Dark matter would have clumped early in the history of the universe, under greater gravitational attraction. The matter and galaxies we see making up our universe would then have followed the greater gravitational attraction of the large clumps of dark matter. At the moment, we do not know what dark matter is, although there are several theories, most involving the existence of new fundamental particles.

Galaxies

Galaxies come in all shapes and sizes. Early galaxies that formed a few hundred million years after the Big Bang resemble blobs of gas. Their spinning meant that, like the Earth, they were not perfectly round but instead a little squashed, which is why they are termed elliptical galaxies.

Galaxy rotation

Most of the visible mass of stars can be found near the center of a galaxy. Other stars should move slower the further they are from this central bulge but they don't. One explanation is that there is unseen dark matter that keeps increasing the force of gravity felt, requiring stars to move faster to stay in orbit in the galaxy.

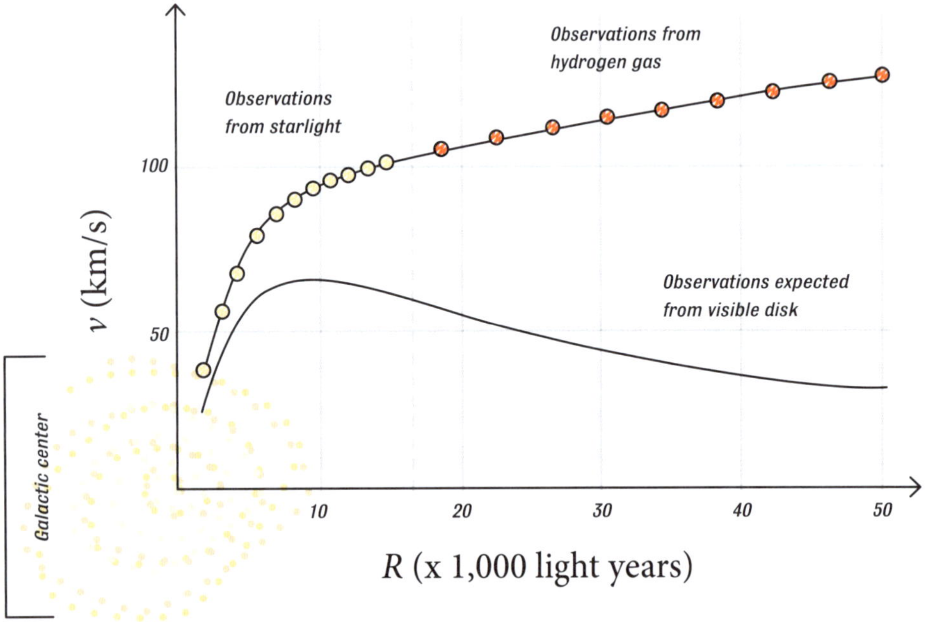

When we look closer to home, where the galaxies are older, they have a very different shape. Billions of years spinning around flings the gas and stars outward from the center of a galaxy until it resembles a spiral. Spinning flattens these galaxies into a thin disk, like a pizza thrower turning a ball of dough to make a pizza base.

Galaxies may collide on their journey through otherwise empty space, and when the universe was smaller, this was far more common. When they hit each other head on, these clouds of stars and gas stir each other up in an oscillating dance that lasts millions of years. When the movement slows, neither galaxy will look as they did before, new galaxies will have been formed and their shape will be irregular. Most irregular galaxies are thought to have formed in this way, although there are other possibilities.

As planets orbit a star and moons orbit a planet, it is thought that stars in galaxies all orbit something far more massive than the biggest of stars—a **supermassive black hole**. In 2019, astronomers took an image of a supermassive black hole for the first time as it was devouring nearby stars. It is not known how exactly they first came to be, but they must have formed early in the history of the universe to guide the rotation of the first galaxies.

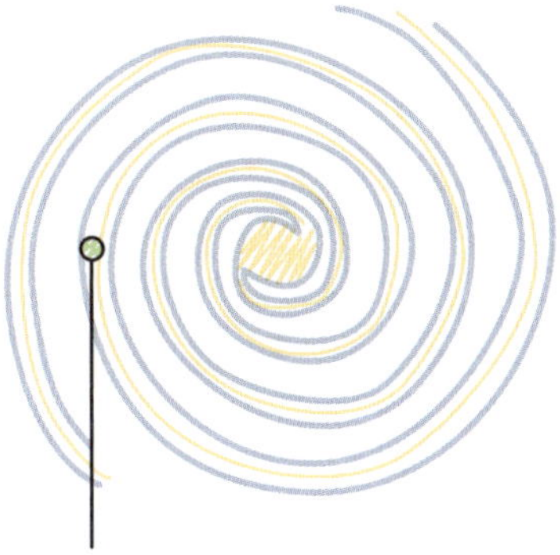

Milky Way

The Milky Way is the spiral galaxy we call home. It contains our solar system, which is 26,000 light years from the center of the galaxy in a spiral arm called Orion.

From reconstructing the positions of our closest neighboring stars, we are able to show that our own galaxy, the **Milky Way**, is a **spiral galaxy**. Looking at this fuzzy, milky streak through a telescope shows it is composed from millions of individual stars. It is about 100,000 light years across and on average just 1,000 light years thick, although it swells to 10,000 light years thick in the central bulge.

Stars

Galaxies are mainly composed of stars. As gas clouds collapse, they fragment into smaller localized clouds that continue to collapse. As the gas collapses inward, it heats up until electrons start tearing themselves free from atoms to form a plasma. This plasma collapses and heats up further, until the positively charged protons that are the former nuclei of hydrogen atoms are traveling so fast they can overcome the electromagnetic repulsion between them to collide. When protons collide, the strong interaction fuses them together to form the nucleus of a helium atom. Light produced in this fusion pushes its way outward through the plasma, fighting against gravity pulling inward. Soon, enough light is produced that its push outward equals the pull of gravity inward and the cloud stops collapsing. The cloud has become a star.

A star spends most of its life turning protons into helium, a period of its life known as its main sequence. Larger stars must produce more light to hold back a larger force of gravity pulling them inward, requiring them to use up their supply of protons quicker. Larger stars therefore lead shorter lives than smaller stars. Larger stars have main sequences lasting millions of years while smaller stars live like this for billions of years.

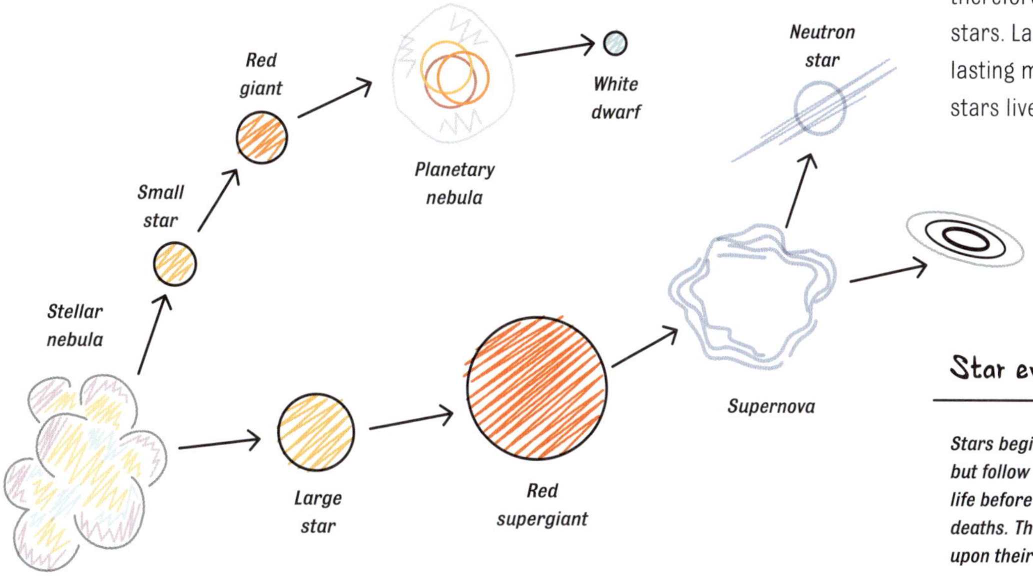

Star evolution

Stars begin their life as a ball of gas but follow very different paths through life before ending in various spectacular deaths. Their route is entirely dependent upon their mass.

Giant stars and dwarfs

When protons become scarce, the rate of fusion slows down. Less light is produced and the star cannot push back with enough force against gravity, causing the plasma to be pulled inward. As it falls, the plasma heats up once again until the center of the star is so hot that the plentiful helium nuclei can overcome the repulsions between each other. When they strike each other, the helium nuclei start to fuse together; three helium nuclei combine to create carbon. Protons a little further out from the center have also heated up to the point that they can now collide to form more helium. These two processes produce far more light than the star emitted in main sequence, and so this light counters and then overpowers the pull of gravity, pushing the star outward. The star swells in size to form a red **giant star**. Low-mass stars will not reach this stage, while medium-mass stars will end their lives here as gravity finally wins.

Red giant

As stars grow older they grow larger because they push out into space with more energy. Our Sun will do this in just over 7 billion years to become a red giant while larger stars will become red supergiants.

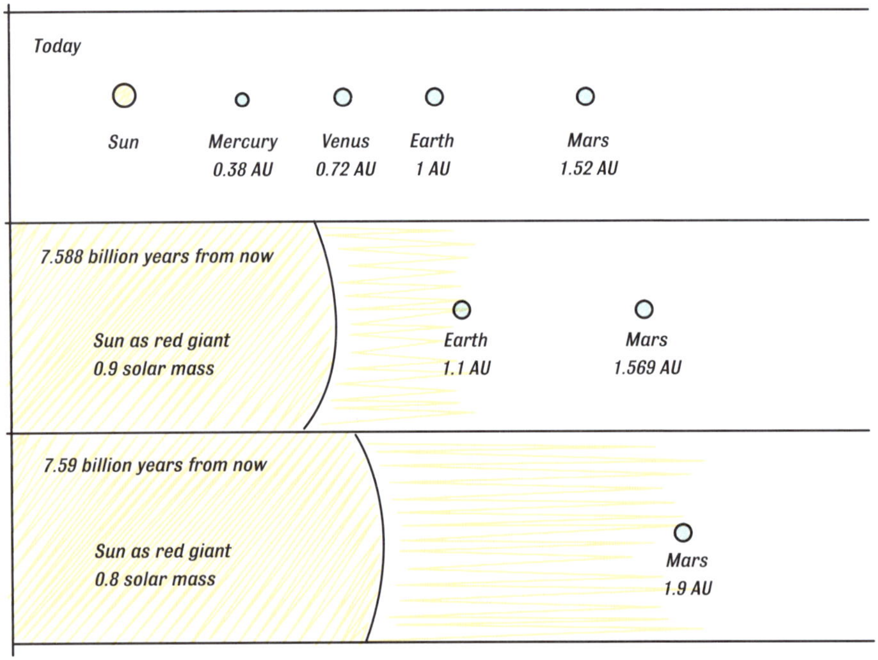

The outer regions of a dying star fall inward, crushing its solid central core. Most of this outer matter bounces off and into the surrounding space, leaving a small dense remnant as the only reminder a star was ever there. Glowing white-hot from its energetic end, this little star is a white dwarf. Electrons in this core have been stacked higher and higher in energy. This produces an outward pressure that pushes back against gravity to halt the collapse, something known as electron degeneracy pressure.

It is thought a **white dwarf** will gradually cool down, glowing yellow, orange, and red before going dark to form a black dwarf. This is only theoretical, because a white dwarf would take longer than the current estimated age of the universe to cool to black, so none should exist yet.

The most massive stars become **supergiant stars**, after repeated cycles of collapse and ignition of new fusion. Each new type of fusion from the collapse and heating of the star results in the synthesis of heavier and heavier nuclei, changing carbon to oxygen, oxygen to neon, and on and on until the fusion forms iron-56. Iron-56 is the most stable nuclei produced in fusion, fusing iron-56 with anything else requires energy. Fusion can no longer release

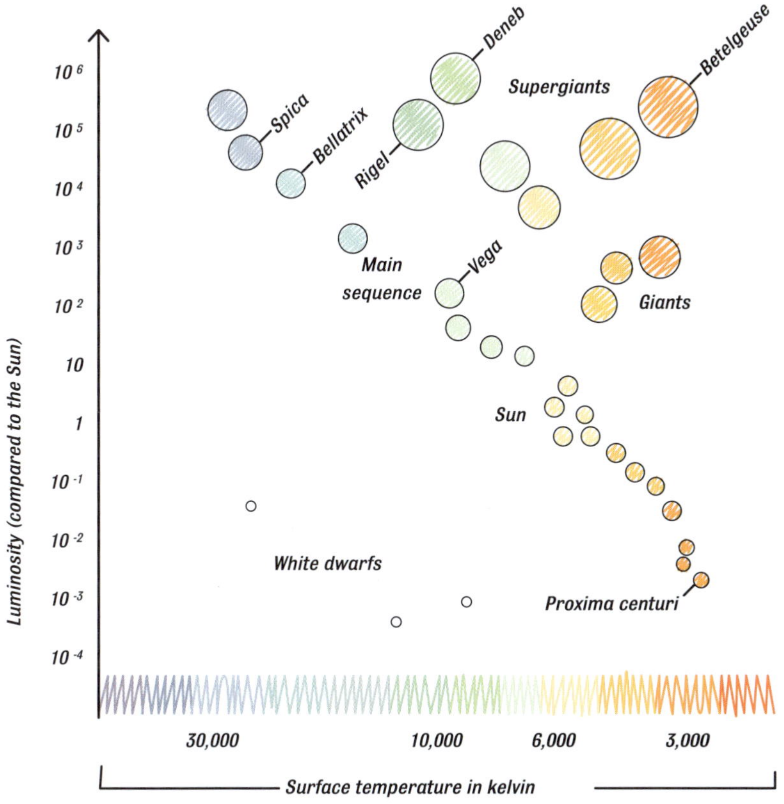

creating the chemical elements up to uranium, which is the heaviest naturally occurring element.

Electrons can only hold up a star of a certain mass. Beyond this, the force of gravity is so large that the supporting stacks of electrons break; they tumble inward and combine with protons to form neutrons, in a process known as electron capture. Neutron stacks are far more stable than electron stacks and if they can stop the collapse then they form a **neutron star**. As neutrons stack up, they create something that resembles a giant atomic nucleus. Just like all atomic nuclei, the neutrons are very densely packed. A neutron star is the densest known material in nature and a teaspoon full of the stuff would weigh as much as the entire Earth.

Categorizing stars

The temperature of a star and the total light it emits can allow us to determine its mass and age on a Hertzsprung-Russell diagram like the one above. The temperature of a star can be measured from the color of light it mostly emits: red stars are colder while blue stars are hotter. Stars in their main sequence line up from the most massive in the top left to the least massive in the bottom right. Giants and supergiants occupy the cool but massive regions at the top right of the picture, while white dwarfs sit at the hot, dim lower left. A few of the brightest stars in the night sky are labeled on the diagram.

energy, the star can no longer produce light and the fight against gravity is finally lost.

Gravity rapidly pulls the outer parts of the star inward until they are traveling so fast that they explode when bouncing from the solid center of the star. This release of energy outshines all other stars in a galaxy combined, for a brief moment it is a super star: a **type II supernova**. The additional energy released in a supernova explosion enables iron-56 to fuse with other nuclei to form even heavier things,

The largest stars, however, will break their neutron stacks and crush their central core with such force that there is no turning back. The fabric of space-time is torn by the force of the collapsing matter, creating a hole so deep that nothing, not even light, can escape. It has formed a **black hole**.

White dwarf stars can become neutron stars, or neutron stars black holes, later on in life. To do this, they have to put on weight, which they do by attracting matter from another nearby star.

Our Solar System

We know that our **Sun** is at least a second-generation star, formed from dust and gas thrown into space by a supernova explosion. Years after the death of a supermassive star, a longitudinal shock wave is thought to have passed through the gas, produced by another nearby supernova explosion. This shock wave triggered gravity to begin snowballing the gas together, eventually leading to the birth of new stars.

Today, the Sun is a common yellow star of average size in its main sequence. It is middle-aged at about 5 billion years old and is predicted to have enough protons in its core to stay on main sequence for another 7 billion years. At this age, it will become a red giant star and end its life just a few million years later. As the Sun spins, the charged particles in its plasma spin with it, forming loops of electric current. A powerful magnetic field is induced by the moving plasma that pushes out deep into space. Electrically charged particles are swept outward along these magnetic-field lines at high speeds as solar wind.

Solar wind

A stream of particles continually blows outward from the Sun along its magnetic field lines; this is known as the solar wind. Where these particles meet the Earth, they are swept around the planet by its own magnetic field keeping everything on it safe.

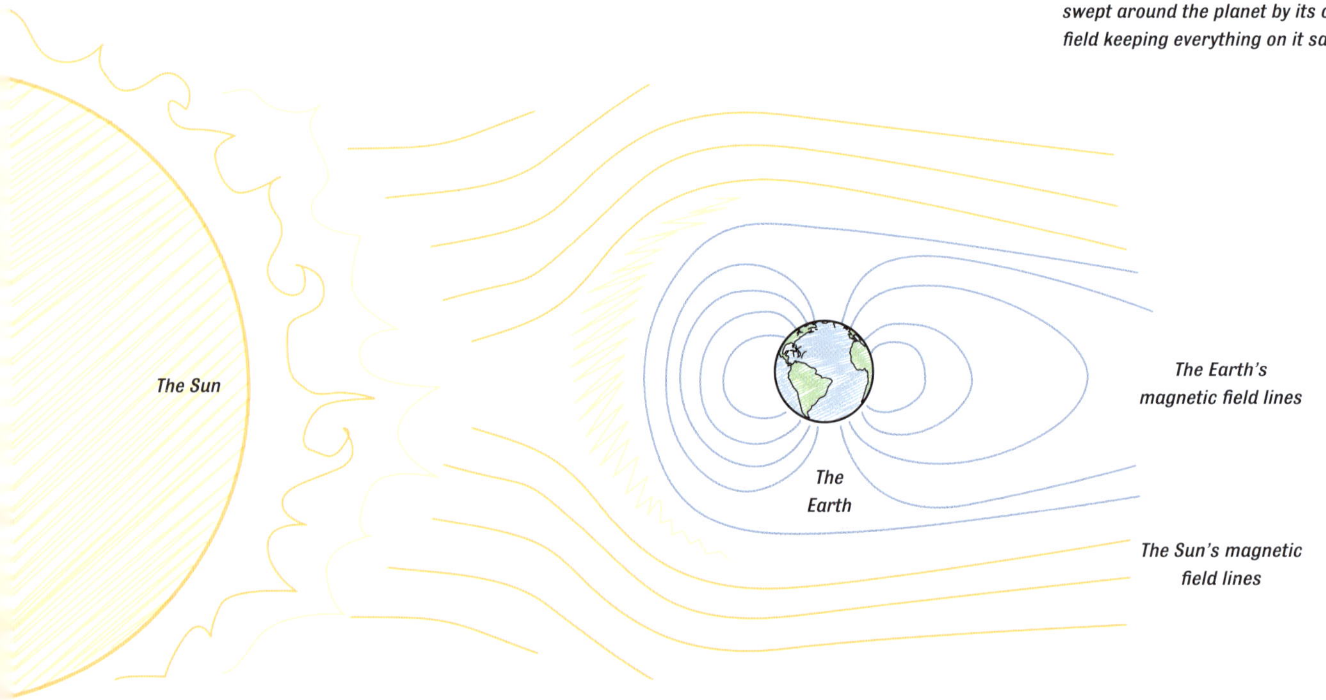

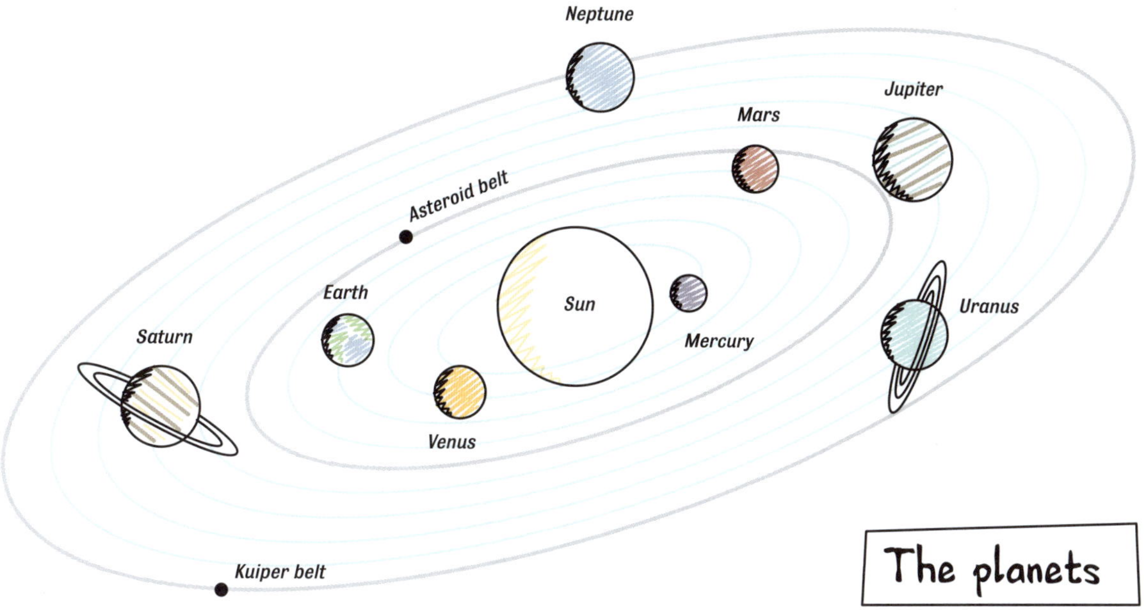

The **solar system** is the region of space containing our Sun and the system of all things gravitationally bound to it. Within this solar system, there are many different objects all with the Sun in common. Our solar system is orbiting about 26,000 light years from the center of our Milky Way galaxy in a spiral arm named the Orion arm, as it also plays host to the three stars that make up Orion's belt in the famous constellation.

Closest to the Sun are a collection of objects that orbit it in a flat-pancake **planetary disk**. Surrounding the newly born Sun was a spinning disk of dust and ice, which gravity clumped together over millions of years. Heat near the Sun only allowed balls of rare molten metal and rock to form. In the colder climes further from the Sun, a collection of more common molecules, which are gases here on Earth, lumped together and formed huge blobs. Collisions between the clumps broke them apart or combined them to form larger and larger clumps. When all of the crashing together was done, four large metal and rock clumps, and four giant gas clumps dominated the landscape, with smaller debris in between.

Solar system

Our solar system contains eight planets. Four inner rocky planets are separated from four gas giant planets by a field of leftover rock called the asteroid belt. Beyond the gas giants lies the Kuiper belt containing leftover frozen gas and dust.

The planets

The largest clumps give their name to the disk: they are the planets. In increasing distance from the Sun, the four rocky clumps of metal and rock are Mercury, Venus, Earth, and Mars, while the four gas giants are Jupiter, Saturn, Uranus, and Neptune. These planets got their name from the Greek word *planan* meaning "wander," as to the ancients they seemed to wander across the night sky. Between the rocky planets and the gas giants lies a graveyard of rock and metal that failed to form planets called the **asteroid belt**. Beyond Neptune is another graveyard of ice and gas left over from the formation of these gigantic outer planets called the Kuiper belt. In these regions also live dwarf planets, such as Pluto in the Kuiper belt and Ceres in the asteroid belt.

KEPLER'S LAWS

The rules governing the orbit of planets were first discovered by German astronomer Johannes Kepler and summarized in his three laws. The first of **Kepler's laws** was that planets do not move in perfect circles around the Sun but instead along elliptical paths. The Sun sits at one focus of the ellipse and as the planet approaches it speeds up, moving fastest where it is closest to the Sun. This is because kinetic energy is being transferred to gravitational potential on this leg of the journey. This motion was explained in Kepler's second law, which stated that an imaginary line between the planet and Sun sweeps out an equal area in an equal period. When far from the Sun, a planet only needs to move a short distance to sweep out a large area. When closer, the line between the Sun and planet is much smaller, and so it must move further around its orbit to sweep out the same area. The third law gave a mathematical relationship between the time a planet takes to orbit once and its distance from the Sun. It stated that the cube of the radius always changes in the same proportions as the square of the time it takes to orbit.

Kepler's laws of planetary motion

From accurate data, Johannes Kepler was able to deduce that planets orbiting the Sun followed three laws of motion: they moved in ellipses; swept out equal areas between the planet and the Sun, in equal time; and had a neat mathematical relationship between their time to orbit the Sun and their average distance from it.

THE EARTH

The location and makeup of our planet has allowed complex life to evolve. Earth formed mainly from a collection of molten iron and nickel metals, and rock made mostly from silicon dioxide. The dense metals sank below the less dense rock while the planet was still liquid. As it cooled, the outermost rock hardened to form a crust, which insulated the rock below, keeping it liquid. Below the liquid rock is an outer core of liquid metal that

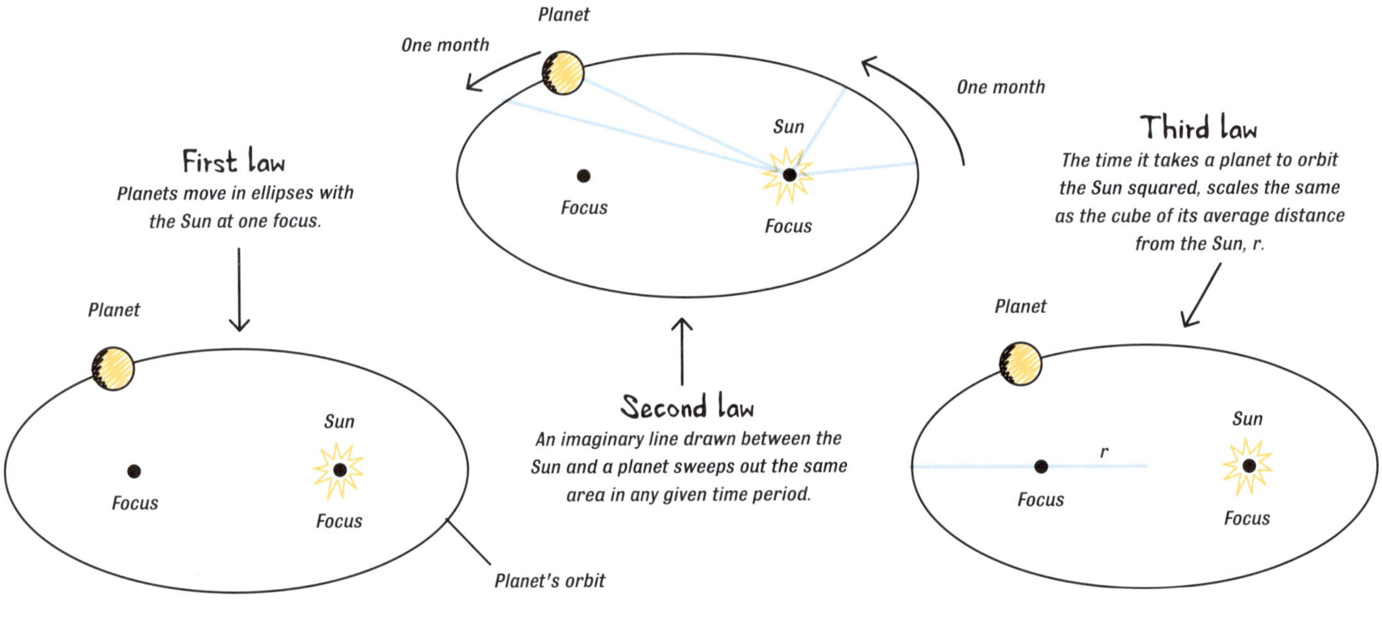

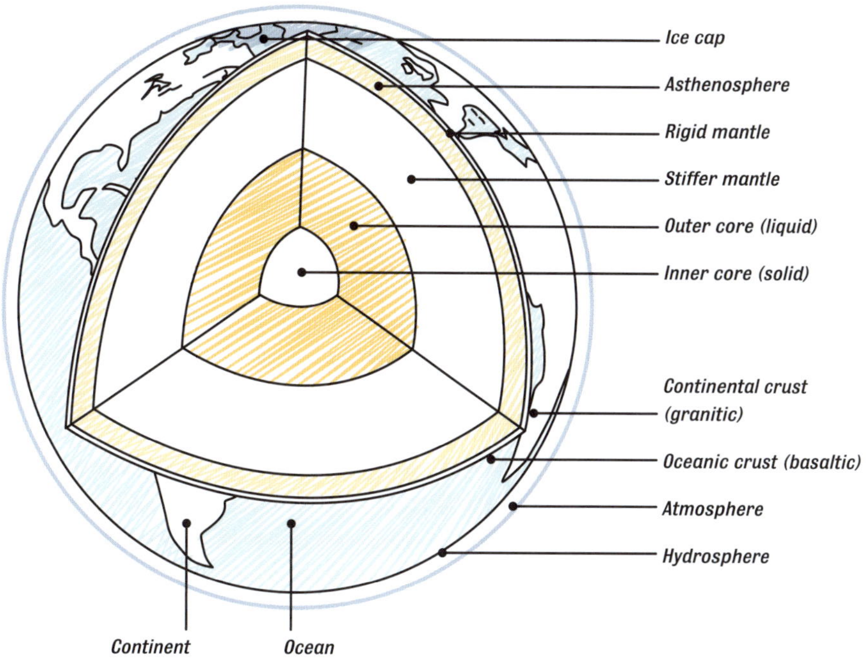

Planet Earth

The Earth is a typical inner planet of our solar system made of metals and rock. Molten metal sank to the center of the planet while lighter rock remained on top, where it has cooled to a solid mantle.

circulates around thanks to convection currents. The circulating metal with free electrons acts like an electric current running through a coil of wire that produces a magnetic field. Earth's magnetic field fights against the Sun's magnetic field to hold back the solar wind. It is powerful enough to keep the harsh solar wind far away from the delicate, thin layer of gas clinging to the surface. This atmospheric shelter protects the Earth from the higher-energy electromagnetic waves emitted by the Sun and is the reason that complex molecules have over billions of years evolved into humans.

Moons

Our **Moon** is the largest in the solar system, as a percentage of the planet size: over one-quarter of the diameter of the Earth. Despite this, it weighs in at just 1.2% of the Earth's mass because it is made almost entirely from the lighter rock found near the surface of the Earth. It is the only celestial body that humans have set foot on; this was during the NASA Apollo missions in the 1960s and 1970s. Apollo astronauts left mirrors on the Moon. By measuring the time it takes for laser light reflecting from these mirrors to make the round trip from Earth to Moon, scientists on Earth can accurately measure the position of the Moon. They have found that it is moving away from us by about 1.6 inches (4 cm) each year, suggesting that the Moon was not captured by the planet's gravity like the moons orbiting other planets.

Moving Moon

Our Moon has been moving away from Earth since its birth billions of years ago.

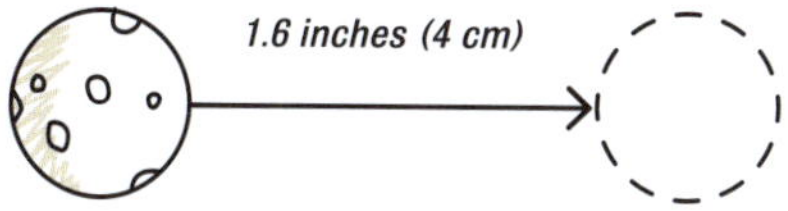

MOON'S FORMATION

The Moon is thought to have formed 4.5 billion years ago, when a smaller clump of molten metal and rock collided with a larger clump. In the impact, molten rock was thrown from the surface of the larger clump out into space, where it cooled to form the Moon; the larger clump then became the Earth. The impact that created the Moon put its orbit at an angle of 5 degrees, which means that a perfect alignment of Earth, Moon, and Sun only happens on occasion. The moon-creating collision is also thought to have knocked the Earth's axis of spin to just over 23 degrees, causing the seasons, as different areas of the Earth receive different intensities of light at different times of the year. Gravitational attraction to the Moon drags the ocean a little to one side of the Earth. This produces the ocean tides: high tide when the Moon is overhead, or on the opposite side of the planet, and low tide everywhere else.

Other **moons** in the solar system are much smaller than the planet they orbit. Most moons are leftover debris from planet formation. Rocks from the asteroid belt or chunks of ice from the Kuiper belt that wandered into a planet's path to be captured by its gravitational field. The planets with the most moons are the gas giants with the strongest gravitational fields. Once in orbit, only a collision with another wandering object can provide a moon with the energy needed to escape.

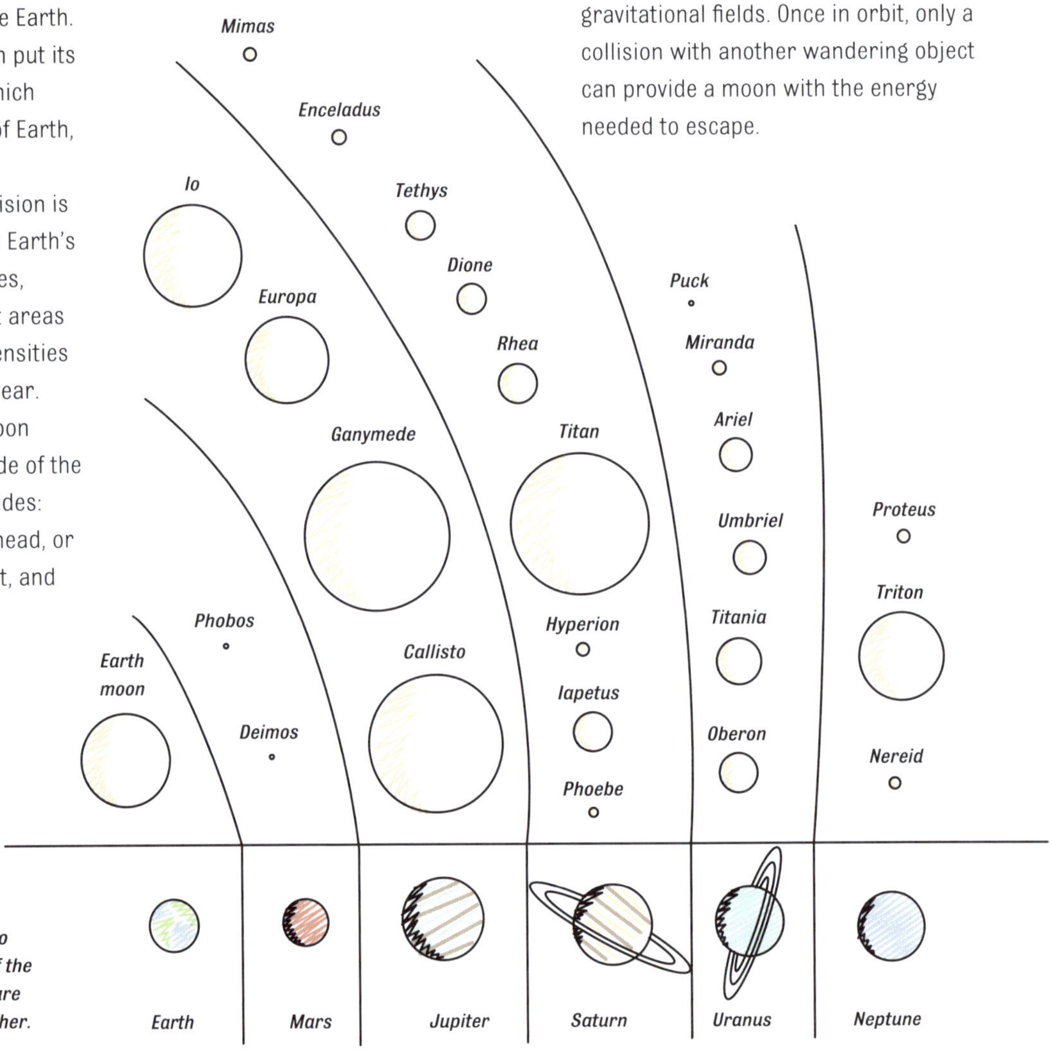

Moons

Moons of the planets that have them, to scale. Only some of the many moons of the gas giant planets are shown. Planets are not to scale with the moons or each other.

COMETS

Chunks of ice in the Kuiper Belt may bounce off each other and be catapulted toward the inner solar system. This turns them into a comet, which takes a highly elliptical path that brings it close to the Sun, before swinging back out beyond Neptune. Comets are usually around 30 miles (50 km) across and made mostly from a mixture of rock dust, carbon-dioxide ice, and water ice. This ice turns instantly to gas as a comet approaches the Sun's heat. This gas is swept out into a tail, which reflects light from the Sun toward telescopes on Earth, where it outshines the comet itself. This tail is not like hair swept back by the motion of the comet, as you might experience when riding a bike very fast. The only wind in space is the solar wind and that only blows in one direction—always away from the Sun. So, the tail of gas does not always point behind the comet to tell you in which direction it is moving; it always points away from the Sun.

METEORS

Asteroids or comets on a planetary collision course are called meteors. As they make their way toward the surface of a planet, friction between the meteor and the planet's atmosphere heats things up. Meteors made from ice or rock will mostly burn up from this heat and vaporize. Meteors containing metal, however, can survive much higher temperatures and can make it all the way to the ground.

If a meteor strikes the surface of a planet then it is a meteorite. **Meteorites** have struck the Earth many times in its 4.5 billion-year past, with some having profound impacts upon its inhabitants. One such meteorite struck the Earth 66 million years ago, kicking up so much dust on impact that it spread across the entire Earth. This dust would have hung in the atmosphere for a long time and killed much plant and then animal life. It is thought that these dark times caused the extinction of the dinosaurs.

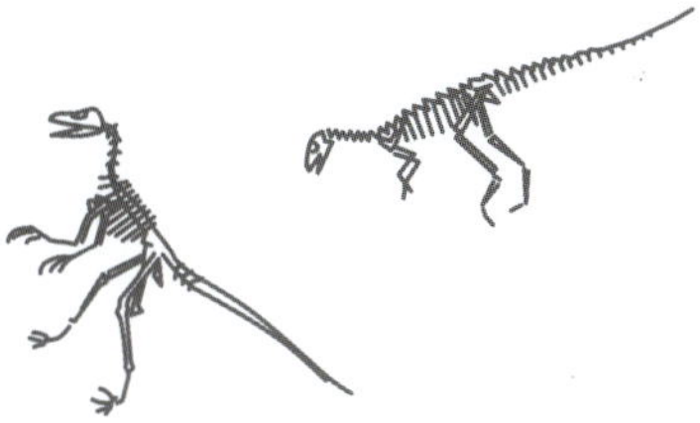

Dwarf planets

The Kuiper belt beyond Neptune plays host to many dwarf planets, each smaller than our own Moon. Some of these dwarf planets themselves posses their own moons. The asteroid belt between Mars and Jupiter also plays host to dwarf planets; the largest is Ceres.

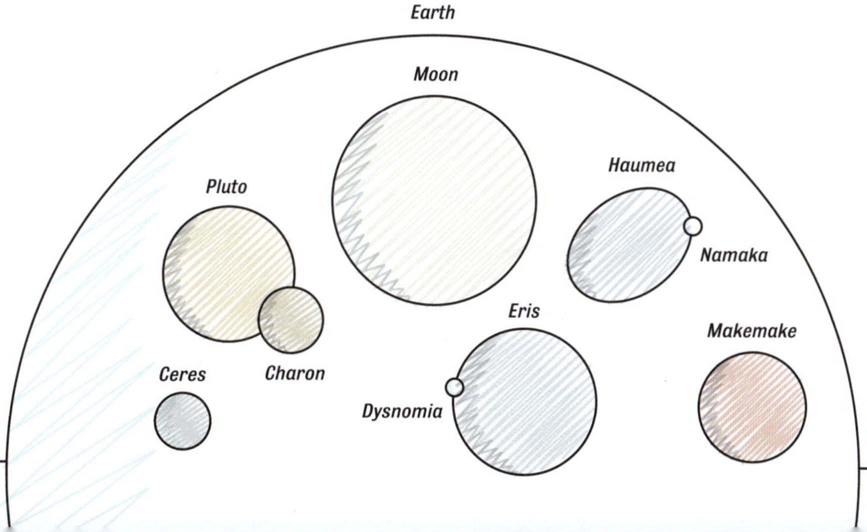

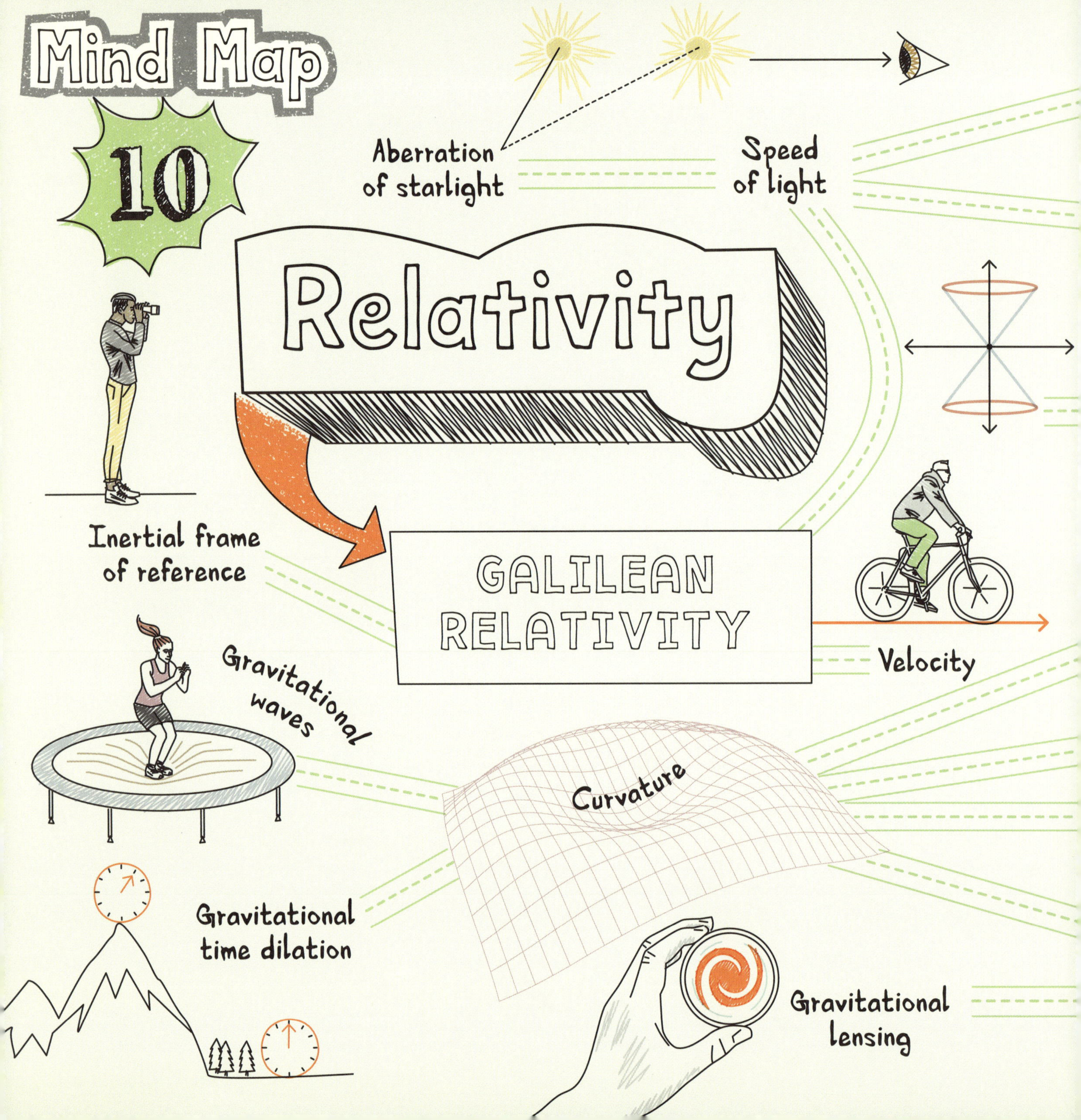
Mind Map
10
Relativity
GALILEAN RELATIVITY
Aberration of starlight
Speed of light
Inertial frame of reference
Velocity
Gravitational waves
Curvature
Gravitational time dilation
Gravitational lensing

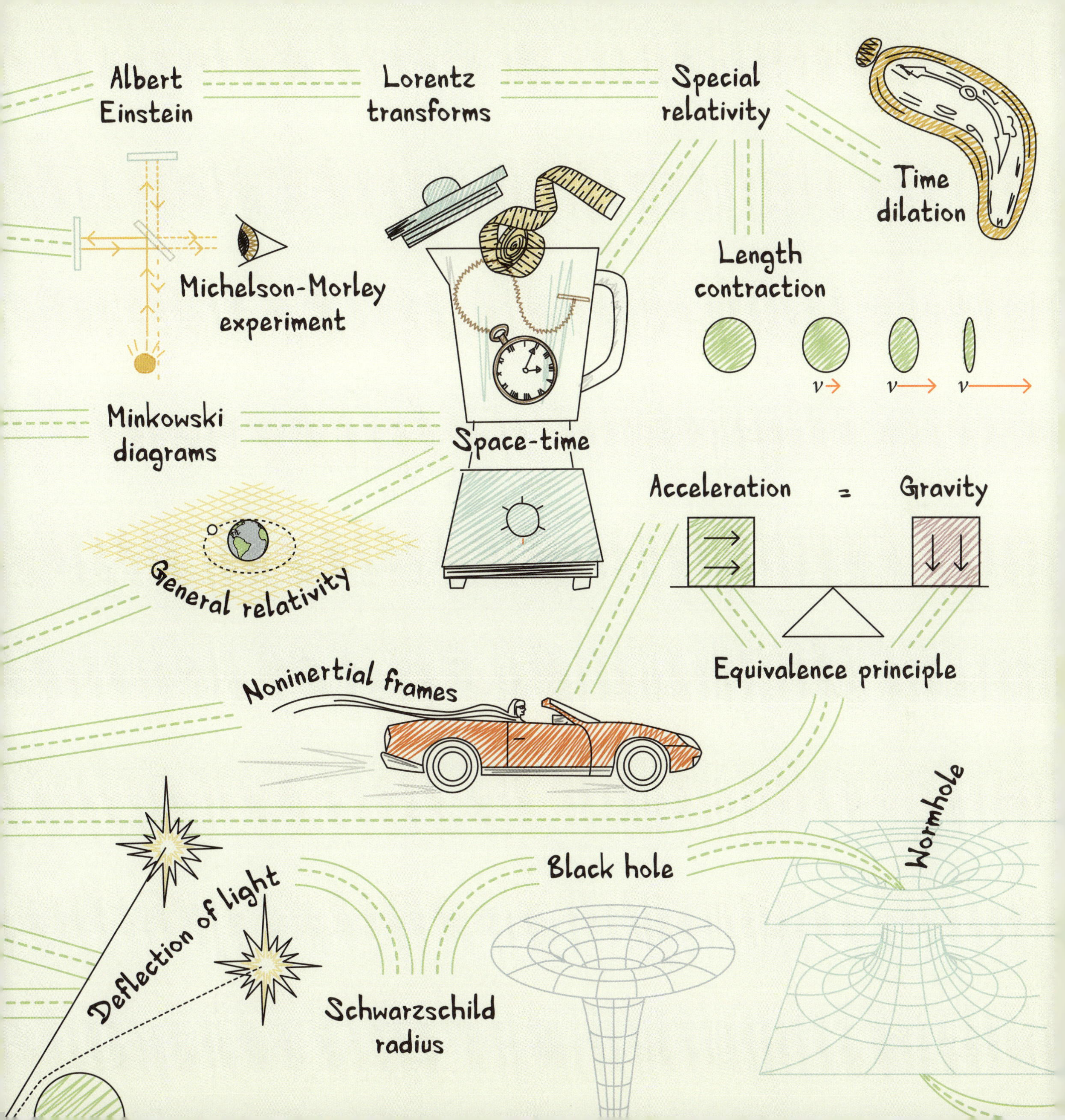

Albert Einstein
Lorentz transforms
Special relativity
Time dilation
Michelson-Morley experiment
Length contraction
v
v
v
Minkowski diagrams
Space-time
Acceleration
=
Gravity
General relativity
Equivalence principle
Noninertial frames
Wormhole
Black hole
Deflection of light
Schwarzschild radius

Relative Motion

Italian physicist Galileo Galilei noticed, as others had before him, that the velocity of an object appears different to someone who is stationary and someone who is moving. Galileo used this to demonstrate that **velocity** is not an absolute that is measured the same by all observers but is instead relative to the velocity of the observer. He codified this understanding, which became known as **Galilean relativity**, in the mathematics of the Galilean transformations.

An inertial frame of reference is a name given to a collection of objects in a region of space that are inert, not accelerating, with respect to each other. When traveling in a moving vehicle we often think of things around us as not changing velocity relative to us; the inside of the vehicle can be thought of as an inertial frame.

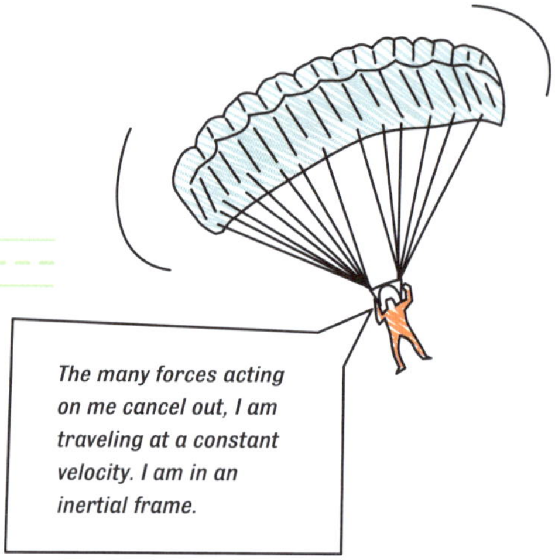

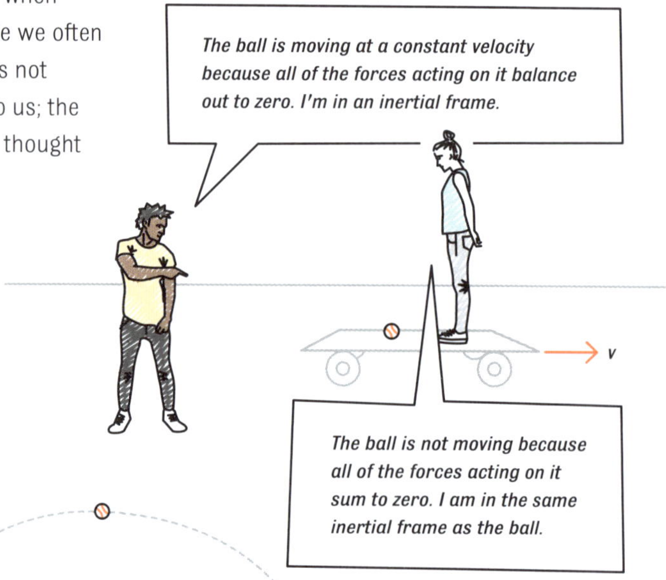

Galilean relativity

Observer A is in a moving inertial frame and observes that a ball thrown in the air travels in a straight line path. A stationary observer B, in another inertial frame, sees the ball follow a very different path: a parabolic curve.

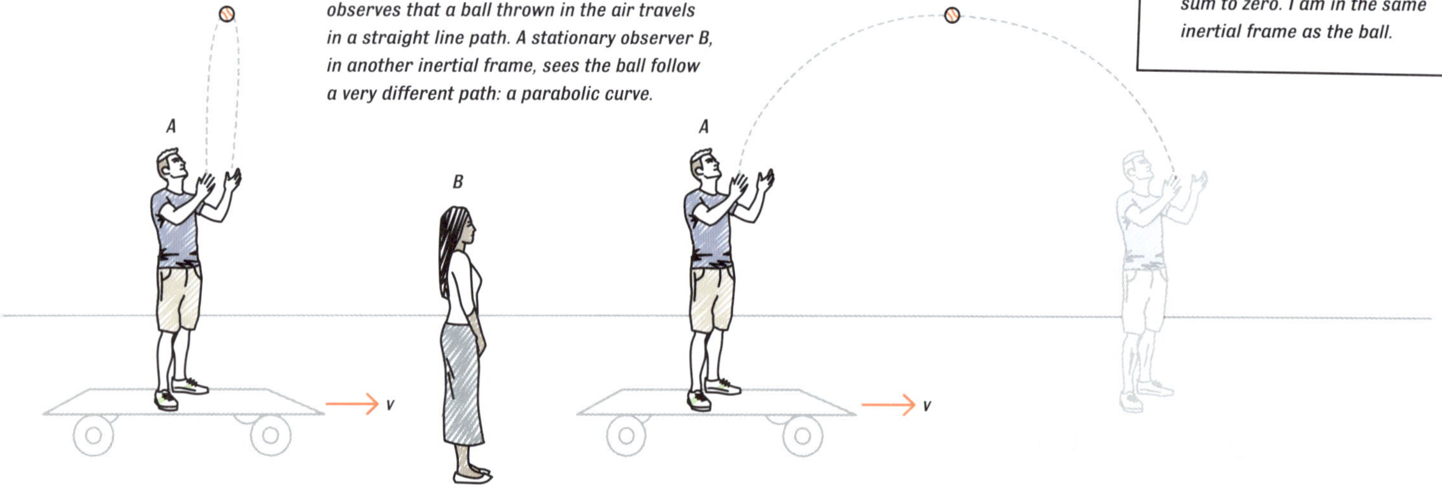

Speed limit

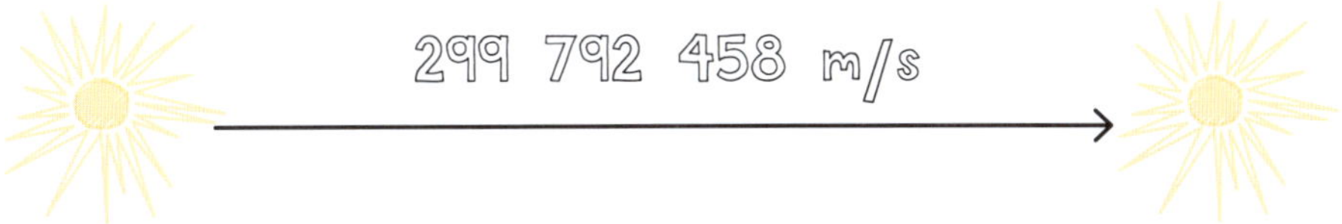

If we shone a beam of light from a torch when in a fast-moving car, the Galilean transformations would tell us that this light would be traveling faster than if we shone the torch when stood still. This was the thinking of scientists in the nineteenth century. It was thought that, as sound waves travel through air, light must also travel through some material termed the aether. The apparent change in the speed of the light would be due to the car traveling at a different speed with respect to the aether and therefore the light. The problem is that this is not true. Every experiment seems to tell us that the **speed of light** is constant; around 186,000 miles per second (300 million meters per second). Strictly speaking, it is the speed of light in a vacuum, where it's not affected by other things, which cannot be exceeded.

Two experiments were conducted to investigate the speed of light. The first was the **Michelson-Morley experiment**, which aimed to detect the speed difference of light traveling down two paths of equal length. One path was pointed in the direction of the Earth's movement around the Sun and the other perpendicular to it. Galileo's relativity would suggest that the light emitted in the direction of Earth's motion would be boosted by its motion around the Sun, while the other route would not be boosted at all. This means there would be a difference in the time taken for the light to travel down each path of identical length.

This time difference would be tiny—30 billionth billionths of a second—so a clock could not be used to measure it. Instead, Michelson and Morley used the principle of interference (see page 50). With no path difference, the light would be as bright as it was when it was first sent on its journey. Any path difference would result in deconstructive interference, which would reduce the brightness of the light. Michelson and Morley saw no evidence of a difference in speed despite their hard work making the experiment sensitive enough that they should have seen one. The only explanation was that, unlike cars on a highway, light was not boosted by the motion of other things—the velocity of light was always constant.

A second experiment looked at light arriving at telescopes on Earth from distant stars. If rain is pouring down vertically, then to keep ourselves dry we point our umbrella to the sky in the direction of the rain. If we start walking through this rain, we must account for our change in velocity relative to the rain by adjusting the angle of our umbrella in order to stay dry. When moving forward, we lower the umbrella to protect the space we are moving into. When moving backward from the rain, we must point the umbrella at an entirely different angle to keep dry. It seems that with relative motion the rain is coming from different directions.

The same is true of starlight. We angle our telescopes to catch the light coming from some distant star. The problem is that we are on a planet that is moving relative to the stars. When moving toward the star, we view it as being lower in the sky and when moving away from it, we view it as being higher in the sky. This causes the position we view a star in the night sky to change throughout the year in an elliptical way as we trace our elliptical path around the Sun; this is called the **aberration of starlight**. The size of the ellipse depends upon the ratio of the relative speed of the Earth with respect to the starlight. In investigating many star aberrations, it seems that light travels at a constant speed no matter the speed of the observer (see page 140).

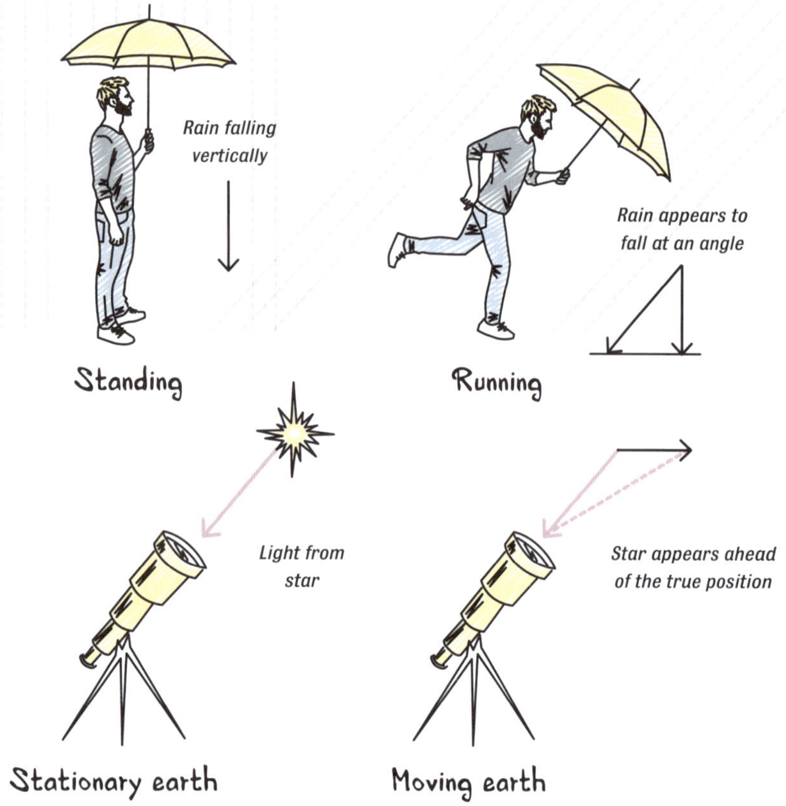

Aberration of light

We have to angle telescopes to catch starlight the same way we must angle our umbrella to protect against rain. The angle depends upon the speed we are moving through the universe.

Lorentz transforms

The Dutch physicist Hendrik Lorentz was a firm believer that light traveled through the aether. He modified Galileo's transformation equations in an attempt to explain the result of the Michelson-Morley experiment. To explain how the light took exactly the same time, **Lorentz transforms** suggested that the motion of the Earth through the aether contracted the length in that direction. This explained why, although traveling on average slower in that direction, the light on that path would still take the same round-trip time as the light traveling faster on a longer path 90° to it. While extending these ideas to ensure that Maxwell's equations of electromagnetism were not changed by movement through the aether, Lorentz and Irish physicist Joseph Larmor realized that for the length to change in motion, then time must also change. Larmor noted that this would require each second for the person moving through the aether to be longer than for a person not in motion. The transforms required physicists to abandon the idea of universal time—that a second measured by one person is the same for every other person in the universe. Relative motion changed the length of a second and therefore the time people would measure if in relative motion to each other.

Special thinking

In 1905, an unknown patent clerk in Switzerland set the physics community ablaze by publishing a series of three papers: his name was **Albert Einstein**. Two papers contributed to the birth of atomic and quantum physics, while the third one laid out a new theory of **special relativity**. He collected a number of different ideas into one theory. The Michelson-Morley experiment demonstrated that there is no aether and therefore nothing to measure velocity against; it is impossible for any person to determine their absolute velocity, only a relative velocity. This experiment helped to demonstrate that the velocity of light is constant, no matter the speed of the source of the light or the person observing it. Einstein also accepted that Lorentz transformations represent the way we transform between two inertial frames traveling at a speed relative to one another. This acceptance required disregarding the idea of universal time and accepting that a second is a different length to people moving at different relative velocities. With these ideas in mind, Einstein reformulated the Lorentz transformations and presented them to the world.

The fact that a change in space required a change in our perception of time, pointed toward a deeper, underlying connection. Where it was previously thought that things were played out on a stage of 3-D space only, with time simply a bystander, it now turns out that space and time are inextricably linked. It is the **space-time** stage upon which everything is played out in nature; and special relativity encodes this in the relationship between motion and our perception of both space and time.

In Einstein's reformulation of the Lorentz transformations, position in the direction of travel and time were modified by the relativity factor. This was given its own symbol—γ, the Greek letter gamma—because it appears so often in special-relativity equations. Sometimes called the gamma factor, it defines the extent to which relativistic effects influence the transformations between two frames traveling relative to one another.

If we were to view something happening in a spaceship traveling past us at a large velocity, we would see things happening on the ship in slow motion.

Experiencing time

Special relativity demonstrates that time is not experienced the same by everyone, it depends on their relative speed. Time experienced by a moving person would run slower than it would for someone standing still, this is called time dilation.

Relativity factor

Definition of relativity factor

$$\gamma = \frac{1}{\sqrt{1-v^2/c^2}}$$

Time dilation increases the length we view each second on the ship by the relativity-factor gamma. Time dilation has been experimentally demonstrated by comparing an atomic clock on Earth with one orbiting the planet in a satellite. The atomic clock whizzing around the planet does indeed tick slower than the clock on the surface of the Earth, something that must be corrected if GPS is to provide anyone with an accurate location.

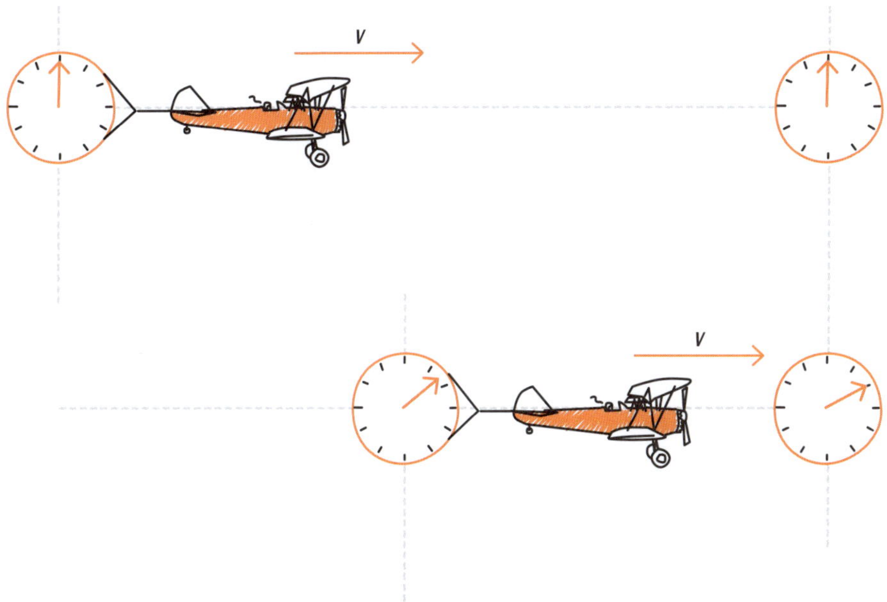

LENGTH CONTRACTION

Another strange result of moving at relativistic speeds is length contraction. An object moving very fast with respect to an observer will appear shorter in the direction it is moving. Of course, in its own inertial frame, the object will not think that anything is different, but will view lengths of objects in other inertial frames to be shorter. Objects are shortened by the relativistic gamma factor and so the faster an object moves with respect to you, the shorter it will seem. As the object is only moving in one direction in space, the dimensions of the object that are not in this direction do not change size.

More than just motion

The German mathematician Hermann Minkowski devised a clever way of making sense of Lorentz transforms. **Minkowski diagrams** have two axes: the vertical representing time and the horizontal representing a single dimension of space. Lines or areas represent the motion of objects through space and time. On a Minkowski diagram, light travels at a 45° angle, splitting the diagram perfectly in half diagonally. A frame that is moving relative to another can be plotted on one of these diagrams by noting that the Lorentz transforms will act to rotate the axes. This is because position in one frame of reference is directly related to position in the other by the relativistic gamma factor. This gamma factor tells us the extent to which the space and time axes of the moving frame are rotated with respect to the stationary frame's axes. The closer to the speed of light, the greater the angle between them. We can then draw parallel lines to show different values on each of these angled axes, the same way we do for any graph. Any object, or event, can be traced back along these lines to read space and time values for the different inertial frames.

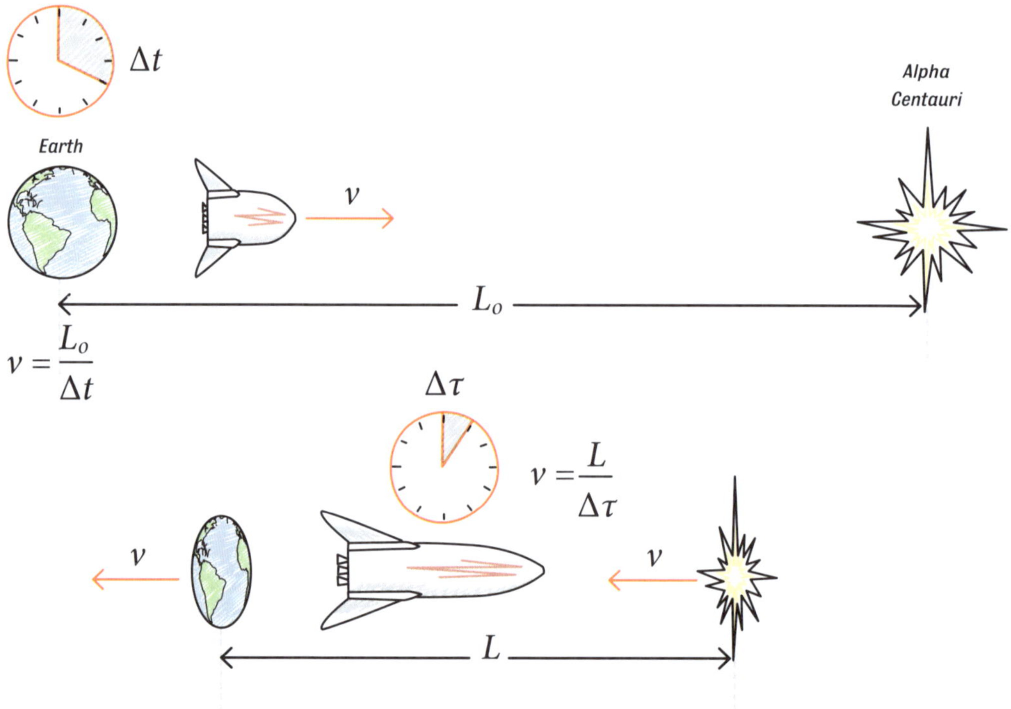

Length contracts

The length we measure an object depends upon the speed it is moving relative to us. Special relativity tells us that length contracts, gets shorter, in the direction an object is moving.

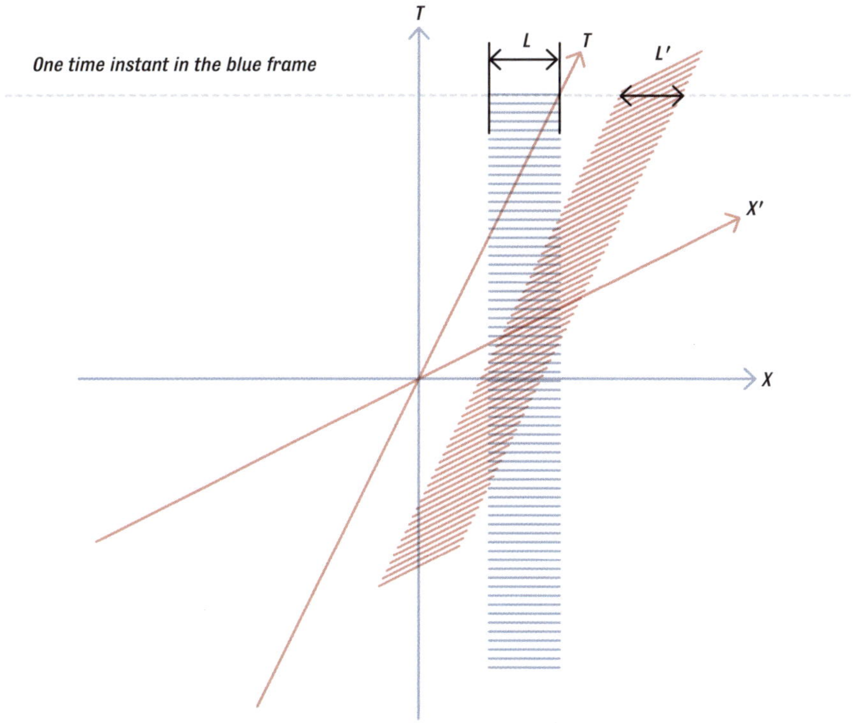

Minkowski diagram

A Minkowski diagram is a plot of space on the horizontal axis and time on the vertical axis. Two frames of reference can be placed on the same diagram, each with its own set of axes. One set of axes represents the inertial frame of an observer (blue). The pink axes are angled with respect to the blue axes because they represent a moving frame of reference.

Two objects of the same length are shown at rest in each of the two inertial frames as lines. The pink line shows an object at rest in the moving frame of reference; this is seen in the blue frame of reference as being much shorter.

J. J. Thomson, discoverer of the electron, noticed that it seemed harder to accelerate an object with an electric charge than one that had no overall charge. Successive physicists attempted to explain the origin of this larger inertia, which they called electromagnetic mass. It was noticed that the electromagnetic mass was not a constant for a given charged object, but increased with the speed of the particle. Hendrik Lorentz used his transforms to derive a formula that linked the rest mass of a particle (its mass in its own inertial frame) with the observed electromagnetic mass.

Albert Einstein extended this idea to derive his most famous formula linking the effective mass of a particle with its energy. He arrived at the relationship $E=mc^2$, where m is the effective mass, using a thought experiment and a rather controversial approximation. This is the relativistic energy equation, sometimes known as the mass-energy equivalence. It tells us that inertial mass and energy are interchangeable, with the speed of light squared as the exchange rate. This formula allows scientists to calculate the energy released in fission of heavy atoms, fusion of light atoms or the stability of different atomic nuclei.

It is incorrect to say that special relativity cannot be used to describe **acceleration** of objects. Special relativistic equations of motion are highly analogous to Newton's classical laws of motion. Within an inertial frame, Newton's laws hold: special relativity allows us to transform this motion between two different inertial frames traveling at different constant velocities. Accelerated motion can be drawn on Minkowski diagrams as curved lines known as hyperbolas. Acceleration in special relativity is absolute—unlike velocity, which is relative—meaning that acceleration of an object, as measured by different frames at the same time, will have the same value.

Thinking Generally

It is not possible in special relativity to translate motion between frames that are themselves accelerating, or **noninertial frames**. In special relativity, space-time is flat. This just means that the intervals between successive time periods and displacements in space are regularly separated. In noninertial frames of reference, this is not the case. As an object accelerates to higher velocity, it experiences differing notions of time and space thanks to time dilation and length contraction. Space-time in noninertial frames of reference is not flat but curved.

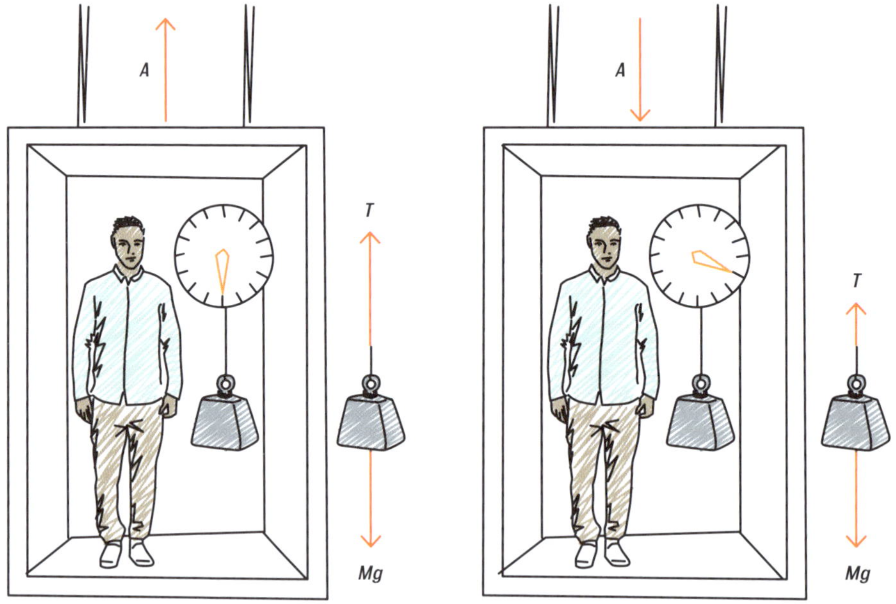

The **curvature** of space-time is a result of being in a noninertial frame. The greater the acceleration of a noninertial frame, the greater the curvature of space-time in that frame. We met the shape of these curves earlier when discussing the shape of lines tracing out accelerated objects in special relativity: the line curves like a hyperbola. A greater acceleration means a more hyperbolic curvature of space-time. Space-time is curved by the presence of energy in any form, including mass.

Massive bodies curve space-time, which has the effect of accelerating objects. This is why objects accelerate to the ground when dropped, because the Earth curves space-time inward to its center of mass. The dropped object is just following this curvature and the associated acceleration.

Noninertial frame

When the elevator accelerates upward, the scale reads a greater value than the weight of the mass.

When the elevator accelerates downward, the scale reads a value less than the weight of the mass.

General relativity is a theory that encompasses all motion, including noninertial frames. One of the biggest assumptions that it makes is the nature of mass. As discussed in Chapter 1, the term mass encompasses inertial mass, which dictates the size of force you need to apply to accelerate an object, and gravitational mass, which determines the strength of attraction felt between two objects through the force of gravity. In setting out his ideas for general relativity, Einstein stated that these two types of mass were in fact the same thing—equivalent; this is known as the **equivalence principle**. In doing this, Einstein also linked the motion of objects in a curved space-time with the effective force of gravity they feel.

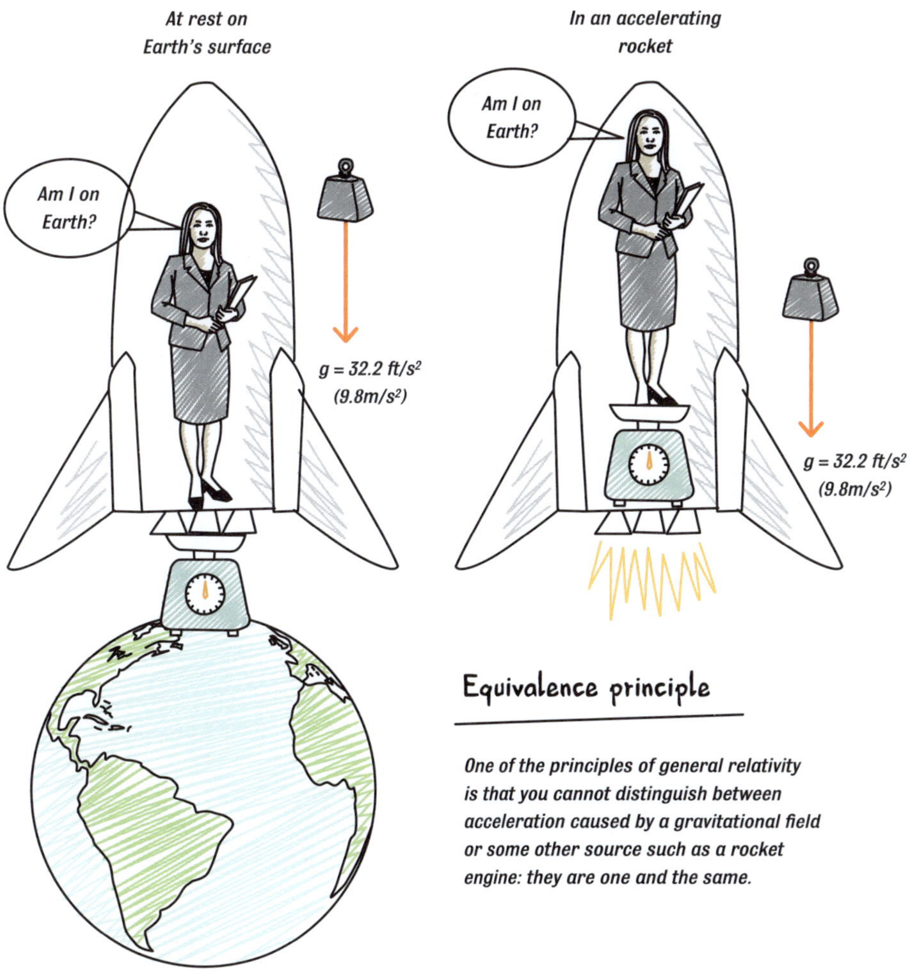

Equivalence principle

One of the principles of general relativity is that you cannot distinguish between acceleration caused by a gravitational field or some other source such as a rocket engine: they are one and the same.

If both inertial and gravitational mass are equivalent, then so too is the acceleration of an object due to **gravity** and acceleration by any other force. Imagine an observer in a sealed box that is accelerating. The observer constructs an experiment to determine the acceleration of their inertial frame, by looking at how much a spring stretches when a mass is hung from it. As the spring obeys Hooke's law (see page 71), the amount it extends is related to the force acting on the spring, and therefore the acceleration. This acceleration will be common to all things in the frame. If the box were in deep space and a rocket engine were providing the box with constant acceleration equal to the acceleration experienced due to gravity on Earth, the person inside the box could not tell the difference from being on Earth. This demonstrates that it is impossible to distinguish between accelerations due to gravity or some other origin. Both result in a curvature of space-time, which dictates the motion of objects that reside there. The degree to which space-time is curved tells us the strength of the gravitational field at that point. Just as with Newton's gravity, this field strength increases as the distance to a massive object decreases, as represented by an increasing curvature in space-time.

Gravitational time dilation

Curvature of space-time leads to a redefinition of the duration of a second or the length of a meter. This is different to the redefinition required for fast moving objects in a flat space-time in special relativity. In special relativity, it is the relative motion that gives rise to the time dilation. For an object in accelerated reference frames, it is the relative difference in the curvature of space-time that leads to a dilation of time; this is referred to as gravitational time dilation.

Curvature of space-time is dictated by the presence of mass (or other forms of energy). The more mass is present, the greater the curvature of space-time and the greater the acceleration experienced by an object wandering by. For this reason, clocks run slower for an observer closer to the heart of a massive object because space-time is more curved. This effect can again be seen using atomic clocks here on Earth: those at high altitude will run faster than those at sea level, because they experience a weaker gravitational pull from the Earth.

The strange behavior of light

The mass–energy relationship is more than just a statement that mass and energy are interchangeable: it states that they are both influenced in the same way by the same laws of physics. Mass is accelerated in curved space-time in the direction of the curvature. If this acceleration is perpendicular to the motion of the object then it changes the direction the object is moving in rather than its speed. The same happens for light, as photons have energy and so are affected in the same way by the curvature of space-time. Curvature of space due to the presence of a gravitational field will cause light to deflect from a usually direct line. This **deflection of light** follows the contours of space-time, and so light curves around a massive body.

Deflection of light

General relativity predicts that light will not follow a straight line when passing close to a massive object like the Sun. In fact, it was observation of the bending of starlight by astronomers that led to the earliest evidence for general relativity. Stars appear to have different positions in the sky during a solar eclipse than they do at night, because their light is curved around the Sun by its gravitational field.

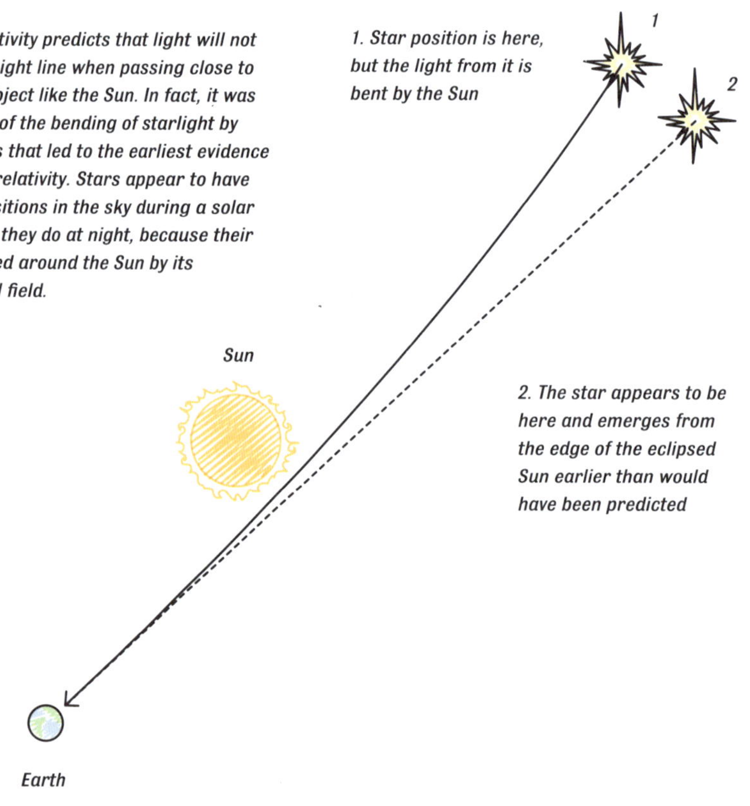

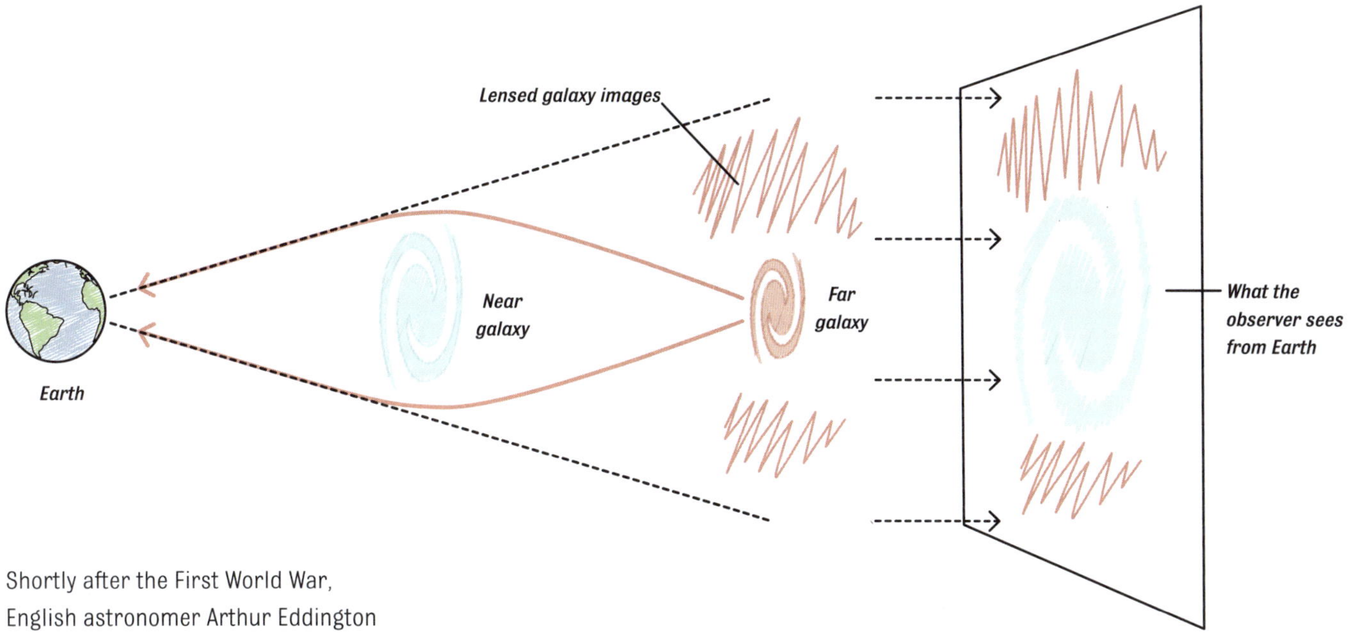

Shortly after the First World War, English astronomer Arthur Eddington traveled to the island of Principe, off the west coast of Africa, to witness a total solar eclipse. Before the eclipse, Eddington exposed photographic plates to the starlight to accurately determine the position of the stars in the night sky. When the time came and the Earth was plunged into darkness as the Moon blocked the light from the Sun, he once again took a photograph of the stars in the sky. When comparing the position of stars close to the Sun with their position in the clear night sky, he discovered they had changed location. This was the result Eddington was searching for. As the light passed by the Sun, its gravitational field would, as Einstein had predicted, curve the path of the light coming from the star and change its apparent position in the sky.

The deflection of light caused by curving space-time is similar to the deflection of light due to refraction (see page 44). Pieces of glass can be shaped into lenses that use refraction to focus light. The curvature of space-time has a similar effect around massive bodies, leading to **gravitational lensing**. Unlike a lens that produces maximal deviation of light at its outer edges, gravitational lenses produce maximal bending of light near the center of the "lens." This means that light is not focused to a point, as with an optical lens, but is instead focused to a line. This leads to images forming as rings, called Einstein rings. If the background light source (galaxy) is not aligned with the gravitational lens (massive object), then only a section of the entire ring will be visible from Earth. Gravitational lensing has been used to detect the presence of otherwise invisible dark matter and planets orbiting around alien stars.

Gravitational lensing

Massive objects that sit between Earth and a source of light, such as a galaxy, can act as a type of lens. They will bend light around them because of their curvature of space-time, which leads to multiple images of the galaxy spread around the lens like a ring. Gravitational lenses do not act as normal optical lenses; they bend the light most near their centers in an opposite fashion to lenses found in spectacles. The closest optical analogy to a gravitational lens is the base of a wine glass; looking at images here produces rings similar to gravitational lenses.

Breaking space-time

If the curvature of space-time is permanently perpendicular to an object's motion, then the perpendicular acceleration will cause the object to move in a circular motion (see page 40). Like a surfer riding along a wave, the object will skirt along the curved edge of space-time. The circularly symmetric curve caused by a spherical planet forces other objects to follow elliptical paths. The distance the object orbits a planet depends upon its velocity and the strength of the gravitational field at that location, which is determined by the degree to which space-time is curved. Objects must move faster to remain in close orbit to a planet. As planets grow larger, they curve space-time more dramatically, and objects must again increase their speed to remain in orbit and not fall downward to the planet.

While serving in the trenches during the First World War, the German physicist and astronomer Karl Schwarzschild received an early copy of Einstein's paper outlying the general theory of relativity. He was able to solve Einstein's equations for the special case of a nonrotating symmetric sphere of mass M. But at certain radius values the equation could not be solved: it gave nonsense answers. This occurred when the radius was zero, as might be expected as the force of gravity would seem infinite, but also at another radius. This radius is the hypothetical radius at which light would orbit the mass, now known as the **Schwarzschild radius**.

Schwarzschild noted that for most objects, the Schwarzschild radius would be smaller than the radius of the object itself, meaning less than light speed is required for an orbit. However, if an object were massive enough, then their Schwarzschild radius would lie outside of the object. Get closer to this object than the Schwarzschild radius and there would be no escaping: it is a **black hole**. The Schwarzschild radius traces out a border between space and the point of no return for light, known as the event horizon. As nothing can escape from this point in space, we can never have any knowledge of an event taking place closer to the black hole. Inside of this is a singularity, a point where the equations of general relativity break down as the curvature of space-time becomes infinite. Infinite curvature in a material is only possible if there is a hole in the material, which is why black holes are often said to cause a rip or tear in space-time.

Surfing space-time

Objects orbit planets and black holes by surfing the edge of curved space-time. Like a surfer riding a wave, if they are not moving fast enough they will fall.

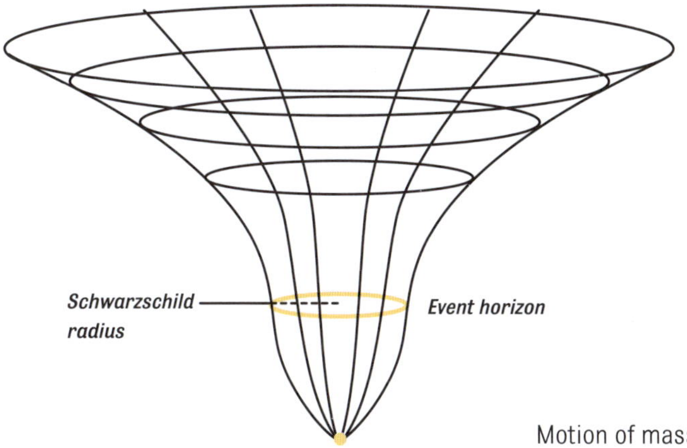

Black hole

Space-time, like any fabric, has a maximum force it can take before breaking. If space-time is stretched too much by a very large mass it can tear and form a sinkhole from which nothing, not even light, can escape. This is a black hole.

While we can never know what goes on beyond the event horizon of a black hole, there are theories that use Einstein's equations to speculate. One theory suggests that the tears in space-time may meet and join together in a connection known as a **wormhole**. Because there would be a continuous bridge between both ends of a wormhole, the opposite end of a black hole is predicted to be a white hole. While a black hole allows matter and light to enter but not exit, a white hole is entirely opposite, only allowing matter and light to exit but not enter.

Motion of massive objects and sudden changes in gravitational strength, such as the merging of two black holes, can send waves through space-time. These **gravitational waves** radiate energy at the speed of light through the cosmos. They are transverse waves that pinch and stretch space in different directions perpendicular to the direction they are moving through space. Interferometers, such as the setup used by Michelson and Morley in their famous experiment, can spot changes in space-time billions of times smaller than a proton. Gravitational waves shorten one arm of the interferometer while stretching the other as they pass through, and were first detected in 2016.

Wormhole

Wormholes are hypothetical connections between different regions of space-time, created when two singularities meet. They would be a gateway to travel vast distances in space and possibly time.

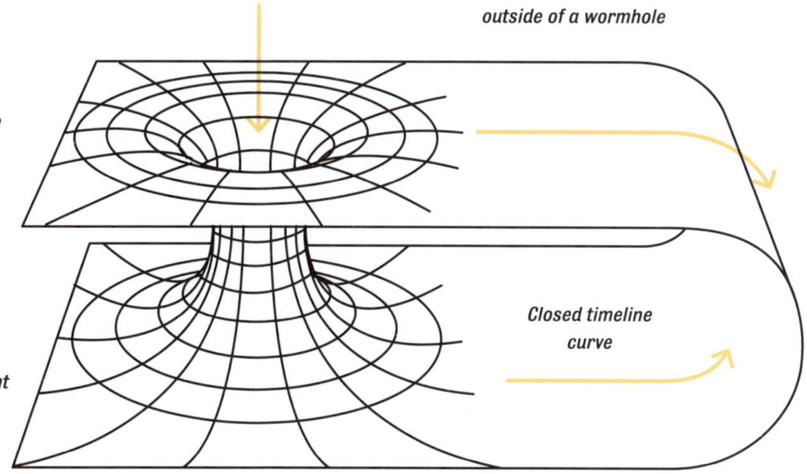

Glossary

Absolute zero The lowest possible thermodynamic temperature.

Accuracy How close a measurement is to its true value as determined by nature.

Amorphous A material with no repeating microscopic structure.

Asteroids Small rocky and/or metallic bodies left over from the formation of the rocky inner planets.

Atom The smallest basic unit of a chemical element. It is comprised of a central nucleus with positive electric charge surrounded by a cloud of negatively charged electrons.

Atomic nucleus The center of an atom where most of the mass is concentrated. It contains positively charged particles called protons and electrically neutral particles called neutrons.

Atomic spectra The various wavelengths of light emitted by atoms.

Band theory A theory that states that the electrons in materials exist in bands. These are either valance bands, where the electrons are bound to atoms, or conduction bands, where the electrons are free to move through the material.

Baryons Composite particles made up of three quark particles. The most common baryons are protons and neutrons.

Blackbody spectrum The various wavelengths of light emitted by theoretically ideal absorbers and emitters of light—blackbodies.

Bosons Particles with a quantum spin that is integer in value, either a 0, 1, or 2. Boson particles exchange the fundamental interactions of nature among other particles.

Capacitance A measure of the reactance of electronic components called capacitors.

Comets Dirty, dusty ice balls that are usually debris left over from the formation of gas giant planets.

Conduction The transfer of heat energy through direct collisions between particles.

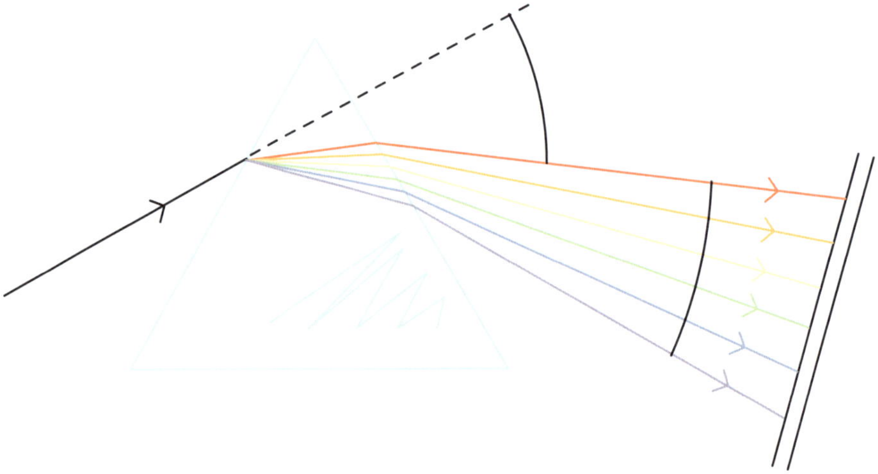

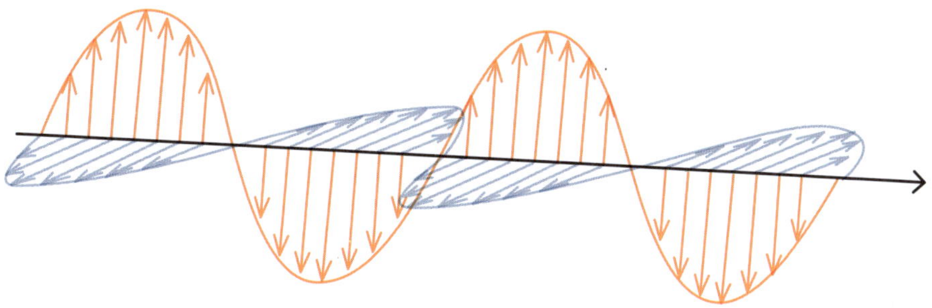

Convection The transfer of particles with energy from one place to another due to a difference in density.

Crystalline A material with regular repeating microscopic structure over large nonmicroscopic scales.

Dark matter Matter that provides gravitational interaction but does not interact with other matter in any other way, e.g. electromagnetism.

Decoherence Interaction between quantum objects and the macroscopic (large scale) environment.

Elastic A material that returns to its original shape when an applied force is removed.

Electric charge A fundamental property of an object that defines its interaction through electromagnetism.

Electric current The flow of electric charge from one location to another.

Electric field An imagined network of lines that begins at an object with electric charge and tells other electric charges the strength and direction of the force they would experience through the electromagnetic interaction.

Electric flux The name given to a group of electric field lines passing through a particular area.

Electromagnetic interaction The generation of forces between objects that possess either an electric charge or a magnetic field.

Electrons Negative electrically charged lepton particles that reside in cloud-like regions around the nucleus of every atom.

Entanglement A connection between wave functions of two or more quantum objects arising from a common origin.

Entropy A measure of the order of a system. Highly ordered systems possess low entropy, while high entropy systems are messy and random.

Fermions Particles with a half-integer spin. Quarks and leptons are all fermions, as are composite baryons such as protons or neutrons. They obey the Pauli Exclusion principle and combine to build more complex forms of matter.

Ferromagnetic A ferromagnetic material anti-aligns its internal magnetic field with an external field, creating an attraction to magnetized objects.

Field A region of space in which an object will experience a force.

Fission The induced splitting of a large nucleus into smaller daughter nuclei usually through capture of a neutron.

Fusion The process where two lighter nuclei combine together to form a single heavier nucleus.

Galaxy A large collection of stars all gravitationally bound to each other.

General relativity A theory that describes the motion of objects accelerating, or in a gravitational field.

Gluons These are bosons and exchange the strong interaction between quark particles, keeping them bound together to form baryon particles such as the proton.

Hadrons Composite particles made up from any number of quarks or antiquarks. Baryons and mesons are both classed as hadrons.

Heat All energy transfers to or from a system that are not work. Heat transfers include conduction, convection, and radiation.

Impedance The vector combination of both resistance and reactance; it is the total opposition to the flow of an alternating electric current.

Inductance A measure of the reactance of electronic components called inductors.

Induction The creation of an electric potential difference from a change in magnetic field.

Inflation The first moments of the universe when everything expanded outward faster than the speed of light.

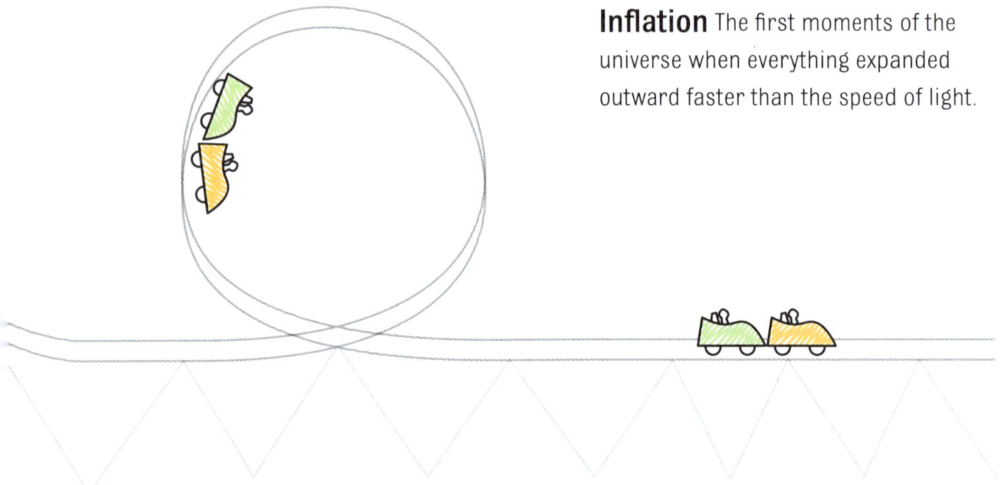

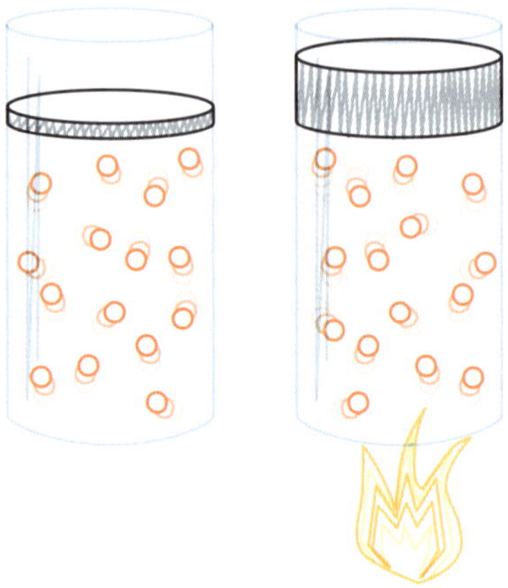

Ions Atoms that have lost or gained electrons to leave them with an overall electric charge.

Isotopes Atoms of a particular element that differ by the number of neutrons present in the nucleus.

Kinetic This relates to motion; kinetic energy is the energy stored in the motion of an object.

Leptons Half of the set of fundamental particles. There are three leptons with an electric charge: the electron and two heavier versions called the muon and tau. There are also three electrically neutral neutrinos each associated with a partner charged lepton.

Magnetic moment The fundamental property of a particle that dictates its interaction with magnetic fields.

Mass Either inertial mass, a measure of how large a force is required to produce a given acceleration, or gravitational mass, a fundamental property of an object that dictates the force it experiences due to gravity.

Mesons Composite particles made from one quark and one antiquark. They are bosons with spin zero and hadrons.

Meteorite A meteor core that has landed on the surface of a planet.

Meteors Light coming from alien objects (asteroids or comets) burning up as they pass through the atmosphere of a planet.

Mole A collection of exactly one Avagadro's number of individual units, usually atoms or molecules.

Multiplicity A measure of all of the different ways a state can exist microscopically, but still have the same set of state variables measurable.

Neutrinos Electrically neutral lepton particles. Each of the three neutrinos are associated with one of the three charged leptons.

Neutron Electrically neutral baryon found in the nucleus of an atom.

Nucleons The collective name for protons and neutrons.

Paramagnetism The moderate misalignment of an atom's magnetic field that results in a weak attraction to a magnetic object.

Photon The name given to the quanta packets of light.

Planet The name given to the large rocky and gassy objects orbiting a star in elliptical orbits.

Plasma The fourth state of matter, composed of dissociated electrons and nuclei.

Plastic A material whose shape is permanently changed when a force is applied.

Potential energy The energy stored in a force field by the position of an object within it, e.g. the position of a mass within a gravitational field.

Precision How repeatable a measurement is; if a method of measurement gives the same answer each time, it is precise.

Pressure Force applied per unit area.

Proton A positive electrically charged baryon found in the nucleus of every atom.

Quantum The theory of the "lumpy" nature of things smaller than the atom.

Quantum numbers Fundamental properties of a quantum object.

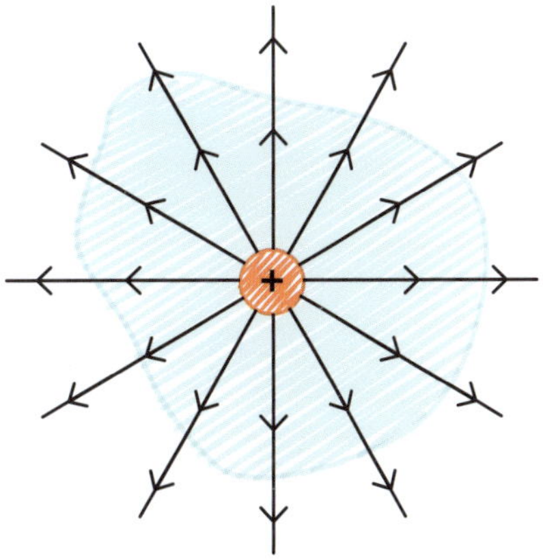

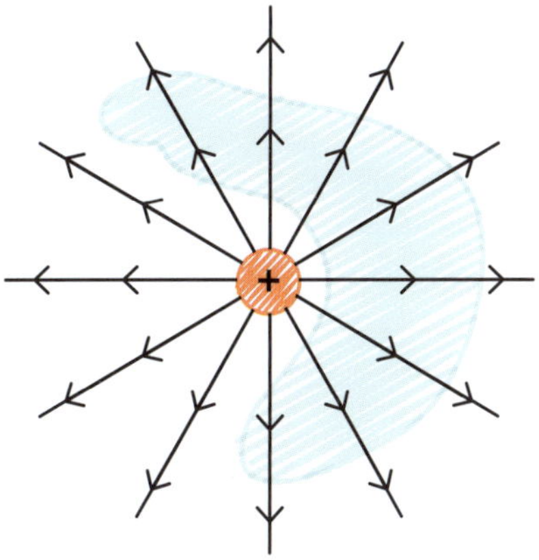

Quantum teleportation The exchange of information over a distance utilizing entanglement between quantum objects.

Quarks Half of the set of fundamental particles in nature. They are fermions and combine into composite hadrons, mesons, or baryons.

Qubits Quantum versions of the classical computing bit.

Radiation Heat transfer through the exchange of electromagnetic waves.

Reactance A different form of opposition to the flow of electric current than standard resistance. Energy from alternating electric currents is stored and released by some electronic components in magnetic and electric fields. The process of energy storage opposes the movement of the electric charges through these components.

Reflection The rebounding of light from a boundary between two materials

Refraction The change of speed and direction when light passes from one material into another.

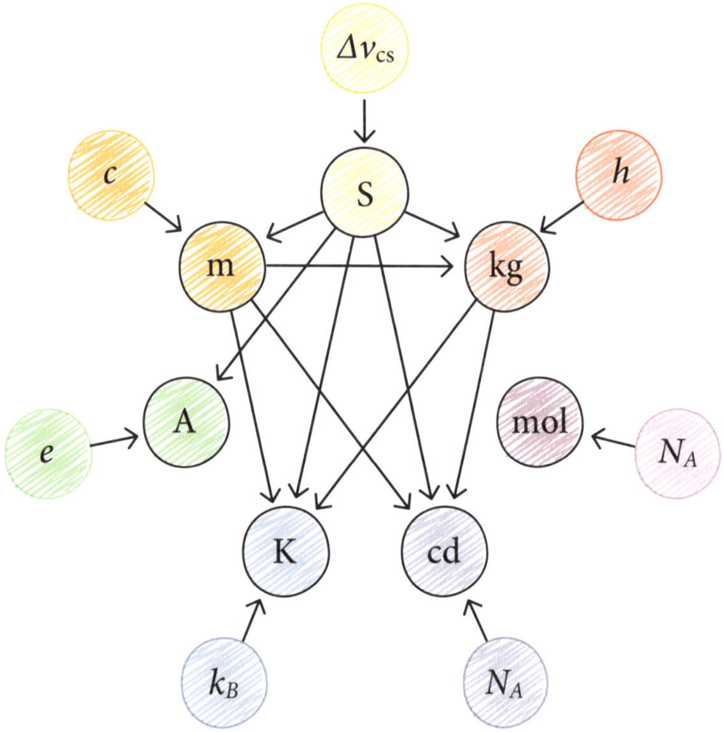

Relativity The speed of an object can only be measured relative to our own speed.

Scalar A measurable quantity with a size only, e.g. time, speed, or energy.

Solar system The region of space containing our Sun and the system of all things gravitationally bound to it.

Special relativity A theory describing how time and space act when objects are moving at very fast constant speeds.

Spin A fundamental property of all quantum particles. Fermion particles have half integer spin ($^1/_2$ or $^3/_2$) while boson particles have integer spin (0, 1, or 2).

Star A giant ball of plasma large enough that its gravitational collapse heats its center to temperatures so hot that nuclear fusion can occur.

Strong interaction Produces a force that binds quark particles together into composite meson and baryon particles. Gluons are the force-carrying boson particles of the strong interaction.

Superconductors Materials in which electric charges can move through the material with zero electrical resistance.

Superposition The combining of two or more waves to form one single wave.

System A collection of objects and their specific properties.

Thermal equilibrium A situation where two objects are at the same temperature; there is zero net heat flow between them.

Uncertainty principle A quantum law that states it is impossible to accurately measure pairs of certain variables, e.g. position and momentum, or energy and time.

Units A way to describe what a number means, e.g. a measure of length, time, or energy, and how they relate to a given number.

Vector A measurable quantity with both size and direction, e.g. velocity, momentum, or force.

Voltage A term given to the electric potential difference between two points; it is the difference in potential energy per unit of charge.

Volume The amount of space a 3-D object occupies.

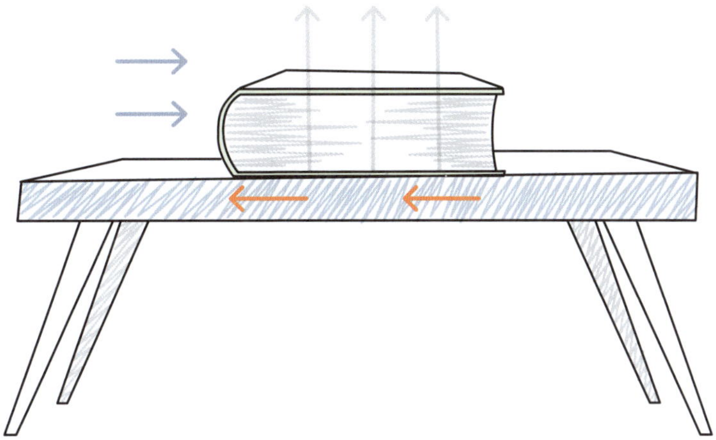

Wave An oscillation of particles or a field that transfers energy but not mass.

Wave function An equation that describes the state of an object that behaves like a wave.

Wave-particle duality When something acts as both a wave and a particle.

Weak interaction A fundamental interaction of nature that does not result in a force but instead transforms particles from one type to another.

Work The energy transferred when a force acts to move a mass through a distance.

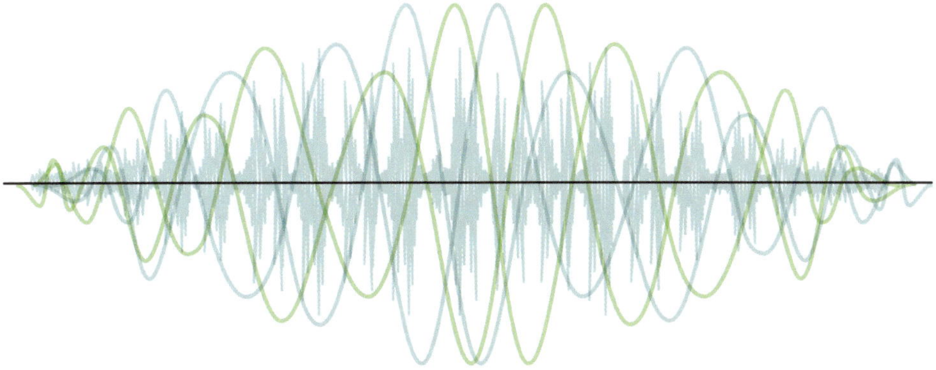

Index

A

absolute zero 57, 77, 81, 83, 85, 89
acceleration 10, 22, 24, 34, 35, 37, 137, 144–5
 angular 10, 23
 electric charge 143
accuracy 10, 13–14
adiabatic processes 80, 92, 93
alpha decay 109, 111
alpha rays 110–12
alternating currents 52, 56
amorphous materials 67, 74
Ampère, André-Marie 18, 64
amperes 11, 15–16, 18, 19
Ampere's law 53, 65
amplitude 39, 40, 41, 50–1
angular acceleration 10, 23
angular displacement 10, 23
angular momentum 10, 23
angular velocity 10, 23
asteroid belt 123, 131
astrophysics 122–35
atomic nucleus 109, 112–15, 119, 121
atomic spectra 94, 98
atomism 110–15
atoms 27, 28, 54, 60, 68, 110
 center 112–13
 nuclear physics 109
Avogadro constant 19

B

band gaps 67, 75
band theory 67, 74
baryons 109, 116, 117, 119, 124
base units 11, 15–16, 18–19
Becquerel, Henri 111
behaviors of waves 38, 43
Bell, John 106
Bell's inequality 95, 106
beta decay 108, 111
beta rays 110–11
Big Bang 26, 33, 120, 122, 124
binding energy 109, 114–15
black holes 123, 126, 129, 137, 148–9
blackbody spectrum 94, 96
blueshift 48
Bohr, Niels 98, 99, 103
Boltzmann, Stefan 90
 see also Maxwell-Boltzmann distribution
Boltzmann's constant 19, 97
Born, Max 102
Born rule 95, 102
Bose, Satyendra Nath 121
bosons 94, 109, 121
 Higgs 109, 121
Boyle, Robert 84
Boyle's law 81, 84
breaking stress 72
brittle materials 67, 72

C

candela 11, 15–16, 19
capacitance 52, 57
Carnot cycle 81, 93
Carnot, Sadi 93
Celsius scale 83
centripetal force 25, 37
Charles, Jacques 84
Charles's law 81, 84
circular motion 10, 22, 38, 40, 148
classical physics 94, 96
closed systems 82, 85
comets 123, 135
communication 38, 46
composite materials 67, 79
compounds 66, 68
compression 66, 70, 72, 79
conduction 80, 86
conduction bands 67, 74, 75
conductors 52, 55
conservation of energy 25, 33, 87
convection 80, 86
Copenhagen interpretation 95, 103, 105
Coriolis force 37
cosmic microwave background radiation (CMBR) 122, 125
cosmological redshift 48
Coulomb, Charles-Augustin de 58, 64
Coulomb's law 53, 58, 59
crystalline materials 67, 73
Curie temperature 67, 78
curvature 48, 136, 144, 145–6, 147, 148

D

Dalton, John 110
dark matter 122, 125–6, 147
de Broglie, Louis 99, 102
de Broglie wavelength 95, 99, 102
decoherence 95, 104, 105
deflection of light 137, 146–7
derived units 11, 16
diamagnetism 53, 62
diffraction 38, 45
diodes 76
direct currents 52, 56
dispersion 38, 44–5
displacement 11, 20, 21, 50
 angular 10, 23
distance 11, 12, 20, 21
domains 67, 78–9
doping 67, 76
Doppler, Christian 47
Doppler effect 39, 47, 48
double-slit experiments 95, 98
drag 24, 30
ductile materials 67, 72
dynamics 25, 34–5, 37

E

Earth 123, 132–4, 135, 139, 140, 145, 146, 147
eclipse 147
Eddington, Arthur 147

Einstein, Albert 97, 103, 105, 120, 137, 140–1, 143, 145, 147, 148–9
Einstein rings 147
elastic limit 72
elastic objects 67, 71
electric charge 52, 54–9, 143
electric constant 53, 59
electric currents 18, 52, 56, 62–3
electric fields 53, 58–9, 65
electric insulators 52, 55, 75
electric potential difference 53, 59, 64, 79
electrical conductors 52, 55
electromagnetic interactions 30, 108, 119, 120
electromagnetic mass 143
electromagnetic spectrum 53, 65
electromagnetic waves 39, 41, 43, 46, 48, 53, 56, 65, 87
electromagnetism 24, 26, 27, 28, 31, 52–65
electromagnets 53, 62–3
electromotive force (EMF) 59, 76
electronic circuits 27
electrons 18, 28, 69, 74–6, 97–100
  astrophysics 124, 127–9
  electromagnetism 53, 54–6, 60–3
  nuclear physics 108, 110–13, 118
  oscillation 87
electrostatic forces 53, 58
elements 66, 68
energy 24–37
  binding 109, 114–15
  conservation 25, 33, 87
  internal 80, 88
  kinetic 25, 36–7, 51, 63, 80, 86, 88–9, 90
  potential 25, 36–7, 53, 59, 62, 63, 80, 88
  relativistic equation 120, 143
  stores 25, 33
  thermodynamics 80, 82, 87
  transfers 25, 33
entropy 81, 89, 91, 93
EPR paradox 95, 105
equivalence principle 137, 145
errors 10, 13, 14
Everett, Hugh 104
exclusion principle 25, 28, 94, 100, 118, 121
expansion 122, 125
experiments 10, 12–14, 23, 26
  double-slit 95, 98
  Michelson-Morley 137, 139, 140, 149

F

Fahrenheit scale 83
Faraday, Michael 64
Faraday's law 53, 64, 65
fermions 108, 118, 121
ferromagnetic materials 53, 61, 62
fictitious forces 24, 37
fields 32–3
  electric 53, 58–9, 65
  force fields 25, 31, 32, 36, 41
  lines 25, 32, 58–9, 64, 130
  magnetic 53, 60–5, 78, 99, 130, 133
  strength 25, 32, 36, 145
fission 109, 114–15, 143
fluids 66, 68, 77
force fields 25, 31, 32, 36, 41
forces 24–37
  elastic objects 71
  material testing 66, 70
Franklin, Benjamin 54
frequency 39, 48
friction 24, 28–30, 37, 52, 55, 77
fundamental interactions 24, 26–33, 109, 119–21
fusion 109, 114, 123, 127–9, 143

G

galaxies 122, 126–7
Galilean relativity 138, 139
Galilean transformations 138, 139, 140
Galileo Galilei 138
gamma decay 108, 111
gamma factor 141, 142
gamma rays 110–11
gas clouds 122, 125, 127
gases 66, 68–9, 77, 81, 84–93, 97
Gauss, Carl Friedrich 59
Gauss's theorem 53, 59, 65
Gauss's theorem for magnetism 53, 64, 65
Gay-Lussac, Louis 84
Gay-Lussac's law 81, 84, 85
general relativity 48, 137, 145, 148
generators 53, 63
Gerlach, Walter 99
giant stars 123, 128–9
gluons 109, 119
gravitational force 18, 30
gravitational lensing 136, 147
gravitational mass 30, 145
gravitational time dilation 136, 146
gravitational waves 39, 48, 136, 149
gravity 24, 26, 30–1, 35, 125, 129, 130, 137, 145

H

hadrons 109, 116, 117, 119
half life 112
hard materials 67, 73
harmonic motion 38–51
heat 80, 85–7
  arrow of time 81, 91
  latent 80, 88
  specific capacity 80, 88
heat engines 81, 91–2, 93
Heisenberg, Werner 101, 102, 103
hidden variables 95, 106
Higgs boson 109, 121
Higgs, Peter 121
homogeneous materials 67, 79
Hooke, Robert 71
Hooke's law 66, 71, 145
hyperbolas 143, 144

I

ideal gases 81, 85, 90, 97
imaging 38, 46
impedance 52, 57
impulses 25, 37
inductance 52, 57
induction 53, 59, 63
inertia 18, 24, 34, 35, 121
  moment of 10, 23
inertial frames of reference 136, 138, 141, 142, 143, 145
inertial mass 30, 34, 83, 145
inflation 122, 124
insulators 52, 55, 75
interference 39, 50, 139
internal energy 80, 88
International System of Units 11, 15
ions 52, 54
isentropic processes 80, 93
isobaric changes 81, 92
isochoric changes 81, 92
isothermal changes 81, 92, 93
isotopes 109, 113, 114

J

jerk 10, 22
Jordan, Pascual 101, 102

K

kelvins 11, 15–16, 19, 83, 85
Kepler, Johannes 132
Kepler's laws 123, 132
kilograms 11, 15–16, 18
kinematics 11, 21

kinetic energy 25, 36–7, 51, 63, 80, 86, 88–9, 90
kinetic friction 29
kinetic temperature 81, 90
kinetic theory 80, 90
Kuiper belt 131, 134, 135

L

Larmor, Joseph 140
latent heat 80, 88
length contraction 137, 142
Lenz, Emil 64
Lenz's law 64
leptons 108, 116, 118, 121, 124
  charged 108, 118
light 19, 43, 120
  deflection 137, 146–7
  diffraction 45
  dispersion 44–5
  early universe 125
  electromagnetic waves 65
  quantum nature 98
  reflection 46
  speed of 18, 43, 44, 124, 136, 139–41
  starlight 136, 139–40, 147
linear motion 10, 22
liquids 67, 68, 77, 88
longitudinal waves 39, 41, 42
Lorentz force 53, 64, 65
Lorentz, Hendrik 64, 140, 143
Lorentz transforms 137, 140, 141, 142, 143
luminous efficacy 19

M

magnetic fields 53, 60–5, 78, 99, 130, 133
magnetic forces 53, 64
magnetic materials 67, 78
magnetic moments 53, 60, 61, 63
magnetism 60–5
malleable objects 67, 72
many-worlds interpretation 95
mass 11, 18, 24, 37, 144–5, 146
  electromagnetic 143
  gravitational 30, 145
  inertial 30, 34, 83, 145
materials 66–79
matrix mechanics 95, 101, 102
matter 66–79, 109, 110
Maxwell, James Clerk 65, 90
Maxwell-Boltzmann distribution 80, 90, 94, 97
Maxwell's equations 53, 59, 65
measurement 10–23
mechanical waves 39, 41, 42
mesons 109, 116, 117, 121, 124
meteorites 123, 135
meteors 123, 135
meters 11, 15, 18
Michelson-Morley experiment 137, 139, 140, 149
Milky Way 122, 127, 131
Minkowski diagrams 137, 142, 143
Minkowski, Hermann 142
molecules 28, 68
moles 11, 15–16, 19, 66, 69, 85
moment of inertia 10, 23
momentum 11, 22, 25, 33, 34, 37
  angular 10, 23
the Moon 123, 133–4, 147
moons 123, 133–4
motion 10–23
  circular 10, 22, 38, 40, 148
  harmonic 38–51
  linear 10, 22
  relative 138–43
  simple harmonic 38, 40, 51
  see also Newton's laws of motion
motor effect 53, 62
multiplicity 81, 89
muons 118

N

neutrinos 108, 118, 121
neutron stars 123, 129
neutrons 27, 28, 54, 109, 112–14, 116, 119
Newton, Sir Isaac 25, 34
Newton unit of force 16
Newton's gravity 24, 30
Newton's laws of motion 30, 34–5, 37, 90, 95, 143
  first law 25, 34
  second law 25, 34
  third law 25, 35
noninertial frames 137, 144–5
normal forces 25, 28–9
nuclear bombs 109, 114
nuclear forces 24, 28
nuclear and particle physics 108–21
nuclear power 109, 115

O

open systems 82
Ørsted, Hans Christian 62
oscillation 38, 40–3, 48, 49, 51, 87

P

p–n junctions 67, 76
paramagnetism 53, 61
particle classification 116–18
particle numbers 81, 83
Pauli, Wolfgang 100
  see also exclusion principle
permanent magnetic materials 53, 61
phase 39, 49
phase difference 39, 49, 50
photoelectric effect 94, 97
photons 109, 120, 121
physical constants 11, 15
piezoelectricity 67, 79
Planck constant 18, 97, 101
Planck, Max 97
planetary disk 123, 131
planets 123, 131–5, 147–8
plasma 52, 54, 67, 68, 69, 77, 122, 124, 127–8, 130
plastic objects 67, 72
Podolsky, Boris 105
polycrystalline materials 67, 74
position 11, 20, 21
potential energy 25, 36–7, 53, 59, 62, 63, 80, 88
precision 10, 13–14
prefixes 11, 17
pressure 81, 84–5, 90, 92–3
progressive waves 39, 49
protons 27, 28, 54, 109, 112–14, 116–17, 119, 127–8
PV diagrams 81, 92, 93

Q

quantum atoms 39
quantum computing 94, 107
quantum entanglement 95, 105, 106–7
quantum mechanics 39, 100–3
quantum numbers 94, 98–9, 100
quantum physics 94–107
quantum teleportation 95, 106
quantum theory 94, 97
quarks 27, 109, 116–17, 118, 119, 124
qubits 94, 107

R

radiation 80, 87, 110–11, 125
radioactive beta decay 27
radioactivity 109, 110, 111–12
random errors 10, 14
reactance 52, 57
redshift 39, 48
reflection 38, 43, 44, 46
refraction 38, 44–5
refractive index 38, 44
refrigerators 81, 85, 92
relativistic energy equation 120, 143
relativity 11, 15, 21, 136–49
  Galilean 138, 139
  general theory 48, 137, 145, 148
  special 137, 140–1, 143, 144, 146
repeatability 13
residual interactions 24, 28
resistance 52, 56, 75
resolution 38, 46–7
resonance 38, 51
resultant forces 26, 28, 34
Röntgen, Wilhelm 111
Rosen, Nathan 105
rotational dynamics 25, 37
Rutherford model 112

S

scalar quantities 11, 21–2
Schrödinger, Erwin 102
Schrödinger's cat 95, 103
Schrödinger's wave equation 95, 102
Schwarzschild, Karl 148
Schwarzschild radius 137, 148
seconds 11, 15–16, 18
seismic waves 39, 42–3
semiconductors 52, 55, 67, 75–6
shear 66, 70, 72, 79
simple harmonic motion 38, 40, 51
snap, crackle, and pop 10, 22
solar system 123, 130–5
solids 67, 68, 70, 88
sound waves 39, 42
space 11, 15, 18, 20
space-time 48, 137, 141
  curvature 48, 136, 144, 145–6, 147, 148
  tears 148–9
special relativity 137, 140–1, 143, 144, 146
specific heat capacity 80, 88
speed 11, 21, 22, 36, 37
  of light 18, 43, 44, 124, 136, 139–41
  waves 39, 49
spin 94, 99, 100, 107, 118, 121
spiral galaxy 122, 127
starlight 147
  aberration of 136, 139–40
stars 52, 54, 114, 123, 125, 127–9, 130, 139, 147
state variables 81, 82
states of matter 67, 68–9
static electricity 55
static friction 29
stationary waves 39, 50–1
statistical thermodynamics 81, 89
Stern, Otto 99
strain 66, 71–2
stress 66, 71–3, 79
strong interactions 24, 26, 27, 109, 119, 124
strong materials 67, 73
the Sun 122, 130, 132, 147
superconductors 52, 57
superfluids 66, 77
supergiant stars 123, 128–9
supermassive black holes 123, 126
supernova, type II 123, 129
superposition 39, 50
system of units 11, 15
systematic errors 10, 13, 14

T

taus 118
temperature 12, 19
  Curie 67, 78
  kinetic 81, 90
  superconductors 57
  thermodynamics 81, 83–5
tension 66, 70, 72, 79
thermal equilibrium 80, 85–6
thermodynamic work 80, 86
thermodynamics 80–93
  first law of 80, 87
  second law of 81, 91
  third law of 81, 89
Thomson, J. J. 97, 112, 143
time 10, 12, 14, 18, 21
  arrow of 81, 91
  dilation 137, 141
  gravitational time dilation 136, 146
  period 39, 48
  space-time 48, 137, 141
  universal 140
torque 25, 37
transducers 79
transistors 75
transverse waves 39, 41
triboelectric series 52, 56

U

ultraviolet catastrophe 96
uncertainty principle 94, 101, 121
unit cells 67, 73
units 11, 14–19
Universal State Formulation 104

V

valence bands 67, 74, 75
Van der Waals' forces 24, 28
vectors 11, 21–3
velocity 21–3, 25, 37, 136, 138, 139
  angular 10, 23
Vickers hardness test 73
viscosity 66, 77
voltage *see* electric potential difference
volume 81, 83, 84, 90, 92–3

W

W+ and W– particles 108, 121
wave functions 95, 100, 102–3, 104–7
wave-function collapse 95, 102–3, 104
wave-particle duality 95, 98
wavelength 39, 45, 48
waves 38–51
  speed 39, 49
weak interactions 24, 26, 27, 108, 119, 120–1
white dwarf 123, 128, 129
work 25, 33
wormholes 137, 149

Y

Young, Thomas 72, 98
Young's modulus 66, 72

Z

Z^0 particles 108, 121
zeroth law 81, 85–6

Acknowledgments

I have to thank my wife Emily for sharing her strength to support me through the writing of this book. Thanks also to my colleagues, friends, and family whose discussion kept me on the right track.
—Ben Still

UniPress Books would like to thank Jon Evans for his assistance.